W9-DGH-970

Children and Emotion

CHILDREN AND EMOTION

The Development of Psychological Understanding

Paul L. Harris

Basil Blackwell

First published 1989

Basil Blackwell Ltd
108 Cowley Road, Oxford, OX4 1JF, UK

Basil Blackwell Inc.
432 Park Avenue South, Suite 1503
New York, NY 10016, USA

British Library Cataloguing in Publication Data

A CIP catalogue record is available for this book from the British Library

Library of Congress Cataloging in Publication Data

Harris, Paul L.
Children and emotion.

Bibliography : p.
Includes indexes.
1. Emotions in children. I. Title.
BF723.E6H37 1989 155.4'12 88–35011
ISBN 0–631–16752–8 (U.S.)
ISBN 0–631–16753–6 (U.S. : pbk.)

Data converted to 11 on 13.5 pt. Sabon
by Columns of Reading

Contents

Acknowledgements

My research on children's understanding of emotion began in Amsterdam. I was fortunate in having two friends and colleagues there, Mark Meerum Terwogt and Tjeert Olthof, whose interest, enthusiasm and criticism stimulated me in that early period and in the years since. I warmly thank them both.

In Britain, I have benefited from the help and ideas of many students. I am especially grateful to Deborah Taylor, Nadja Reissland, Gaby Guz, Dale Tiller, Mark Lipian, Rosemary Jordano and Maria Dias.

Judy Dunn was a marvellous editor. To the extent that I have successfully followed her advice, the book is more readable than it might have been. I would also like to thank all those people who reviewed the content of individual chapters. In particular, I received helpful comments and suggestions from Simon Baron-Cohen, Mark Bennett, Philip Carpenter, Larry Fensom, Fabia Franco, Damian Gardner, Robert Gordon, Dana Gross, Charlotte Hardman, Debbie Hutton, Jenny Jenkins, Carl Johnson, Mark Meerum Terwogt, Arietta Slade, Ross Thompson, Pascale Torracinta, Arlene Walker-Andrews and Michael Westerman.

I am also indebted to the children and staff in schools and hospitals who were willing to participate in our research and make this book possible.

This book is affectionately dedicated to Viru, Sophie and Olivia here, and to Nicholas, Walker and Phoebe over there.

P. L. H., Oxford

Series editor's preface

What kind of insight do children have into their own emotional state – and how well do they understand other people's feelings? Does children's grasp of the causes of emotions affect their ability to cope with upsetting or frightening experiences? How do their strategies for coping with such experiences change with age? The questions with which this book is concerned are clearly of practical importance in the lives of children. They are also currently of great interest to developmental psychologists: the issue of when and how children begin to develop a concept of mental life, and how this relates to their understanding of the behaviour, intentions and emotions of other people is unquestionably important for our understanding of children's development – cognitive, moral, social or emotional. Paul Harris brings together the findings of important and innovative research – largely his own – to consider these questions, setting his argument in a broad framework that includes evidence from widely differing cultures, from experimental and naturalistic studies, and ideas from psychology, anthropology and sociology. The scholarship is impressive and substantial, but always clear and intelligible.

In his distinctive approach, children's imaginative capacities are given a central role in the growth of social understanding. It is an analysis that has implications not only for current theories of children's conception of mind, but also for our ideas on the development of moral judgement, and on the social construction of emotions – here Paul Harris provides an integration of ideas that are more commonly set in opposition to one another. The book highlights the development of children's insight into the complexity of 'mixed-feelings', their understanding of deceit, and of the significance of cultural rules concerning the display of emotions, and their growing grasp of the strategic control of emotional expression. Perhaps most important of all, the argument makes connections between the theories and systematic research of developmental psychologists, and children's real-life emotional experiences, difficulties and developmental problems. To establish such links, and to encourage psychologists to set out the implications of their research for the lives of children and adults in classroom, hospital and at home is the central aim of the series *Understanding Children's Worlds*, in which this volume appears.

Judy Dunn

Introduction

Several of the ideas developed in this book began with a collaborative research project that I carried out in the Netherlands together with Tjeert Olthof and Mark Meerum Terwogt. We were intrigued by the notion that children would gradually gain more insight into their emotional lives, and as a result be better able to cope with distress and anxiety. At the time, we were guided by work on the development of memory showing that older children understand how their memory operates to a greater extent than younger children, and therefore control their memory capacities more effectively. We wondered whether a similar picture might emerge for emotional development; children might be better able to cope with their emotions to the extent that they gained insight into the causes of those emotions (Harris, Olthof and Meerum Terwogt, 1981).

The results of that initial investigation were surprisingly orderly. We found that younger children (around the age of six) usually conceived of emotion in terms of an emotionally charged situation that provokes a visible emotional reaction. At this age, children rarely referred to the mental processes that might re-direct an emotion or its manifestations. By ten years of age, the pattern of replies was different. Children were more likely to refer to the mental processes that intervene between a situation and the emotional reaction that it provokes. For example, they argued that one could be cheered up by *thinking* positively about a situation – or *forgetting* about it – even if the situation itself remained unaltered.

Similarly, older children were more likely to refer spontaneously to the gap between the emotion that one might express to other people and the emotion that one covertly experienced. We concluded that children shift from a behaviouristic concept of emotion to a more cognitive or mentalistic concept (Harris and Olthof, 1982). A series of follow-up studies has shown, not surprisingly, that our description requires modification, although it is not completely wrong.

As in many other areas of developmental psychology, we have discovered that our characterization of younger children was uncharitable. If we ask not whether they appreciate that an emotional reaction can be re-directed by mental processes, but whether its initial instigation depends upon mental processes, we immediately uncover a rich and inherently mentalistic conception. Specifically, young children grasp that people's emotional reactions differ depending on the beliefs and desires that they have about a situation. Even when two people are confronted by the same objective situation, they may appraise it differently depending on what they want or believe. As a result, a situation that upsets one person may delight another and young children realize this. Their mentalistic stance is also revealed in more probing questions concerning the difference between hidden and expressed emotion. By the age of six, children grasp that the emotion displayed on one's face may not correspond to the emotion that one really feels, and that onlookers may be unaware of the discrepancy.

If such conceptual subtleties are beyond the reach of a crude behaviourist, we immediately confront new questions. In particular, what concept of mental life does the young child possess and where does it come from? One recent answer to the first question is that children have a truly theoretical concept of mind. They postulate inter-related, unobservable entities (notably, beliefs and desires) and they refer to those entities in both explaining and predicting behaviour (Astington, Harris and Olson, 1988). In answer to the second question, some authors have argued that children are probably born with a theory of mind – not the entire theory, admittedly, but at least the capacity to impute beliefs and desires – 'the rudiments of commonsense Intentional Realism' as Fodor (1987) puts it.

I shall argue that both of these claims are wrong. Young children are not born with, and do not acquire, a genuine theory of mind. First, they do not need to 'postulate' beliefs and desires because they have beliefs and desires and they can report their content from around two years of age. Second, they can predict other people's reactions not by recourse to a set of generalizations linking beliefs, desires, emotions and actions, but by virtue of their imaginative capacity. Specifically, children can imagine the beliefs and desires that other people may have, even if they themselves do not share them. They can then use such make-believe premises to reach new conclusions (Dias and Harris, 1988). For example, if they examine a situation in the light of the beliefs or desires that another person brings to it, they can proceed to simulate the intentions or emotions of that person. Moreover, their predictions about the other person will be increasingly accurate as their simulation improves. This argument is presented in chapter 3 and elaborated in later chapters.

The argument borrows from Craik (1943), who suggested that we use working models in our head to make predictions about reality. By feeding in various inputs to the model, and observing its outputs, we can extrapolate from the model to predict what will happen in reality. We may apply this account to our predictions about other people in the following way. First, we each possess a working model of the other person (namely the psychological machinery that governs the relationships between beliefs, desires, actions and emotions in our own mind); we feed in various make-believe or pretend inputs to this model; we observe its outputs, and base our predictions about the other person on those outputs.

Admitting that young children have a conception – if not a theory – of mental life, how does this change in the course of development? Our research has continued to show that older children are much more likely to mention mentalistic or cognitive strategies in trying to *change* their emotional reactions. Unlike five- and six-year-olds, children of eight years and upward frequently refer to the need to stop thinking about, or forget about situations that are distressing. Implicit in their formulation are two key notions: first, that one can deliberately set out to suppress or re-direct the thoughts triggered by an emotionally-charged situation; and second, that the contents of thought are finite – thinking about one situation precludes thinking about another. As a result, worrying thoughts can disrupt concentration on other tasks, but mercifully the reverse can also be true: the distraction afforded by an absorbing activity can block out anxious or sad thoughts. These strategies for coping with homesickness and distress are described in chapters 7 and 8.

Finally, I consider ways in which the child's conception of emotion can be disrupted. In chapter 8, the impact of a highly charged event, namely hospitalization, is described. In chapter 9, the syndrome of autism is reviewed and interpreted in light of the claim that autistic children cannot engage in the imaginative simulation that enables normal children to enter into the emotional lives of other people.

1

Facial expression in infancy

How does the child come to understand that another person is feeling happy or sad, angry or afraid? An understanding of the feelings of other people is something that we expect of any normal human being, but the origins of that understanding are not obvious. It is one part of a more general capacity to make sense of other people's thoughts, desires and beliefs. In developmental psychology, we have only recently begun to wonder about the origins of that general capacity.

It could be argued that the emotional life of another person provides a natural starting point for children seeking to understand other people's mental states. Children can easily know what people feel because feelings are often visible in the face. Emotional states are in that sense transparent, whereas beliefs and desires are not. One of the earliest careful observers of human infants, Charles Darwin, came to that conclusion. In his classic book *The Expression of the Emotions in Man and Animals*, Darwin (1872) was struck by the similarity in the facial expressions of various nations. From these similarities, he argued that there is an innate, universal basis to our emotional expressions, and this simple, bold hypothesis continues to inspire current research on emotion and emotional development.

Darwin went on to make a further claim, less well substantiated, and often neglected by his commentators, but directly relevant to any discussion of how we come to identify another person's feelings. He believed that we have an innate ability to recognize facial expressions of emotion. By this he meant not simply that the young infant can see that one facial expression is different from another, but that the infant instinctively knows the meaning of the facial expression. He also noted that such instinctive recognition produces an emotional reaction in the observing infant. Darwin gives the following illustration from his son aged just over six months.

> His nurse pretended to cry, and I saw that his face instantly assumed a melancholy expression, with the corners of the mouth strongly depressed; now this child could rarely have seen any other child crying, and never a grown-up person crying, and I doubt whether at so early an age he could have reasoned on the subject. Therefore it seems to me that an innate feeling must have told him that the pretended crying of his nurse expressed grief; and this through the instinct of sympathy excited grief in him. (1872, p. 368)

It is important to notice that each of Darwin's claims are connected with one another. Specifically, if there were not a universal repertoire of emotional expressions – if facial expressions were produced according to mere convention – there would be no possibility for nature to equip the infant with foreknowledge of how to interpret any particular expression, just as there is no way to equip the child with foreknowledge of the English or Chinese lexicon. Moreover, if there were no capacity for innate recognition, there would be little immediate likelihood of any emotional transmission from adult to infant, since the expression would be opaque and meaningless in the eyes of the infant. In the remainder of this chapter I shall examine Darwin's claims about the innate basis for the production and recognition of emotional expressions in more detail, beginning with his claim that facial expressions are universal.

Cross-cultural similarity

In order to obtain evidence for the universality of particular facial expressions, Darwin wrote to various informants and asked them to supply a description of the facial movements associated with particular emotions. He was at pains to sample across the globe and wrote to informants in Australia, New Zealand, Borneo, Malaya, China, India, Africa and North and South America. Darwin was especially concerned to obtain information about people who had little contact with Europeans, and achieved some success. For example, he obtained reports of isolated Australian aborigines, and of Malays in the interior of Malacca. He was also scrupulous in trying to obtain accurate and unbiased reports from his informants, although his introductory remarks show that he trusted some of his informants more than others. Mr J. Scott, for example, a curator of the Botanic Gardens in Calcutta, is singled out: 'No one has sent me such full and valuable details . . . The habit of accurate observation gained by his botanical studies, has been brought to bear on our present subject.' Nevertheless, we cannot be certain that even the best descriptions were not biased, at least to some degree, by the context in which they had been made. Perhaps there are universal beliefs about how certain emotions are conveyed, but no actual universality.

Recent studies of Darwin's cross-cultural hypothesis have been strongly influenced by the work of Paul Ekman and his colleagues (Ekman, 1973; Ekman, in press). One study, in particular, has been especially influential. After a discouraging field-trip to Borneo and New Guinea, where equivocal results had been obtained (Ekman, Sorenson and Friesen, 1969), Ekman and Friesen (1971) returned to New Guinea in order to test adults and children of the Fore – a linguistic-cultural group from the South East Highlands. Many had had contact with foreigners but some had not. Ekman and Friesen concentrated on the latter group. These people had seen no films, neither spoke nor understood English or Pidgin, had not lived in any of the Western Settlement or Government towns, and had never worked for a Caucasian, at least according to their own report. Ekman and Friesen concentrated on these isolated members of the group because contact with foreigners, be it direct contact or through watching films, might have enabled them to learn to interpret a different, non-indigenous set of facial expressions.

Ekman and Friesen made use of a simple but informative task. They asked the Fore to listen to several short stories that described an emotionally-charged episode. Following each story, the listener picked out a picture displaying the emotional expression appropriate to the episode from a set of photographs. The photographs showed Western adults and children producing various expressions of emotion. For example, one story described the arrival of friends; we would expect the listener to select the happy facial expression to show the emotion that would be provoked by the episode. Another story described an encounter with a wild pig. Here, we might expect the listener to select the fearful facial expression. In all, there were stories intended to evoke six different emotions: happiness, sadness, anger, disgust, surprise and fear.

The results were quite straightforward and convincing. The adults listening to the stories accurately chose pictures of faces that were appropriate to the episode for four expressions: happiness (92 per cent), anger (84 per cent), disgust (81 per cent) and sadness (79 per cent). They were less accurate for surprise (68 per cent) and poor at discriminating fear from surprise (43 per cent), but could correctly distinguish fear from the other three negative emotions (80 per cent). Very similar results were obtained from children. To some extent, the children performed even better than the adults, but the experimenters had simplified their task by offering them only two facial expressions to choose between.

These results show that for certain facial expressions the case for universality is hard to resist. Given the isolation of the people tested by Ekman and Friesen (1971), it seems unlikely that their choices were based on any learning of how foreigners express their emotions. It must have been based on their ability to see some similarity, and moreover a common meaning, between the facial expressions that they were asked to choose among and the facial expressions that members of their culture would normally produce in the situations described in the stories.

The Fore adults were also asked to pose the facial expression that the story episodes would provoke – to mimic, for example, the broad smile that a friend's arrival might provoke or the expression of disgust that a rotting carcass might induce. When Ekman and Friesen returned to the USA with films of these posed expressions, US judges correctly interpreted them (Ekman, 1973). So, whether we examine transmission from Westerners to isolated New Guineans, or the transmission from those same New Guineans back to Westerners, there is a consensus on the characteristics and meaning of particular facial expressions.

There is, however, one problem in interpreting these results. Ekman and Friesen (1971) made use of the fact that adults can easily pose a particular facial expression, although the pose may not correspond exactly to the spontaneous expression. Many of the photographs that they took to New Guinea consisted of a deliberate pose rather than a spontaneous expression, and, of course, they returned from New Guinea with film of local tribesmen simulating the expression they would make when encountering a bad smell, or the arrival of friends. The results, therefore, testify inadvertently to the widespread ability to copy certain facial expressions. This is important because Darwin, and following in his footsteps Ekman and Friesen, take the universality of facial expression as evidence that they are innate. Strictly speaking this does not follow. It is just conceivable, albeit unlikely, that people in different countries and cultures learn to convey particular emotions by copying the signals they see others displaying in certain situations. Admittedly, for these signals to have the universal meaning that Ekman and Friesen have confirmed, we would need to postulate a time before their isolation when cultures such as the tribe studied in New Guinea were in contact with the wider world, but there is nothing inherently implausible about that.

In order to rule out this copying hypothesis and to provide a stronger case for the nativist claim, we need to know whether facial expressions are produced spontaneously in the appropriate circumstances during childhood, or are copied from others. As we shall see, there is evidence to suggest that Darwin was correct in supposing that particular facial expressions are not only universally produced but also have an innate basis.

Developmental evidence

Developmental studies of emotional expression in infants have benefited considerably from the analytic work undertaken with adults. Ekman and Friesen (1978) describe a coding system that allows observers to record and identify all visible changes of the facial musculature. In total, 58 different features or movements are listed, some of which are characteristically associated with a particular emotion, whereas others are not tied to any particular emotion. Simpler coding systems, which allow the observer to compare a set of movements with templates for each basic emotion have also been developed (Ekman and Friesen, 1975; Izard, 1979). For example, the presence of arched brows, rounded eyes and opened mouth corresponds to the critical configuration for surprise.

What have these systems revealed about the development of the expression of emotion during infancy? A study by Carroll Izard and his colleagues in Delaware offers a good starting point (Izard, Huebner, Risser, McGinnes and Dougherty, 1980). They first asked whether babies produce discriminably different facial expressions. To check this, they filmed babies of one to nine months engaged in various activities, playing with their mother, receiving an inoculation, being approached by a nurse, etc., and made up a set of slides that offered good examples of various emotions: happiness, sadness, surprise, interest, fear, contempt, anger and disgust. They then asked judges to look at the slides and identify the emotion expressed in each. Their success rate was good; it ranged from 81 per cent for happiness to 37 per cent for disgust, and it also improved with a short training session in which the various features of each facial expression were highlighted.

This study shows that babies can produce discrete, recognizable facial expressions. However, it relied on the selection of examples from a large footage of film. Were these examples more or less random configurations that happened to resemble certain adult facial expressions? Several experiments have now been carried out in which the baby is put in a situation likely to provoke a particular emotion. The baby's facial expression is then carefully observed. These studies demonstrate that, far from being random movements, the baby's facial expression is tied in a psychologically meaningful way to immediately preceding events.

In one of the first and most comprehensive studies, babies of 10 to 12 months were presented with six different situations (Hiatt, Campos and Emde, 1979). Two were expected to produce happiness: a peek-a-boo game and a game involving a collapsing toy. Two were expected to produce surprise: an object that unexpectedly changed its identity or vanished. Two were expected to produce fear: placement at the edge of a table (the so-called visual cliff test) and the approach of a stranger. The experiment was a partial success. During the two games, the babies looked happy: they smiled, and wrinkles appeared under the eyelids as they do in adults. These facial movements were much less common during the fear and surprise episodes. For these episodes however, the babies reacted in a less specific fashion.

These results are encouraging but not as strong as one would like. Particularly critical is the question of whether the infants were simply displaying facial expressions that were globally positive or globally negative rather than displaying the discrete facial expressions postulated by Darwin and by Ekman. Two key negative emotions – anger and distress –

have been clearly distinguished in later studies. For instance, anger was provoked in seven-month-old infants by frustrating them: they were repeatedly presented with a teething biscuit to suck on for a few seconds, which was then withdrawn (Stenberg, Campos and Emde, 1983). Using the coding system devised by Ekman and Friesen (1975), several of the components of anger were identified after the biscuit had been withdrawn: the babies' brows were joined together and a vertical line appeared between them, the eyelids were tensed and the mouth was compressed or squared.

Babies' expressions of distress were studied when they were receiving a painful inoculation (Izard, Hembree, Dougherty and Spizzirri, 1983). The dominant initial reaction among 2–8-month-olds was distress. Strikingly, the movements were the same as those identified a century earlier by Darwin (1872): '[The] eyes are firmly closed, so that the skin round them is wrinkled, and the forehead contracted into a frown. The mouth is widely open with the lips retracted in a peculiar manner, which causes it to assume a squarish form, the gums or teeth being more or less exposed.'

A final study shows that selective facial expressions can be observed even in newborns (Ganchrow, Steiner and Daher, 1983). Shortly before or after their very first feed, they were given liquids that were slightly sweet or very sweet, slightly bitter or very bitter. The baby's facial expression changed depending on the liquid: sweet tastes evoked a slight parting of the lips, rhythmic licking and sometimes a slight smile, whereas bitter tastes evoked a closed or open mouth with the corners down, repetitive pursing of the lips, and a quick blink of the eyes. When observers tried to identify the babies' reaction to the liquids from their expression (without knowing which liquid was being tasted) they judged that the babies disliked the bitter tastes, and enjoyed the sweet tastes. In addition, the observers could tell when the babies were tasting the more concentrated liquids, as opposed to the mild ones. Apparently, newborns can display not just distinct facial expressions, but more or less intense expressions.

In summary, these studies confirm that the young infant can produce several discriminably different facial expressions in appropriate circumstances. The range and selectivity of the baby's expressive repertoire has not yet been established but there can be little doubt that expressions of happiness, anger and distress are systematically produced. It is worth underlining this systematicity. Recall that the universality of facial emotions does not in itself establish their innateness, because it is conceivable that children everywhere learn to copy what has become a universal code for the expression of discrete emotions. Yet the fact that infants in the first months or days of life produce appropriate and discriminably different emotional expressions casts doubt on the copying hypothesis and suggests instead, as Darwin supposed, that there is a direct unlearned link between particular emotional states and particular facial expressions.

Still, it could be argued that even the observation of infants cannot rule out the copying hypothesis. Recent evidence suggests that neonates are very good at imitating facial movements so that, in principle, they could learn how to produce particular facial expressions through imitation. Several experiments have shown that they can copy lip and tongue movements (Meltzoff and Moore, 1977; 1983). Some investigators have even suggested that babies who are only two or three days old can imitate facial expressions, although the findings are controversial (Field, Woodson, Cohen, Greenberg, Garcia and Collins, 1983; Field, Woodson, Greenberg and Cohen, 1982; Kaitz, Meschulach-Sarfaty, Auerbach and Eidelman, 1988; Reissland, 1988a).

Babies might look happy or angry not because such facial expressions are an innate and universal signalling system, but because they have observed other people, be they adults or children, producing such expressions and they reproduce them by means of imitation. If we look at the copying hypothesis more carefully, however, it is not very plausible, even if we allow that facial expressions can be imitated from early infancy. Consider, for example, the angry face that Stenberg and his colleagues (1983) observed when they repeatedly removed a teething biscuit. No doubt seven-month-olds have seen an angry face from time to time in one of their caretakers; they may even be able to imitate that facial expression, but it is implausible to suppose that they have seen their caretakers look angry at the removal of a teething biscuit. The copying hypothesis can explain how the infant could come to copy a particular facial expression at some point in time, but it cannot explain how the infant comes to produce that expression in appropriate circumstances. Again, consider the reactions of newborn babies: we cannot seriously suppose that they have had time to observe that adults produce different expressions in response to different flavours and copy them in an appropriate fashion. It is much more parsimonious to suppose that there are particular elicitors that more or less automatically elicit particular emotional expressions. Admittedly, for the facial expressions of sadness, surprise and fear, we still lack systematic evidence for their connection to particular elicitors but my guess is that we have not yet demonstrated the full range of the infant's repertoire. Meantime, the limited repertoire that has been established provides good support for Darwin's assertion that human beings have an innate, universal repertoire of facial expressions.

Recognition of emotion

As I pointed out at the beginning of this chapter, Darwin's observations led him to the conclusion that babies not only produce facial expressions on an innate basis, but recognize and react to them on an innate basis also. Darwin's evidence quoted earlier was that when his son aged six months saw his nurse pretend to cry, 'his face instantly adopted a melancholy expression, with the corners of the mouth strongly depressed.'

In order to investigate the baby's capacity to recognize different emotional expressions, recent investigations have made use of the fact that babies are quite selective in what they look at. I will describe two representative and well-designed experiments. In the first, babies ranging from four to seven months were given pictures of four women to look at; each picture portrayed a different woman, but they all expressed the same emotion, either happiness or surprise (Caron, Caron and Myers, 1982). In the course of this series of pictures, the babies gradually looked less and less, but the older babies increased their attention if they were unexpectedly shown a picture of a woman portraying a *new* expression (i.e. surprise for those who had seen happiness, and vice versa). Thus, the older babies gradually lost interest so long as the various pictures expressed the same emotion but could identify a change of emotion and renew their interest.[1]

A second study shows that babies can go even further. Not only do they treat different versions of the same facial expression as belonging together, they also appreciate that a given expression goes with a particular tone of voice. Arlene Walker-Andrews (1986) presented seven-month-old babies with two films side-by-side; one showed a face making an angry expression and the other showed a face making a happy expression. At the same time, the babies could hear a soundtrack of either a happy or an angry voice. Presented with this situation, infants tended to look at the face that matched the voice: they looked more at the happy face if they could hear a happy voice, and more at the angry face if they could hear an angry voice. Apparently, babies do not simply respond to features that recur across different examples of a given facial expression – such as the rounded eyes of surprise – they can also connect quite disparate signs of the same emotion. Their 'concept' of an emotional expression seems to include a particular type of facial movement such as a smile or a frown on the one hand and a completely different stimulus in a different modality on the other hand.[2]

Can we interpret these intriguing results as support for Darwin's claim of innate recognition? The findings that infants can group different examples of the same expression together, and also know which facial expression goes with which tone of voice are certainly consistent with Darwin's position but fall well short of establishing it. The main weakness of the experiments is that they tell us virtually nothing about the meaning of the expressions for the infant. Consider a somewhat far-fetched analogy. We might measure babies' visual attention to show that they can distinguish red from blue. We might even be able to show that they treat various hues of red as a group and various hues of blue as a group. Yet we could scarcely conclude from these tests of categorization that the babies would correctly interpret red to indicate hot and blue to indicate cold. Similarly, from the fact that babies can group together the various manifestations of a given emotion, no matter how disparate those manifestations (even if they range over different modalities and different persons), we cannot conclude that the baby recognizes that a given expression implies a particular emotion – that a smile conveys happiness whereas a furrowed brow and tight lips convey anger.

How can we get back to the claims that Darwin made and study the meaning that the baby attaches to a particular emotional expression? One obvious technique is to study the spontaneous reactions that the baby shows to one expression as compared with another, just as Darwin did. If we find that the baby responds differently and appropriately to an angry as compared with a happy expression, it must to a limited extent interpret the meaning of those expressions correctly.

Everyday contact with young babies certainly gives us the impression that they respond to changes in emotional expression. For example, if a parent holds a six-month-old in a face-to-face position, attracts its attention, smiles and talks in an animated and positive tone, the baby will frequently respond in an 'appropriate' fashion with a smile or positive vocalization (Cohn and Tronick, 1987). However, these observations of an emotional 'dialogue' between parent and baby are difficult to interpret. In particular, it is hard to identify what aspect of the dialogue the baby is responding to. One plausible interpretation is that babies rapidly come to expect their caretaker, and indeed adults in general, to behave in an animated fashion and enjoy it when they do so. Such animated behaviour will, of course, typically include smiling and a friendly tone of voice, but any type of movement or animation might please the baby. Certainly, this possibility is consistent with the fact that babies become wary or upset if an adult stays inexpressive or motionless in front of them (Cohn and Tronick, 1983; Field, Vega-Lahr, Scafadi and Goldstein, 1986; Gusella, Muir and Tronick, 1988). To study the baby's recognition and reaction to emotional expressions we need to break up the flow of normal interaction and compare the baby's reaction to one discrete expression versus another.

Some of the earliest work on the recognition of facial expression did use this technique. Charlotte Bühler (1930) and her colleagues in Vienna spent hundreds of hours watching a group of infants who were being temporarily housed in the *Kinderübernahmstelle*, a reception centre for children who were to be adopted or placed in another institution. Based on these observations, they subsequently devised a test schedule that covered various aspects of infant development including social development. The test items for five months probed for a differentiation by the baby between happy and angry behaviour. The description given by Bühler is as follows: 'Experimenter bends over the child, brings her face close to his (10 in. away), smiles and addresses him in a friendly fashion for 30 seconds. Suddenly she changes her tone, wrinkles her brows, and talks to the child angrily.'

The child is scored for 'smiling and positive expressional movements in answer to the friendly attitude, negative expressional movements in answer to the angry attitude.' At six months, the test requires that the experimenter hide from the child, and speak in friendly and then angry tones. A correct response is scored in terms of the expressive movements of the face to the experimenter's voice, so that imitation is easily ruled out. At seven months, the experimenter remains silent and simply produces a friendly facial expression, followed by an angry one. Credit is again awarded only for selective responding provided it is not imitative, although in this case imitation is harder to rule out. Bühler (1930) reports that, between five and seven months, babies respond selectively to the two types of expression, although from eight months on, the infant begins to treat the angry face as a game or joke, and responds positively rather than negatively.

This early work is very suggestive. Bühler's observations lead us to expect that from five months and possibly earlier the infant will respond appropriately to different facial expressions, especially if these expressions are accompanied by variations in tone of voice. Recent experimental studies have begun to provide solid support for these expectations.

Jeanette Haviland and Mary Lelwica (1987) asked mothers to engage in a miniature dialogue with their ten-week-old babies. The mothers sat facing their babies and displayed each of three emotions: happiness, sadness or anger. For each emotion, mothers adopted the appropriate facial expression and talked in the relevant tone of voice, be it happy, sad or angry. Each emotion was presented repeatedly, with rest periods. The babies' facial reactions to these three emotions were then filmed and analysed.

The babies clearly distinguished between the three emotions in their reactions, particularly when they were presented for the first time. For example, in response to their mother's expression of happiness, they looked happy; in response to her anger, they looked angry, or remained still; in response to her sadness, they did not look sad but they often engaged in mouthing, chewing and sucking. Parallel results were obtained by Termine and Izard (1988). Mothers were asked to look and talk in either a happy or a sad fashion as they sat face-to-face with their nine-month-old babies, and then to maintain that same expression while the babies were given several different sets of toys to play with one after another. Overall, the babies did seem to discern their mothers' expressed mood. When the mother appeared happy, the baby often looked at her, and expressed interest and happiness. When the mother appeared sad, the baby looked at her less often - although still expressing interest, and also expressed more anger and occasional sadness. These differential effects carried over to the play period when the toys were introduced. If the mother expressed happiness rather than sadness, their babies spent more time playing with the toys.

Taken together, these results are very important. From about ten weeks, babies appear to react differently and appropriately depending on the emotion that the mother expresses. More work will be needed to establish just how sensitive the baby is, but in the meantime we have evidence supporting Darwin's claims that babies recognize and respond to the meaning of a caretaker's expression.

Before turning to look at further evidence from older infants, we should briefly consider one objection. Perhaps the young infant is just a good mimic. We have already mentioned some evidence showing that even newborn babies can engage in selective imitation of a model's facial movements. Perhaps, young babies do not really grasp the meaning behind a smile or an angry expression; rather they simply try to reproduce such an expression when they see one. This interpretation has a superficial plausibility, but it does not fit the detailed results described above. For example, Haviland and Lelwica (1987) noticed that the babies were much less mobile when they were confronted by their mother displaying anger: yet their mothers were no less animated in their display of that emotion. It seems more plausible to suppose that this immobility is akin to the freezing response that is seen in toddlers and indeed in older children when they see or hear an adult expressing anger (Cummings, 1987; Cummings, Iannotti and Zahn-Waxler, 1985; Jordano, 1986). Similarly, Termine and Izard found that the babies were more likely to look away from their mother and played less with their toys if she looked sad; these reactions do not suggest that the baby is simply engaged in a detached copying of the mother's expression with no sensitivity to its meaning.

Social referencing

So far we have looked at the way in which an emotional dialogue can be arranged between adult and baby. The caretaker expresses an emotion and the baby responds appropriately. We now look at a more complex type of communication, one in which the adult does not communicate directly with the infant but expresses an emotional stance toward some object or event in the environment. If the baby can interpret that stance correctly, we might expect the baby to respond differently to the object or event in question. An example will make this clearer: father and baby encounter a stranger. The father looks at the stranger and greets him in a positive way with a smile and a happy tone of voice. Cued by this emotional stance, the baby may be more disposed than usual to approach the stranger. Evidence for this cuing function of an adult's emotional expression is now quite firm. The phenomenon has come to be known as social referencing

It was first identified in some detail by Mary Klinnert and her colleagues in Denver (Klinnert, Campos, Sorce, Emde and Svejda, 1983). They noticed that towards the end of the first year of life infants who are faced with an object that they are uncertain about often look toward their mother as if for guidance. The mother, in turn, can provide that guidance by offering an encouraging smile or an anxious frown.

Mary Klinnert (1984) carried out an illustrative study. Babies of 12 and 18 months were tested on three different trials. On each trial a toy was introduced, at some distance from the baby. Once the baby looked towards the mother, the mother adopted a particular facial expression: a smile for one toy, a fearful face for another toy and a neutral face for the remaining toy. Mothers held this expression for the next minute so that the baby could look away and back at her face several times, and would always be exposed to the same expression. The results were clearest for the smiling and fearful expressions: initially – that is to say for the first toy –

expression had no effect. When the second and third toys were presented, however, the infants tended to respond to the fearful face as opposed to the smiling face by approaching the mother more quickly, by remaining close to her and by touching her more.

These results are exciting because we again have a selective and appropriate response to different expressions. The babies were emboldened by their mother's positive reaction but inhibited by her apparently fearful reaction. In addition, their reactions were obviously not imitative: they changed their position relative to the toy but their mothers did not do so. So, by 12 months, we can conclude that infants not only react within a social dialogue in an appropriate manner to an emotional expression, they are also guided by an adult's emotion in their behaviour toward objects or events in the environment.

How exactly does the adult's expression exert its regulatory effect on the baby? One possibility is that the adult's expression directly influences the baby's tendency to move away or to stay close. A positive expression encourages the baby to move away whereas a negative expression, makes the baby stay close. This possibility is neatly ruled out by an experiment of the Denver investigators (Sorce, Emde, Campos and Klinnert, 1985). They looked at the impact of the mother's facial expression on whether babies would crawl over what appeared to be a fairly sharp drop (the so-called visual cliff). When the drop was of an intermediate height so that the babies were uncertain whether to cross or not, most of them crossed if the mother smiled, but none did so if she looked fearful. Since the mother was on one side of the cliff and the baby on the other, a positive expression encouraged exploration by drawing the baby *towards* the mother. Conversely, a fearful expression discouraged exploration, and left the baby hesitating at some distance from the mother. Clearly, the mother's facial expression does not directly regulate the probability that the baby will move towards or away from the mother.

An alternative interpretation is that the mother's emotional expression influences the baby's general level of exploration. To make this suggestion more concrete, we may borrow from the ideas of John Bowlby (1973). He argued that the infant's behaviour is organized into distinct systems. There is an attachment system which ensures that the baby maintains secure contact with the mother, and there is an exploratory system which guides the investigation of novel objects in the nearby environment. Accordingly, we can think of the adult's facial expression as a signal that activates or suppresses the exploratory system. It could achieve this impact by shifting the baby's mood towards either confidence or wariness. This interpretation allows us to explain the baby's behaviour facing a novel toy or the visual cliff: encouraged by its mother's positive expression the baby will confidently explore the toy or cross the cliff; inhibited by its mother's fearful or angry expression it will hesitate or stay still.

A third and final interpretation incorporates the notion of predication. Suppose that the infant can figure out which object the mother is directing her emotion towards. The baby might do this by noting the mother's line of regard. We know from other evidence that by about nine months babies can detect the mother's line of regard because they will re-direct their own gaze if she turns to look at an interesting object (Butterworth and Cochran, 1980; Scaife and Bruner, 1975). Having noted the mother's object of attention, the baby might treat her emotional reaction as a predicate or comment that is directed towards it and it alone. This account implies that the mother's emotion will have a highly selective effect on the baby's behaviour. It will not regulate the global amount of exploration, rather it will regulate approach to specific objects.

Recent evidence supports this last interpretation. The baby does treat the adult's facial expression as a commentary about a particular object or event. For instance, in one study mothers were asked to express delight, disgust or neutrality (i.e. silence) towards a particular toy when it was introduced (Hornik, Risenhoover and Gunnar, 1987). Other toys were scattered about the room. Their children aged 12 months responded appropriately but selectively: they stayed further away from the designated toy and played less with it if the mother expressed disgust, but behaviour towards the other toys and overall mood was unaffected. A similar pattern was also found a few minutes later, even though at this point the mother remained neutral. Indeed, the Denver group found that fifteen-month-old infants hesitated to touch a particular object if the experimenter had looked and sounded angry when they had approached it some 30 minutes earlier (Bradshaw, Campos and Klinnert, 1986). In conclusion, an adult's emotional reaction does not simply have a global effect on the baby's current exploratory behaviour; it influences the baby's exploration of a particular object and it exerts that influence for some time.

Origins of recognition

The evidence described so far shows that quite early in the first year of life, babies adjust their social behaviour to the emotion expressed by their caretaker. By the end of the first year of life, they extend this selectivity to objects in the environment; they seem to recognize that adults do not simply express emotion, rather they express emotion in a targeted fashion toward particular objects. Babies approach or avoid an object in terms of the emotional message that an adult conveys about it, or did convey at some earlier point in time.

How does the baby arrive at this understanding of emotional expression? We can fall back on Darwin's nativist interpretation: 'an innate feeling' that tells the infant what emotion is being expressed and perhaps an instinct of sympathy that arouses the same feeling; but other alternatives are available.

One possibility is that the facial expressions of the caretaker are followed by different consequences; a smiling face is followed by desirable consequences, a frightened face is followed by frightening consequences, and so forth. Since the consequences elicit the appropriate emotion in the baby, the expressions that signal their arrival would gradually come to be associated with the consequences and also with the emotions that they elicit.

A second possibility is that imitation does play a key role, but not through detached copying. Suppose that from an early age the baby selectively imitates particular facial expressions. Suppose, further, that the production of a particular facial expression is sufficient to elicit the emotion typically associated with that facial expression in the baby. There is some research with adults suggesting that this type of feedback from the muscles of the face to emotional state does occur (Laird, 1974). The upshot would be that the infant should eventually come to associate the appropriate emotional state with a particular facial expression. To take a concrete case: the baby would, at first, observe its caretaker smiling but attach no meaning to that expression. It would, however, come to imitate the smile; the feedback resulting from the smile would elicit feelings of happiness; after several repetitions of this sequence, happiness would come to be associated with the perception of a smile whether the baby imitated that smile or not.

These two accounts depart radically from Darwin in supposing that each emotional expression that the baby perceives is initially quite neutral: it carries no affective meaning at all, and it acquires meaning by dint of an association mediated by either external consequences or by imitation. Despite the radical differences among the three interpretations, they do share one important feature: they each assume some mechanism whereby the emotion displayed by a caretaker is aroused in the observing infant. Recall that Darwin postulated both an innate recognition device and also an 'instinct of sympathy'.

I prefer to avoid postulating any such mechanism for the generation of sympathetic or contagious emotion. In my view, there may well be an innate recognition of the significance of emotion by the young infant, along the lines proposed by

Darwin, but with no correlated arousal. The recognition device would lead the baby to attribute meaning to an emotional expression without either triggering or depending upon correlated arousal of the same emotion in the infant. Indeed, as we shall see in the next chapter, this latter type of contagious excitation could yield only a limited understanding of another person's emotion. In their second year, children definitely move beyond that limited understanding. They react appropriately to another person's emotion even if they show no obvious sign of sharing that emotion.

Summary and conclusions

At the beginning of this chapter, I asked how children start to understand the mental states of other people. Emotions are often expressed facially and vocally by those who feel them, and for that reason one might suppose that very young children find them easy to understand. Darwin (1872) made two relevant claims. He argued first that human beings have a universal, innate repertoire of discrete facial expressions, and second that such expressions are endowed with meaning for the infant by an innate recognition device. Cross-cultural studies, particularly those by Paul Ekman and his associates, have provided evidence for the universality of facial expressions. Recent research with babies also provides considerable support for Darwin's nativist claim concerning the production of facial expressions, at least for the expression of distress, of happiness, and of anger. It seems likely that future research will extend these findings to other negative emotions, particularly fear, sadness and surprise.

The case for innate recognition of the meaning of particular facial expressions is more difficult to establish and may remain so. Yet we do have good evidence for early if not innate recognition of meaning. Infants' social behaviour changes appropriately and non-imitatively in response to the different facial expressions of their caretaker from ten weeks and upward. By the end of the first year, babies can even attach emotional meaning to a particular object in the environment. If the infant's caretaker expresses a positive rather than a negative emotion towards an object the infant is less likely to retreat from or avoid the object.

How exactly the caretaker's emotional expressions come to regulate the infant's social and exploratory behaviour is still uncertain. Darwin could be right to postulate an innate recognition device, but other interpretive mechanisms remain plausible. Whatever the explanation, it is now clear that the one-year-old infant has a rudimentary capacity to attach meaning to particular emotional expressions and to see them as making reference in a selective fashion to particular objects. In the next chapter, I shall ask when infants appreciate the meaning of an emotional expression in terms of what it signifies about the person expressing it.

NOTES

1 As Caron, Caron and Myers (1985) subsequently pointed out, it is difficult to be sure that infants are really focusing on the different emotional configurations being expressed rather than isolated features that often accompany those configurations. For example, perhaps the infants were noticing that in all the happy faces the person's teeth were visible, or that in all the surprised faces the eyes were rounded and the whites more noticeable. Even when films of moving faces rather than pictures of still faces are used (e.g. Caron, Caron and MacLean, 1988) this problem of interpretation arises. From the work of Ekman and Izard described earlier, we know that happy faces will have several component movements in common, as will surprised faces, so that the infants may respond to these movements, gradually habituating to their repeated presentation, and then showing more interest when new movements are presented. Hence, this type of selective attention shows only that the baby can see that several happy (or surprised) expressions have something in common with one another; it does not show that babies are recognizing a complete facial configuration. Nevertheless, the results are important in showing that young infants can identify recurrent components of a facial expression despite the presence of irrelevant, variable features.

2 Surprisingly, Walker (1982) and Spiegler and Caron (1986) use these results to argue that babies are sensitive to information which is invariant across the two modalities. This seems to force a Gibsonian interpretation on the data when it may be inappropriate, because the one obvious invariant that could have cued the infants – the temporal synchrony between movements of the voice and changes in the sound of the voice – was ruled out. Walker-Andrews (1986) found that infants tended to look at the matching facial expression even if the lips were covered and invisible, or when sound and lip-movements were desynchronized (Walker, 1982). Similarly, Spiegler and Caron (1986) using a habituation technique found that six- and seven-month infants who heard a happy or angry tone of voice could subsequently identify the facial expression that matched the tone of voice that they had heard. Since no sound-track was available during this post-test, detection of synchrony could not have helped the infants to match.

Although there are some alternative candidates to temporal synchrony that have not yet been investigated (e.g. tempo) it may be more appropriate to interpret the results as showing that infants can treat quite disparate types of information as belonging together rather than to insist that they must be detecting some invariant information common to both facial expression and tone of voice. Such grouping might be based on the concurrent experience of particular facial expressions and particular tones of voice, or on innate mechanisms, similar to those postulated for the recognition of certain phonemes by both ear and eye (Kuhl, 1987; Kuhl and Meltzoff, 1982).

2

Hurting and comforting

By the end of the first year of life, children respond selectively and appropriately to their mother's facial expression. This selective responding, for example the tendency to approach or retreat from an object depending on whether the mother smiles or looks fearful, is a major step in the understanding of emotion. It implies that the infant can grasp at some level whether the person's emotional stance is positive or negative – whether it signals encouragement or discouragement. It also implies that the infant understands the intentionality of the person's emotion – the fact that it is directed towards one particular object rather than another. Still, no matter how appropriate these reactions, the baby makes no deliberate effort to bring about any change in another person's emotion. The baby reacts to emotion but does not seek to bring about emotion.

In the course of the second year, an important change takes place. First, children begin deliberately to comfort other people. Their efforts may be tentative or clumsy initially, but they are qualitatively different from anything that can be observed in the first year of life. This change should not, of course, be taken to suggest that little children become paragons of virtue. Although they become more adept at comforting and relieving distress, they also become more adept at provoking distress by teasing, hurting and annoying other children and adults. From a theoretical point of view, this combination of increased sympathy and spite is particularly interesting. It suggests that young children are beginning to identify the conditions or actions that will start or stop an emotional state in another person. Their efforts to change another person's emotional state constitute a clear advance on the type of behaviour that we see around 12 months of age. Children are beginning to have some appreciation of how an emotion fits into a causal sequence. Below, I take a closer look at this remarkable change.

Comforting

Judy Dunn and her colleagues asked mothers in Cambridge, England to keep a record of the behaviour of their eldest child towards a younger brother or sister (Dunn, Kendrick and MacNamee, 1981). The older children ranged from two to four years and the younger siblings were 8 or 14 months. Mothers reported that about a quarter of the older children 'frequently' comforted their sibling if he or she was upset during the first month; about one third did so 'occasionally' and another third did so only 'rarely'. Most children, then, were helpful toward their brother or sister, although some helped more often. It was also clear that the distress of the younger sibling did not always elicit help. Sometimes, the elder children remained neutral; sometimes they seemed to positively enjoy their younger sibling's distress or made it worse; and a frequent reaction was simply to become upset themselves.

The older children's efforts to comfort were apparently not in vain. By 14 months, almost one-third of the younger children went to their older siblings for comfort. This was more likely to occur in families where the elder child often tried to comfort the younger one, did not mind sharing his or her toys, and where fights were infrequent. By 14 to 16 months, several of the younger siblings had begun to reciprocate by comforting their older brothers and sisters when they were upset. At this age, children also comfort their parents. For example, a father describes the following incident involving his 14-month-old son J.:

> When we came home this afternoon, I slipped and fell and came down really whacking my nose. I was in real pain and sat down in the rocker in J.'s room, holding and rubbing my nose. J. was very sympathetic. He acted for me the way I do when he hurts himself. He hugged and patted me and even offered me his blanket that he uses when he's hurt or tired. He seemed very upset, whether for me or because of me. (Wolf, 1982)

The above findings were all based on parental reports. Does direct observation of family interaction corroborate this picture? When Judy Dunn and Carol Kendrick made home visits in Cambridge they observed helpful or sympathetic actions by 80 per cent of the older siblings (Dunn and Kendrick, 1979). These incidents included those in which the younger child was upset and the older child offered food or toys, or the younger child was frustrated and received help. Dunn and Kendrick also spotted the occasional use of more unconventional strategies, particularly by younger children. For example, they describe the following episode involving Len, a stocky boy of 16 months with a big stomach, who often amused his parents by approaching them and pulling up his T-shirt to reveal a splendid stomach: Martin, Len's three-year-old brother, had fallen off the climbing frame and was crying vigorously. Len watched his brother. He then went up to Len, pulled up his T-shirt to show off his stomach, vocalized and looked expectantly at Len.

A longitudinal study by Carolyn Zahn-Waxler and Marion Radke-Yarrow (1982) gives a bit more detail about how reactions to distress change from 10 to 30 months. Mothers were trained to keep records of what children did when someone was distressed in their immediate vicinity. In addition, the children's reactions were observed when their mothers or the investigators feigned mild distress.

Various stages in children's reactions could be seen. Between 10 and 12 months, children remained unresponsive bystanders about one-third of the time; they either showed no discernible reaction or they simply watched. In about half the incidents, the children showed some sign of distress themselves: they frowned, looked sad or cried. At this age, however, the children scarcely ever sought to comfort the person in distress. Over the next 12 months, children showed fewer signs of distress themselves but active interventions became increasingly common: children approached the person in distress, and tentatively touched or patted him or her. Beginning at around 18 months these initiatives were translated into more complicated efforts to offer comfort: children brought objects to the distressed person, made suggestions about what to do, expressed sympathy in words, sought the help of a third party, and even attempted to protect the victim.

Often the child's behaviour revealed not just a diagnosis of the other person's distress, but an understanding of what the other person was distressed about. For example, a child of 20 months sees its mother hurt her foot. The child expresses concern, runs over to the mother, says 'hurt foot', and rubs the mother's foot. Another child, also aged 20 months, has upset its mother by making a mess. The child tries to placate the mother, saying: 'I want Mommy', hugs her, says, 'I wipe it up' and proceeds to do so.

By the age of 20 to 24 months, children responded on about one-third of those occasions in which they saw someone in distress (Zahn-Waxler, Radke-Yarrow and King, 1979). One might have expected that children would respond differently depending on whether they had or had not caused the distress. In fact, this was not the case. Whether they had simply witnessed or had instigated distress, they intervened just as often. On the other hand, there were dramatic individual differences in reactions to distress. Some children responded to more than half the incidents, whereas others responded to only about one in twenty.

A classic study of the 1930s carries the story forward from two to four years, and out from the home into the nursery school. Based on 100 days of direct naturalistic observation, Lois Murphy (1937) observed children to help others in distress, to protect and defend them, and to punish whoever had caused the distress. She also saw instances where one child's distress led another child to laugh, to attack, or simply to watch. A substantial minority of the children, approximately one-quarter of them, were never seen to show sympathy to another child.

Pulling together the evidence from these various studies, we arrive at the following picture. In the course of their second year, young children begin to try to alleviate distress in another person; they comfort their parents and siblings at home, and later they comfort other children in the nursery school, particularly if they are hurt. These attempts to give comfort are not unsuccessful, because children will go to their brother or sister if they are upset, especially if that sibling has been well-disposed in the past.

Children's reactions to another person's distress change with age. Until the end of the first year, they usually remain bystanders. Admittedly, they are not always passive bystanders -they often become upset themselves, but they do not make any active attempt to comfort somebody else in distress. Active interventions become increasingly common in the second and third year. They usually involve gestures or words of sympathy and the sharing or retrieval of appropriate objects, but more idiosyncratic approaches are also tried.

Reactions to another person's distress vary enormously from child to child. Whether children are observed at home or in the nursery school, some children prove to be very responsive to another's distress, whereas others rarely respond. Moreover, the ways in which children respond to distress remain fairly stable in these early years; some often respond with concern whereas others often respond with indifference or even aggression (Cummings, Hollenbeck, Iannotti, Radke-Yarrow and Zahn-Waxler, 1986). Later, I shall examine possible explanations for these individual differences. First, however, it will be helpful to get a more balanced picture of how children behave towards their siblings and parents.

Hurting

When mothers are asked to report on episodes in which older children upset a younger brother or sister, such episodes turn out to be just as prevalent as attempts to comfort (Dunn, Kendrick and MacNamee, 1981). Moreover, it is the older child of three years and upward who is more likely to start the fight than the younger child (Abramovitch, Corter and Lando, 1979; Abramovitch, Corter and Pepler, 1980). The asymmetry can be quite pronounced. For example, Dunn and Kendrick (1982) report that in some families as many as 85 per cent of the interactions involved the younger child acting in a friendly fashion and the older child behaving in a negative fashion.

Despite the overall tendency for the older sibling to be more aggressive, the amount of harmony or conflict varied enormously from family to family as indexed by the proportions of mutually friendly and mutually hostile episodes (i.e. where both siblings behaved in a hostile or friendly way). The proportion of mutually hostile encounters ranged from zero to 50 per cent, and the proportion of mutually friendly encounters ranged from zero to 85 per cent

Hitting, poking or pinching a brother or sister may not involve a deliberate attempt to cause distress. One could conceivably argue that two- and three-year-olds strike out in a more or less involuntary fashion when they are frustrated, with no intention to hurt anyone. However, a close look at the pattern of behaviour shows that this is too charitable an interpretation. When children are confronted by a brother or sister in distress, they are especially likely to do something to exacerbate that distress if they provoked it in the first place. Such repeated aggravation is obviously part of a deliberate strategy (Dunn and Munn, 1986). Moreover, children often use techniques that are planned rather than involuntary. This is particularly clear in the case of non-violent ploys. Consider, for example, the following episode reported by Dunn and

Kendrick (1979): Gary persists in reaching for and handling the magnetic letters which three-year-old Tracey is playing with. Tracey repeatedly, albeit gently, says 'no'. Gary persists. As a last resort, Tracey carries the letters to a higher table out of Gary's reach. Gary, who is angry and starts to cry, goes to the sofa, picks up Tracey's rag doll (a comfort object) and holds it tight while looking at Tracey. She, in her turn, now starts to cry and comes to retrieve her doll. In a study of conflict between toddlers, Dunn and Munn (1985) describe an equally deliberate stratagem by C. C.'s mother explains to the interviewer that Amy (C.'s sister) is frightened of spiders. There is one toy spider that Amy particularly hates. Overhearing this remark, C. runs to the next room, searches in the toy box, finds the toy spider, and pushes it toward Amy, who starts crying.

In line with the developmental changes that we saw for comforting, such teasing becomes increasingly frequent during the second year (Dunn and Munn, 1985). By 16 and 18 months, most incidents involve the removal of the older sibling's comfort object, or destruction of some favourite possession. By 24 months, however, more subtle techniques are deployed. For example, one child teased her sister by pretending to be her imaginary friend.

Teasing is not directed only at siblings; it is also directed at the mother. Moreover, just as teasing of siblings increased in frequency during the second year, so did teasing of the mother, although the strategy was suitably altered. It usually consisted in looking at the mother and smiling or laughing while carrying out a forbidden act.

Individual differences in comforting and hurting

We have seen that children in the home often comfort their siblings but they also often hurt or irritate them. Recalling the enormous individual differences among children in their readiness to hurt or comfort, how do these individual differences come about?

First we may ask whether the variation in these two types of behaviour fits together in any way. Two interesting possibilities come to mind. First, there might be a positive correlation between the two types of behaviour, particularly in their more deliberate and planful manifestations. Children who comfort more might also hurt and tease more. This kind of association would come about if children varied along what might be called an engaged to detached continuum in terms of their relationship with their sibling: the more engaged children would display a combination of positive and negative behaviour, whereas children who have a more distant, less involved relationship would neither comfort nor provoke their siblings very often. Some support for this expectation is to be found in the study by Lois Murphy (1937) mentioned earlier. She found that children who were inclined to express sympathy were also likely to express aggression, and she put this down to a factor of general sociability that encompassed negative as well as positive behaviour. Such a pattern might also come about if children vary in terms of their social insight, being more or less adept at figuring out what would upset or soothe another child. This interpretation presupposes that such insight is morally neutral; it is a mere tool which can be used for good or bad ends depending on other factors at work in the child.

A second possibility is that there is a negative correlation, so that siblings who often hurt rarely comfort, and siblings who often comfort rarely hurt. This kind of result has an obvious intuitive appeal. It would fit in with the everyday notion that some children, either because of their temperament, or perhaps because of an orientation to social relationships that they have built up, are both hostile and unsympathetic.

In dealing with this question, Dunn and Kendrick (1982) are careful to point out that 'many children showed both friendly social behaviour and some physical aggression', just as Murphy might have expected. Nevertheless, they also report data suggesting that for some children the second model may be more appropriate. None of the children who responded to a younger sibling's distress with glee, or deliberately increased their distress ever comforted that sibling. These results suggest that there is a group of children who know how to upset or hurt another child, but lack the ability or motivation to sympathize.

How should we explain this patterning? Children might learn from the way in which their parents react to distress or express anger. They might also vary in their ability to imagine themselves in the shoes of another child. Investigators have begun to look at this issue and have produced some striking results.

Explaining individual differences

When one child upsets another, parents can intervene in various ways. They can comfort the victim; they can scold the child who has caused the distress; and they can encourage that child to make some type of reparation. Carolyn Zahn-Waxler and her colleagues argue that mothers play a considerable role in offering their children an interpretation of another person's distress (Zahn-Waxler, Radke-Yarrow and King, 1979). This is especially true when it is distress that the child has caused. In such cases, mothers are more likely to draw attention to the child's role and to adopt a moral tone. Specifically, they found that when children (aged 20 to 24 months) had caused the distress, as opposed to merely witnessed it, mothers were more likely to offer an explanation, more likely to moralize ('You made Doug cry. It's not nice to bite'), and more likely to suggest a positive intervention ('Why don't you give Jeffrey your ball?'). On the other hand, when the children had not caused the distress but merely witnessed it, mothers were more likely to do something for the victim (e.g. to pick him or her up, and to offer comfort), to reassure the child who was a witness, or not to react at all.

Do these reactions have any impact on children? Zahn-Waxler and her colleagues divided mothers into two groups: those high and low on a given technique, and checked to see whether their children differed in what they called reparation, i.e. attempts to comfort or help their victims. Some maternal behaviours did appear to be effective. Specifically, statements of principle by the mother (e.g. 'People are not for hitting'; 'You must never poke anyone's eyes'; 'You can talk about biting but you cannot ever do it') were associated with more reparation by the child both in the same time-period, and in a second time-period, approximately four or five months later.

The mothers' reactions also influenced children's behaviour when the children were witnesses rather than instigators of distress. There were some indications that explanations to the child promoted altruistic reactions, whereas unexplained prohibitions (e.g. 'Stop that') reduced them.

Some of the most dramatic evidence for the role of parents comes from the study of children who have been subjected to physical abuse. When such children are observed in a preschool setting, they are frequently more aggressive than other children. They are also less likely to help or share with another child than children who come from the same social background but have no known history of abuse (George and Main, 1979; Hoffman-Plotkin and Twentyman, 1984; Trickett and Kuczynski, 1986).

The work of Mary Main and Carol George (1985) is particularly informative in showing how abused children respond to distress in another child. They compared two groups of children from one to three years of age. One group came from disadvantaged families, in several of which fathers were absent and mothers were living on welfare. The other group of children came from similarly disadvantaged homes, but in addition the children had been abused and battered. The severity of the maltreatment ranged from severe punishment to skull and bone fractures and severe burns. None of the children in the first group had any known history of such maltreatment.

Observation of these two groups of children responding to another child's distress during day-care sessions revealed clear differences. Abused toddlers never responded with obvious concern for the distressed child. At best, they mechanically patted or attempted to quiet the crying child, or they simply looked on. More often, however, they responded in a negative fashion. Some became hostile and made threatening gestures (both verbal and facial) or direct physical attacks on the crying child. Alternatively, they became upset and showed fear or distress or a mixture of the two. In complete contrast, non-abused children never displayed this latter type of upset, and only one made a threatening gesture. Their most common response was to look at or mechanically pat the crying child and, in response to about one-third of the episodes of distress, they displayed a more active concern. Recall that this figure for active concern is the same as the one obtained by Zahn-Waxler and her colleagues (1979) from mothers' reports on children in the home.

In some of the most disturbing incidents (involving three abused toddlers) an alternation between comforting and attacking the distressed child was seen. For example, one toddler pursued and tormented another child precisely until the child exhibited distress, and then mechanically comforted the child, smiling at the same time.

These data are both reassuring and disturbing. First, on the positive side, it seems that the type of concerned comforting found in intact, stable, working-class families (Dunn and Kendrick, 1982) or in middle-class families (Zahn-Waxler, Radke-Yarrow and King, 1979) is also found among children in a day-care setting, even when the children come from stressed, disadvantaged homes, where as often as not there is a single parent living on welfare. On the negative side, abused children respond to another child's distress as normal children might respond to displays of anger (Denham, 1986; Strayer, 1980); they become upset, or they ignore the distress or occasionally they respond with aggression; they rarely make comforting or helpful gestures unless requested to do so. Abusive parents appear to transmit an abusing style to their very young children long before these children have any parental responsibilities placed upon them. The mode of transmission is not clear. Do abusing parents inhibit and distort an inherent empathic tendency? Do they offer an abusing model to infants who start off with no inherent tendencies either toward empathy or hostility when faced with distress? Do they fail to reason with the children when they hurt or upset another child? Certainly there is evidence that abusive parents are much more likely to punish their children than to reason with them when the children are aggressive or act selfishly toward other children. Non-abusive parents, by contrast, use reasoning just as often as punishment (Trickett and Kuczynski, 1986). Finally, it is conceivable that abusing parents pass on a genetic pattern of hypersensitivity to and aversion from distress in others, irrespective of how they treat their children. Whatever the final interpretation of these findings, they show that empathic concern for another child's distress is not ineluctably wired into the emotional repertoire of a young child.

Cognitive factors

So far we have approached the question of individual differences by considering the impact of the family. We can also ask about cognitive differences among children. Once a child has seen or heard another child in distress, what mental processes lead one child to offer comfort and another child to turn away or even to become aggressive? It seems reasonable to suppose that children differ in the extent to which they can put themselves in the shoes of the other child, so as to appreciate both what led to the other child's distress and what might alleviate it, even when they themselves feel little or no distress.

An interesting study by Robert Stewart and Robert Marvin (1984) provides some support for this idea. Stewart (1983) had noticed that when three- and four-year-olds were left by their mothers in a waiting room, about half of them acted to provide comfort or reassurance to a younger sibling. He then set out to explore the source of this variation. Children aged three to five years were given two tests of perspective-taking. In one, they were told about the preference of some imaginary child for a particular outcome such as not getting dirty or climbing very high. Notice that the preference is slightly idiosyncratic – it is not likely to be universally preferred. Children were then asked to say which of two activities the imaginary child would prefer. One of the two activities would lead to the desired outcome and one would not. To answer correctly, they had to keep the child's somewhat idiosyncratic preferences in mind, rather than choose egocentrically between the activities in terms of their own preferences. In the second task, children were assessed for their appreciation that two other people might know the location of a hidden object even if they themselves had closed their eyes when it was hidden. Although different in content, both tasks required that children distinguish between their own preference or knowledge and that of another person. Based on their performance on these two tasks, the children were classified into two groups: good and poor perspective-takers.

In a separate part of the study, the children were left alone with their younger sibling in a waiting room. All the younger siblings responded to the departure of their mother with varying degrees of distress and within ten seconds of their mother's departure about half the older children turned to their younger brother or sister and offered some type of comforting response, such as approaching and hugging the infant, offering verbal reassurance of their mother's eventual return, or offering toys as a distraction. The remaining children responded to their sibling's distress by turning away and concentrating on their own play, by singing or talking loudly, or by covering their ears and moving away.

To what extent was there a link between the perspective-taking ability of the older siblings and their readiness to comfort their younger sibling? The relationship was by no means perfect but there was a clear association: the majority of the children who did well on the perspective-taking task promptly comforted their younger sibling, whereas the majority of those who were poor at perspective-taking did not.[1]

Both mothers and younger siblings behaved differently if the older child was good at perspective-taking. Specifically, when mothers made their departure, they were more likely to ask older siblings who scored well on the perspective-taking tasks to look after their younger sibling.[2] The younger siblings, for their part, were much more likely to approach an older sibling, treating him or her as a secure base, if the older sibling was good at perspective-taking.

These results suggest that cognitive factors are associated both with the actual behaviour of offering comfort to a younger sibling, and with the expectation by other people that such comfort will be offered. Of course, it is important to stress that we do not know how these interconnections are established. Do mothers who request that their elder child look after a younger child promote the perspective-taking ability of the elder child? Alternatively, are mothers simply responding to individual differences over which they have little influence? We cannot be sure. For the moment, the important point to underline is that cognitive factors, particularly the ability to look at a situation from another's perspective, appear to be intimately connected with the willingness to offer comfort. This perspective-taking ability may help because children are often called upon to offer comfort in situations that they themselves do not find distressing. If they cannot understand that the other child may nevertheless have good reason to be distressed, they may react with indifference. Indeed, it is clear from the results of Stewart and Marvin (1984) that the majority of children who comforted their younger sibling were not themselves upset when their mother left. Perspective-taking skill would be needed, therefore, to grasp that although they were not upset by their mother's departure, the same might not apply to their younger sibling. Similarly, observational studies of children in preschool settings show that a hurt child will often elicit help or concern from another child but there is no indication that the young Samaritan must feel distressed in order to intervene (Denham, 1986). These results underline the fact that understanding another's distress and taking remedial steps, may not necessarily involve feeling distress yourself.[3]

Moral and conventional rules

We have looked at children's strategies for upsetting and comforting other children. Such actions are not, of course, morally neutral. Most children will be told at some point that it is good to help, comfort or share with other children and bad to upset them. When do young children begin to attach such moral evaluations to their acts of comfort and provocation? Recent research shows that they are quite sensitive to issues of right and wrong, whatever their behaviour might lead one to expect. Moreover, as I shall try to show, it is likely that their understanding of the emotional reactions of other children plays an important role in that sensitivity.

Consider the results of this next study by Judith Smetana (1981). Three- and four-year-old children were told about a child who engaged in various transgressions, such as hitting another child, taking another child's apple, putting toys away in the wrong place, and not saying grace before a snack. The children were then questioned about these transgressions. As will be apparent, some could be seen as moral transgressions whereas others simply involved deviation from the norms or conventions of the preschool where the children were tested. The children were quite sensitive to this difference. They judged the moral violations as more serious than the conventional violations. For example, whereas they judged that it is 'very bad' to hit another child, they judged that it is only 'a little bit bad' to put toys away in the wrong place. They also maintained that it would be wrong to engage in the moral transgressions even if there were no rules about such actions; for the conventional transgressions, on the other hand, they were more likely to say that such actions would be permissible if they were not proscribed by rule. Taken together, the results suggest that very young children realize that some actions involve a serious breach of a fixed moral code, whereas others merely involve a minor breach of contingent, local rules.

Given the impact of family environment described earlier, one might expect children's sensitivity to the distinction between moral and conventional rules to vary depending on their family background. Take, as an example, children who have been the victims of neglect: it is highly likely that such children will be left to their own devices quite often, and rarely disciplined for quarrelling with other children or hitting them. Faced with such parental indifference, a neglected child might well conclude that hitting or upsetting other children is not a serious offence. To assess the plausibility of this idea, Smetana and her colleagues tested three- to five-year-old children from different family environments: one group had suffered physical abuse; a second had suffered neglect; and a third was a control group of non-maltreated children (Smetana, Kelly and Twentyman, 1984). Despite these differences in family background, the children and their families were comparable on other potentially confounded dimensions such as parental income, education of the mother and intelligence of the child. As in the earlier study, the children were asked to judge the seriousness of various types of transgression. The results were striking. All three groups reached very similar conclusions. They all judged that violations of social convention (e.g. leaving class without permission) were minor offences; more serious offences were respectively: not sharing resources fairly; distressing another child; and being physically aggressive towards another child. There was very little impact of family background to be seen in children's judgements. Rather there was a clear-cut consensus about what constituted a minor as opposed to a major transgression.

These results are very puzzling so long as one focuses on the child's parents as being the main source of information about the difference between moral and conventional rules. Children do have other sources of information, however. In particular, the reactions of children themselves to various types of transgression may be instructive. To find out how children do respond to different types of transgression, Judith Smetana (1984) observed young children playing at their preschools. The reactions of the children, and also of their teachers, were noted whenever a rule violation occurred, such as physical aggression, not sharing toys, making a mess, working in the wrong place, and so forth. The teachers reacted to both moral and conventional violations; if anything, they responded somewhat more often to violations of convention. Their most frequent reaction, in each case, was to issue a command. The reactions of the children, by contrast, were highly selective: they *never* responded to violations of convention, whereas they responded to about a third of the moral violations. Moreover, their reactions to moral violations were potentially highly instructive. As victims of aggression, poaching or aggravation, children expressed (either verbally or non-verbally) the pain or loss that they felt.

Is this pattern also found in the home? Do parents react to a variety of transgressions, moral and conventional, whereas children confine themselves to moral outrage? Judy Dunn and Penny Munn (1987) went into children's homes and kept a record of the disputes that erupted either between the children, or between mother and child. Observations were made when the younger child was 18 months, two years and three years. At each point, the children became embroiled in disputes on a variety of topics: politeness rules (e.g. saying 'please' and 'thank you'), house rules about what to do in which room and when it could be done ('You can't eat that now, it's not tea-time'), rules about possession, sharing and turn-taking, and about disorderly or disruptive behaviour. However, the disputes showed a different focus depending on the protagonists: disputes between mother and child were concentrated on disorderly behaviour and on house rules, whereas squabbles between siblings were concentrated on rules about possession, turn-taking and sharing. Moreover, when the children were only 18 months old, it was conflicts over these latter issues that were especially likely to end in tears or anger. Assuming that the older child was the wrongdoer in such cases, he or she would undoubtedly receive conspicuous feedback from the younger sibling.

Detailed naturalistic observation shows that young children are sensitive to such expressions of emotion in turn-taking disputes. Children who start to appropriate a toy from another child and then see that child look angry or sad as a result will often desist (Camras, 1977). Even a fairly subtle change – a raising of the inner corners of the eyebrows – is sufficient to convey sadness, and to stave off the intervention (Camras, 1977; 1980).

In summary, if we focus not on adult reactions but on the way that the victims themselves react, young children are offered a clear indication that moral transgressions are more serious than violations of convention: even if adults make no clear differentiation for the wrongdoer between a moral breach and a conventional breach, other children certainly do. From such feedback children might be able to work out that even if all adult prescriptions about hitting, snatching and tormenting other children were suddenly suspended – if there were no rules – the reactions of the victims would remain much the same.

Various pieces of evidence support this interpretation. First, if young children are asked to justify a moral rule – to explain why it is wrong to hit other children or take their possessions – they mostly refer to the consequences of such actions for the victim, particularly the harm or distress it will cause (Davidson, Turiel and Black, 1983). On the other hand, if they are asked to justify a conventional rule, they rarely refer to anyone's welfare. Children can also start to categorize an action as morally wrong, rather than conventionally wrong, if they learn that it causes distress: if, for example, they are introduced to some novel activity in a story, and told only that when a story character engages in this activity, it makes other children cry, they judge the action as violating a moral rule rather than a conventional rule, and they back up their judgement by referring to the distress the action causes (Smetana, 1985).

Pursuing this argument, it seems likely that children will vary in their differentiation among transgressions depending on the extent to which they have played with other children. At one extreme, we can imagine an only child who has spent little time with other children. Such a child will be exposed to the somewhat undifferentiated dictates of adults whether he or she commits a moral or a conventional offence. On the other hand, a child who has spent a lot of time with other children, particularly in small unsupervised groups, will have been exposed to a good deal of information about what does and does not constitute a serious breach. Michael Siegel and Rebecca Storey (1985) conducted a study which provides an interesting test of this line of speculation. They compared preschool 'veterans' (four-year-olds who had already had about nine months at preschool) and preschool novices (four-year- olds who had had only about three months at preschool) using the same type of transgressions as Smetana and her colleagues. Both groups judged moral transgression as quite serious; they differed, however, in their conclusions about conventional transgressions. The novices regarded these too as quite serious. Their more nonchalant veteran colleagues, on the other hand, judged the same transgressions as minor. The implication of these results is that the novice arrives at preschool with a considerable excess of moral baggage, convinced that sitting in the wrong place is as serious a crime as poking his or her neighbour. The hurly-burly of the preschool allows the child to cast off some of this excess baggage, by teaching him or her that although adults may take certain conventional violations quite seriously, their classmates often do not care a fig.[4]

If we accept this conclusion, it has several implications. First, it implies that the child's moral intuitions are inextricably bound up with an understanding of emotion. A child who does not understand that someone is distressed nor what caused it will scarcely conclude that the action that caused it is wrong. This does not, of course, mean that the toddler is a moral utilitarian weighing up the happiness or distress that various courses of action will lead to. It is only to suggest that the child is sufficiently sensitive to the reactions of other children to use them to make a broad division between minor (and essentially local) offences and serious transgressions.

The second implication is that adults may be indiscriminate instructors because they are concerned that children adhere to a whole range of rules, some weighty and some petty. This, however, is no bad thing because children can arrive at a distinction between moral and conventional prescription during their encounters with other children. Whether they come from abusive, neglectful or supportive homes will make little difference. Third, it implies, at least for the relatively immediate emotions that are caused by physical aggression, a failure to share, wrongful appropriation, and so forth, that small children everywhere, irrespective of culture or class, will arrive at roughly the same conclusions about what constitutes a serious moral breach. Recent cross-cultural studies provides some support for this conclusion. For example, preschool children in Korea all claim that hitting another person would be wrong whether or not there was a rule proscribing it, whereas they typically acknowledge that eating with one's fingers would be acceptable if there were no rule. Moreover, like their Western counterparts, they went on to explain that hitting another child was wrong because it would upset or hurt the child (Song, Smetana and Kim, 1987).[5]

Finally, there is a paradox to be considered: we have seen that young children irrespective of their family background realize that certain actions, particularly hurting or distressing another child, are wrong. On the other hand, there is also good evidence that children vary a lot in their willingness to abide by these precepts, and some of that variation can be attributed to the child's family background. Abused children, for example, are known to be more aggressive than normal children. How can we square the apparent universality of children's intuitions about right and wrong with the marked variation in aggressive or prosocial behaviour? My guess is that for toddlers, like the rest of us, it is quite easy to appreciate that an action will be distressing, particularly if they are in the role of an observer who sees one person upsetting another. It is more difficult for them to use such knowledge to guide their own actions. The impulse to tease, to strike back and to hurt will often override or distort their knowledge of right and wrong. Judith Smetana and her colleagues (1984) observed this type of egocentricity among three- to five-year-old children who thought that other children's rule violations were more serious and more worthy of punishment than their own. So, we should not expect to see a very close relationship between children's knowledge of right and wrong and their willingness to flout such prescriptions. I shall return to this issue in chapter 4, where children's understanding of guilt and pride will be discussed.

Summary and conclusions

In the second and third year of life, children actively comfort and hurt other people. They no longer simply react to another person's current emotion; they can anticipate the possibility of bringing about a different emotion. Nor do they simply use another person's emotional state as a moderator of their own current exploration; the other person's emotional state becomes a goal in itself, a goal that they actively seek to bring about. To achieve that goal, they will try various techniques in succession, showing some appreciation of the type of event or object that can bring about or alleviate distress. These behavioural changes strongly suggest that there is a major shift in the way that the young child thinks about the nature and causes of emotion. We shall look more closely at those cognitive changes in the next chapter.

Although there appear to be major behavioural changes starting in the second year of life, the particular interventions that young children make do not show a clear-cut, universal pattern. Especially when confronted by another's distress, children show markedly different reactions. In part, these differences appear to reflect their family history. Some parents give their children clear prescriptions about what they should and should not do after they have upset another child and these prescriptions appear to have an effect. They foster the young child's tendency toward reparation or comforting when faced with another child's distress. At the other extreme, parents who physically maltreat their children have children who are disturbed by another child's distress to the point where they exhibit fear or aggression, and those two patterns predominate over or preclude the tendency to comfort. Finally, there is evidence showing that some children are better at taking another child's perspective and more ready to comfort another child as a result.

Despite these variations among preschool children in their willingness to upset or comfort another child, there is a widespread appreciation among three- and four-year-olds, whatever their family background, that actions which cause distress are intrinsically wrong. It seems likely that the emotional reactions of other children to being provoked or tormented bring about that understanding.

NOTES

1 There is a long tradition of empirical work on the relationship between perspective-taking and prosocial behaviour. A recent meta-analysis shows that there is a small but significant relationship between altruism and measures of the capacity to diagnose and predict another person's thoughts and actions, even when the potential contribution of age is partialled out (Underwood and Moore, 1982). Significant relationships are often weak or inconsistent among preschool children (e.g. Zahn-Waxler, Radke-Yarrow and Brady-Smith, 1977). The study by Stewart and Marvin (1984) is unusual in finding a strong relationship. However, their study has several noteworthy features. First, they assessed perspective-taking with tasks that required children to distinguish carefully between the preferences and knowledge of another person and their own; second, they assessed prosocial behaviour in a setting where the emotional reaction of the child receiving comfort was likely to differ from that of the child offering comfort; and third, they conceptualized

perspective-taking as a cognitive prerequisite rather than as a continuum (cf. Denham, 1986).

2 It might be argued that perspective-taking children comforted their sibling more often, simply because they had more often been asked to do so by their mothers. This argument is undermined, however, by the fact that the majority of non-perspective-taking children who received such requests from their mothers failed to comply.

3 Are those children and adults who are empathic (i.e. feel distress) when seeing another person in distress more likely to volunteer help and comfort? A recent meta-analysis of the considerable literature on this topic suggests that when empathy is assessed by asking people to describe their emotional reactions to a distressing film or to a laboratory simulation of distress (as opposed to less life-like materials such as a picture or a story) a modest correlation is found between such reports and the tendency to offer help or comfort, at least for adults, who are probably more accurate in their self-report than children (Eisenberg and Miller, 1987). Even this research, however, fails to demonstrate a simple link between felt distress and altruism. The most analytic work in the area suggests, rather, that it is feelings of concern for the other that prompt an intervention; feelings of distress, if they do not include a component of concern for the other, do not prompt an intervention (Batson, 1987).

4 I have deliberately remained vague about the exact way in which children's reactions might be instructive. Three different possibilities can be distinguished. First, children might learn from observing how the victims of their own transgressions react. Second, they might learn from being victims of other children's transgressions. Third, they might learn from being bystanders to conflicts and disputes between other children. One possible interpretation of the effectiveness of experience in the preschool (Siegel and Storey, 1985) is that, unlike the family where the child will often be a protagonist or victim, it offers considerable opportunity for being an objective bystander.

5 The claim that some rules are rapidly identified as merely conventional is obviously provocative and, not surprisingly, it has been attacked. Shweder, Mahapatra and Miller (1987) claim that young children and indeed adults from the temple town of Bhubaneswar, in Orissa, India do not acknowledge a conventional domain. My position would be that such an acknowledgement is made under very specific circumstances: it is made only for rules whose violation produces indifference among peers, and it is made only if children are exposed to that iconoclastic indifference. If children are questioned about practices whose breach is emotionally repugnant to peers and adults alike, or if they are constantly in the company of older children who act as substitute parents (which is common in India), they may not acknowledge that some rules are merely conventional.

3

Beliefs, desires and emotion

The subjective is made over to others, it is ejected into the individuals of the entourage.

Baldwin (1891)

So far, I have mostly described the behaviour of the baby and toddler in response to another person's emotion. In this chapter, I shall speculate about the way in which the young child conceives of emotional states and situates them within a larger conception of the mind. Rather than concentrating narrowly on emotion, I shall indicate how the child grasps the relationship between beliefs, desires and emotion. My argument will be that children understand other people's mental states by relying on a distinctive type of imaginative understanding.

The imagination, particularly as it is manifested in early pretend play, has often played an equivocal or marginal role in theories of cognitive development. Among psychoanalysts, notably Freud, it has been seen as a means for wish-fulfilment or drive satisfaction, but not as a tool for understanding. Among child psychologists, it has been seen as a faculty that leads the child to escape from or distort reality. For example, despite his careful analysis of the development of pretend play, an analysis which has guided most later research on the topic, Piaget wrote: 'Play enables the child to relive his past experiences and makes for the satisfaction of the ego rather than for its subordination to reality' (Piaget, 1962). I shall argue that the imagination, and more specifically the capacity for make-believe, does allow the child to escape from his or her current reality but that such an escape is functional. It allows the child to entertain possible realities and, what is especially important, to entertain the possible realities that other people entertain. It is a key that unlocks the minds of other people and allows the child temporarily to enter into their plans, hopes and fears.

The first two chapters have underlined an important paradox. It is tempting to suppose that in arriving at a reading of another person's emotion, the infant ends up by experiencing that same emotion through a kind of sympathetic contagion. In chapter 1, we saw that Darwin postulated something akin to this contagion in his six-month-old son. The son looked sad when his nurse pretended to cry and Darwin concluded that 'an innate feeling must have told him that the pretended crying of his nurse expressed grief; and this through the instinct of sympathy excited grief in him.' Yet much of our everyday understanding of emotion scarcely requires such emotional contagion or congruence. Admittedly, we may sometimes feel an empathic concern if we see that someone is upset. However, we can also understand another person's emotion without feeling the same emotion. We may discern their feelings of anxiety or pride and feel no such emotion ourselves. Even when we comfort someone in distress, we are likely to do so out of a feeling of concern for the person, rather than because some equivalent distress has been aroused in us. Recall from the last chapter that the same holds in early childhood. When preschoolers comfort their younger sibling upon the departure of their mother, they do not often exhibit the distress that is almost universal in their younger siblings.[1]

Indeed a moment's reflection shows that this conclusion is not only true of emotion. In order for you to understand my beliefs and assumptions, you need not share them. You may readily know what I believe and why without believing it yourself. Conversely, I may appreciate what you intend or perceive at this moment, but I scarcely need to intend or perceive the same thing.

What does my understanding amount to in such cases? One way to state it is as follows: if I appreciate what you feel or perceive at the moment then I can *imagine* what you feel or perceive. I do not actually experience a mental state like yours.

Imaginative understanding does not involve a contagious transmission of mental states from observed to observer. Rather, when you feel embarrassed or proud, I observe this and imagine what emotion I would feel were I in your shoes. As a result, I generate an 'as if' or pretend emotion. Unless I have contributed to or in some way shared your success or discomfiture, I do not feel any genuine pride or embarrassment myself. Similarly, if I am a spectator at tennis, I can appreciate, by an act of imaginative projection, what you perceive as you receive a service. I can imagine myself in your position with the ball coming towards me, and if my imagery is vivid enough, I may even generate, again in an 'as if' mode, some of the sensations that you experience: the effort of trying to reach the ball, the recoil of the racquet, and so forth. I can imagine all of these sensations without actually having them.

Often, my appreciation of your current emotional state will also require that I imagine, not just what you feel, but what you believe and what you want. Thus, I must imagine what you believe to have occurred (which need not correspond to what has actually occurred). I must also situate that assumed course of events in relation to what I imagine you to want. I can then appreciate why you are now happy or sad, relieved or disappointed.

Can young children achieve this type of imaginative understanding or role-taking? I shall argue that it is possible and in the course of this chapter I describe both a mechanism for its achievement and evidence for that mechanism. The argument builds on ideas advanced by the philosopher Robert Gordon (1986; 1987).[2] Briefly, I shall claim that children are aware of their own mental states, and can project them on to other people using a mechanism that depends crucially on the imagination. There are several pieces to the argument. I will focus briefly on each piece, and then go back and attempt a more detailed description of the supporting evidence. The argument is necessarily tentative at this point. Many details are almost certainly wrong, but if its main lines are correct it will require a re-evaluation of the role of the imagination in early childhood.

Self-awareness The first assumption is that preschool children are aware of their own mental states. They know when they want something, or expect something; they know when they have made a mistake, or feel sad (Johnson, 1988). The most straightforward indication of that self-awareness is to be found in young children's utterances. There is now considerable evidence that very young children can appropriately report their desires, beliefs and emotions. Moreover, they comment on their own psychological states before they comment on those of other people.

The capacity for pretence The second assumption is that young children have a powerful imagination. One obvious index of children's imagination is their pretend play. From about the age of 18 months, children start to endow physical objects with pretend properties, and thereby create a make-believe situation. For example, they pretend that an empty cup has some tea in it or that the tea is too hot to drink. Crucial for the case that I want to establish is the fact that children also start to endow dolls with mental states: desires and plans that may or may not come to fruition within that make-believe situation.

Distinguishing reality from pretence The third assumption is that although children occasionally mix the world of reality and the world of pretence, they do not show any systematic confusion between the two worlds. They know that dolls really cannot run, or feel thirsty, or want a glass of water, or say 'ouch'. So, from an early age, children can construct a make-believe world, yet it is not confused with the real world. The pretend desires, beliefs and emotions with which the child endows its dolls and imaginary characters are not confused with real desires, beliefs and emotions. Equally, the mental states that the child imputes to other people are not confused with the child's own mental states.

Desires, beliefs and emotions The fourth assumption is that the ability to pretend allows children to engage in an imaginative understanding of other people's mental states. Given their capacity for pretend play, children can imagine wanting something they do not actually want. They can also imagine believing something they do not actually believe. On the basis of such simple pretend premises, they can proceed to imagine the emotional reactions of another person who does have such a desire or belief.

A concrete example will make the argument clearer. Children seeing their younger sibling's distress upon mother's departure can imagine wanting her to come back, which is what their younger sibling actually wants. By appraising the status quo in the light of that pretend premise, they can understand the distress that their sibling experiences when that desire is not met – when she does not come back. In addition, by imagining her return, they can proceed to imagine the relief that their sibling would experience. Thus, they can appreciate both why their younger sibling feels sad when mother does not return and why it is reassuring to be told that she will return. In each case, their appreciation of the emotional world of their sibling depends upon taking a make-believe desire as a starting point, and appraising the changing circumstances that might confront their sibling in the light of that premise, so that they can imagine an emotional state that is akin to what their sibling is actually experiencing, or might experience.

Children also attribute to other people beliefs that they do not share, beliefs which they may know to be false. They can conjure up the possible world that another person takes to be the real world. This mode of pretending enables children to endow other people with beliefs and plans that are directed neither at current reality, nor at some as yet unrealized reality, but at a reality that flies in the face of known reality. For example, in their play children can act out the part of both the hider and the seeker. To take on the latter role, they must temporarily set aside what they know to be the case (i.e. the place where the hider is concealed) and pretend that, like the seeker, they think the hider is somewhere else.[3]

Let us now look at the evidence for each of these claims in more detail.

Self-awareness: reports of mental states

Although it is quite possible that children are aware of their mental states before they can talk about them, their emerging ability to talk explicitly about their mental states provides convincing evidence of awareness. Inge Bretherton and her colleagues have found that at about two years of age, children start to describe themselves and other people as creatures that can perceive, feel emotion, have desires, and enter into various cognitive states (Bretherton, McNew and Beeghly-Smith,1981). For example:

> 'I *see* a car' (20 months).
>
> 'I *wanna* take a nap now' (20 months).
>
> 'Et [name for self] is *happy* now' (21 months).
>
> 'I'm *sad* I popped it' (about a balloon; 25 months).
>
> 'I don't *believe* it that Brian went to A . . .' (tries to say Arizona; a neighbour had left for Arizona the previous night; 26 months).

By about two years, words for perceptual (e.g. 'see') and volitional states (e.g. 'want') are produced by almost all children; references to emotional states (e.g. 'happy'; 'mad') are a bit less prevalent but still made by most children; and references to cognitive states (e.g. 'know'; 'think') are made by about one- to two-thirds. Especially important for my argument is the finding that references to the self are more frequent than references to others. This pattern holds for each of the various types of mental state just mentioned: perception, volition, emotion and cognition. It also holds for those statements which discuss the cause, object or consequence of a mental state (Bretherton and Beeghly, 1982).[4] The general lag between statements about the self and about other people is important since it fits the claim that children are initially aware of their own mental states, and subsequently interpret the behaviour of other people by projecting their own mental states on to others.[5]

Recall that in discussing comforting and teasing in chapter 2, it became clear that children have some knowledge of what will activate or alleviate an emotional state. Specifically, in the case of comforting they know something about what might relieve distress, or might have provoked it. In the case of teasing or hurting, they reveal their knowledge of what might cause distress or exacerbate it. This causal reasoning is directed at both the past causes of distress, which they seek to rectify, as well as the future instigation or alleviation of distress.

It is striking therefore that children's remarks about the causes of psychological states show the same preoccupation with the causes of existing distress, both in themselves ('Me fall down. Me cry') and in others ('Grandma mad. I wrote on wall' 'You sad Mommy. What Daddy do?') and its future alleviation ('I cry. Lady pick me up and hold me') or instigation ('Will it be scary?'). Indeed, Bretherton and Beeghly (1982) comment that a large proportion of children's causal utterances were concerned with pleasure and pain, or with pleasant or unpleasant physiological states (being hot, cold, warm, hungry, thirsty, sick, etc.).

The emergence of pretend play

For most children, pretend play emerges between 12 and 24 months of age. As Alan Leslie (1987) has pointed out, pretending is in some ways a very odd sort of ability. From an evolutionary point of view, one might expect there to be a high premium on maintaining an accurate and objective view of the world. A child who acts as if dolls have genuine feelings or as if there were monsters lurking in a dark hallway is scarcely acting upon a veridical picture of the world. Yet such pretend play emerges at an early age, and it becomes more complicated and elaborate during development. It is not a temporary retreat from reality that is quickly abandoned as the child gets older.

It is not easy to define pretend play, but certain key features have been identified. Leslie picks out three of them. First, the infant makes one object stand in for another, different object. Consider the following episode described by Dennie Wolf and her colleagues (Wolf, Rygh and Altshuler, 1984): 'J. (at 24 months) finds an enclosure made from blocks. He picks up a small figure with a wide-brimmed hat on: "Farmer want a bath. Gonna give Farmer a bath."' Here, J. uses the enclosure made from blocks to stand in for the bath. A second feature of pretend is evident in the next episode. Where necessary, the child not only makes one object stand in for another but also creates an imaginary object with no props at all. The narrative continues: 'J. pretends to turn on imaginary faucets at one end of the enclosure.' The third feature of pretend play – the attribution of pretend properties – now appears: 'He swishes the figure round briefly, then says: "Oh no, sooo hot. Gotta put some cold in."' Here, we have not just an imaginary object, namely water, but the attribution of imaginary properties to that water.

Children who took their pretence too seriously, who momentarily forgot that they were engaged in an act of pretence, would do considerable violence to their normal thinking about objects. An ordinary set of blocks would suddenly be credited with quite inappropriate features (faucets, water, etc.). If these thoughts were not only taken literally but also remembered, the child would rapidly end up with a distorted view of the world. To avoid such distortion of everyday reality, children must know how to separate assertions made during pretence from assertions that are true. Although J. pretends that the blocks are a bath with faucets, such a claim should not be taken literally. At the same time, the child must be capable of acting as if such a claim were temporarily true, so that the Farmer can take a bath, the imaginary faucets can deliver water, and the water may turn out to be too hot, just as it often is in reality.

As this example illustrates, there is little doubt that two-year-olds engage in pretend play as defined by Leslie; even a single episode may contain all the prototypical features that he emphasizes: object substitution, object creation and property attribution. Nevertheless, there is another crucial feature of pretend play that rapidly becomes elaborated: the creation and attribution of mental states as opposed to purely physical objects or properties. Dennie Wolf and her colleagues (1984) have eloquently documented this development. They watched children playing with their toys and dolls, and noted whether the children treated them as passive recipients to be fed, washed, towelled, and so forth or whether they were regarded as persons with their own independent plans and desires.

Three phases were especially clear across all the children. At around 18 months, children begin to treat dolls as representations of human beings, but these human beings are not credited with any power to act and feel independently; they remain the passive recipients of the child's ministering. They are fed or washed or put to bed.

Between two and two and a half years, children begin to endow dolls with a capacity for action and experience: the dolls are made to talk and act independently, and eventually credited with desires, sensations and emotions. The episode from the pretend play of J. (aged 24 months) illustrates these attributions. 'Farmer want a bath,' says J. and then, having swished the Farmer in the imaginary water, J. makes the Farmer announce how it feels: 'Oh no, sooo hot. Gotta put some cold in.'

Later still, at around three and a half to four years, children begin to endow dolls with more explicit thought processes and intersecting plans. One character might be made to voice a plan to hide something or a character might be explicitly described as wondering about the whereabouts of other characters.

These phases illustrate that the child's capacity for make-believe quickly moves beyond the realm of physical objects. Children do not confine their pretence to the substitution of one object for another, nor to the creation of make-believe objects and properties. They begin to conjure up animate beings. At first, these beings have no mind of their own, but gradually children begin to entertain make-believe mental states and to project them on to these beings. Here, we see good evidence for the projective mechanism I argued for earlier.[6]

The contrast between reality and imagination

Confronted by the growing complexity and vivacity of children's make-believe, one might be tempted to argue that, far from revealing the child's sophisticated capacity for pretence, it reveals the child's inability to distinguish pretence from reality. One might claim that children do not studiously bracket off their pretend world from the real world. Rather, they get carried away by their play to the point where they take it to be true. Do they come to think of their dolls as having human qualities in some attenuated form similar to those that they might attribute to a pet, or would they readily admit that their doll feels nothing, even when an older brother runs off with it, and bangs it on the floor?

There are some indications that young children, particularly one- and two-year-olds, are sometimes confused by pretence. For example, Judy DeLoache and Beth Plaetzer (1985) noticed that children aged 15 to 30 months were sometimes confused by their mother's interventions when she joined in their play, even though her support usually led to more complicated play. Their confusion was reflected in a sudden shift from a pretend to a literal mode. For example, one mother was pretending to hold up an umbrella, and suggested that her 30-month-old son hold up his hands in order to 'feel the rain'. He did what she suggested, but then turned the palms of his hands to his face and looked at them, apparently checking to see if they were wet. Similarly, a 15-month-old peered into the cup her mother had just 'poured tea' into, as if expecting to see some actual liquid. A 30-month-old knocked his cup over. His mother said: 'Uh-oh, you spilled your tea. You better wipe it up.' The child picked up a sponge and looked at the area surrounding the cup, asking: 'Where?' DeLoache and Plaetzer point out that the child appeared to be looking for real tea, not imaginary tea, and when he could not find any, he did not switch back into make-believe and pretend to clean up imaginary tea instead.

Such confusions between pretence and reality are not confined to those occasions when the mother produces an act of pretence that is too sophisticated for the child to grasp. It sometimes occurs between playmates as well. For example, Arietta Slade (1986) quotes a two-year-old who, in the midst of pretending to make a meal at the stove, turned to his companion and said, somewhat anxiously: 'This is pretend, right?' Another two-year-old whose symbolic play was quite impoverished, seemed to lose track of his own self-generated make-believe: while dressing a baby doll, he put into words a fantasy that she was hurt, and then began undressing himself. Similarly, a three-year-old who pretended to be a monster began to make growling noises, and then burst into tears saying that he was afraid of the monster (DiLalla and Watson, 1988).

Despite such occasional doubt and confusion, three-year-olds can make a distinction between the real world and the world of the imagination. Some of the best evidence for that ability comes from the work of Henry Wellman and David Estes (1986). They gave preschool children stories in which either a real or an imaginary entity might appear. For example, a real creature might be introduced into the story like this: 'Judy likes kitties. She didn't have a kitty, but then her father brought home a new kitty, so now she has a kitty.' By contrast, an imaginary creature might be introduced in the following way: 'Judy likes kitties. She doesn't have a kitty, but right now she is pretending to have a kitty.' Even three-year-olds were able to distinguish the imaginary objects from the real objects. They realized that the imaginary object – the kitty that was only part of Judy's pretend world – could not be seen or touched, unlike the real kitty.

Young children can even maintain a distinction between fantasy and reality if they are asked to imagine more equivocal creatures such as ghosts and witches. For example, we have found that three- and four-year-olds who are asked to 'make a picture in their head' of a monster, and then imagine the monster chasing after them know perfectly well that the monster is not real and is not publicly visible (Harris, Marriott and Whittall, 1988).

Do young children think of imagined or pretend entities in purely negative terms, as invisible, intangible and unreal? Wellman and his colleagues went on to show that preschoolers know that imagined objects can be deliberately transformed (Estes, Wellman and Woolley, in press). The children were again questioned about different sorts of entities: for example, a real balloon; a balloon hidden in a box; and a mental image of a balloon. For this last sort of entity, children were first shown a balloon, and then asked to close their eyes and 'make a picture of it' in their head. The three-year-olds realized that the shape of the imagined balloon could be changed just by thinking about it, whereas a real balloon, whether visible or hidden, could not be so transformed.

Children's spontaneous remarks also show that they can mark the distinction between an imagined reality and an actual reality (Shatz, Wellman and Silber, 1983). Here, for example, are some remarks made by Abe, a child whose conversation was recorded about twice a week between the ages of 28 and 48 months:

> 'I thought it was an alligator. Now I know it's a crocodile.'
>
> 'Do you know these people are the targets? But they're not real O.K. I'm just pretending that there's an airplane doing that.'

'I was teasing you. I was pretending 'cept you didn't know that.'

In these examples, Abe sets up a contrast between the real world and the mental world of pretence or thought. In the first remark, a contrast is set up between the real creature, a crocodile, and the putative creature, an alligator. The last two comments are more complicated. Abe draws an implicit distinction between the pretend world that has been created and the real world in which the pretence does not actually obtain. At the same time, he appears to be aware that, for an onlooker, this distinction may not be obvious: the pretend world may be taken for the real world.

A final index of children's ability to contrast the imagined world with the real world is their emerging facility with the syntax for referring to hypothetical events. In English, there are two major types of hypothetical reference: future hypothetical reference containing a modal auxiliary such as *would*, *could*, or *might* (e.g. 'And I *would* say giddy up horse and he *would* go whee-ee' – Abe at three years seven months) and past hypothetical reference containing a modal auxiliary, the auxiliary *have*, and a tensed main verb. (e.g. 'If you *would have eated* all that turkey, your tummy *would have kersploded*' – Abe at three years eleven months)

Stan Kuczaj and Mary Daly (1979) found that initially the appropriate markers such as the modal *would* or the auxiliary *have* are omitted. Nevertheless, at three and four years of age, appropriate marking is more and more frequent, showing that the child is aware at some level of having entered the hypothetical world as distinct from the real world. The emergence of this marking is not just a question of learning the correct syntactic form. Children start to refer to hypothetical future events much earlier than hypothetical past events. It seems likely that the difference between the two hypothetical forms has a cognitive basis. Future hypothetical reference sets up an implicit contrast between 'What could happen' (hypothetical) and 'What will happen' (prediction), whereas past hypothetical reference sets up an implicit contrast between 'What could have happened' (hypothetical) and 'What did happen' (actual). Unlike a reference to the future, a reference to the past requires that the child temporarily sets aside or 'undoes' an event that really happened. Kuczaj (1981) confirmed the extra burden of that mental undoing: children find it easier to cope with hypothetical references to a fantasy character, than to their own parents. Fantasy characters unlike parents have not really done anything, so that no mental undoing is needed to think hypothetically about them.

To sum up the conclusions that we have reached so far, one- and two-year-old children engage in symbolic play, but they may not always maintain a distinction between the real world on the one hand and the pretend world that they have created or been drawn into by another person. The prevalence of such confusion is not yet known because investigators usually make the assumption, which may be wrong, that the child is not confused unless he or she produces evidence to the contrary. Nevertheless, by three to four years, it is clear that children can distinguish between the real world and the mental or pretend world. They know which objects inhabit which world. They admit that entities in the mental world cannot be seen or touched but they can be transformed simply by imagining the transformation; on the other hand, entities in the real world can usually be seen and touched but they cannot be transformed by thought alone. Second, children spontaneously talk about the contrast between the mental world and the real world; they contrast what is pretend or imaginary with what is real, and they contrast an assumed (but counterfactual) state of affairs with what is known to be really the case. Finally, they increasingly mark the contrast between the hypothetical realm and the actual realm with appropriate syntactic forms. Movement into the hypothetical realm is undertaken more easily at this age, when it is untrammelled by knowledge of a countervailing reality. The child finds it easier to travel into the hypothetical future than into the hypothetical past.

Desires and emotions

If the child is capable of conjuring up a hypothetical world and keeping it quite distinct from actual reality, how might this help the child to understand other people? Earlier, I proposed that children's awareness of particular mental states, and their ability to pretend, enables them to imagine being in a particular mental state. For example, the child can imagine wanting something: recall the episode of pretend play described earlier when J. announced: 'Farmer *want* a bath.'

The next step for the child is to examine reality to see whether it matches what is desired. If there is a match, then the child can generate not an actual emotion but an 'as if' or pretend emotion of happiness. If, on the other hand, there is not a match, if the simulated desire is not fulfilled, then the child can generate an 'as if' sadness or discomfort. These simulated or pretend emotions can then be attributed to the other person. Notice that the generation of these 'as if' or pretend emotions depends on the bringing together of a pretend desire and an outcome, but young children are adept at carrying off such conjunctions. During a play episode, they may pretend that a doll wants to go for a ride or take a bath, and they also look around for something to satisfy that desire – a horse or a bath. Of course, during pretend play children are able to satisfy the desires of their doll characters by fiat. For example, J. continued the pretend episode described earlier by adding water from the imaginary faucet. Yet such inventions clearly show that the child knew what outcomes would and would not satisfy the desire to have a bath.

Does children's understanding of emotion require this complex mechanism? Much of the available evidence suggests instead that they operate with a simple empirical list specifying the links between particular situations and particular emotions. I will describe that evidence but then I shall describe some new findings showing that the mechanism that I have described is needed.

We may begin by looking at a pioneering study carried out by Helen Borke (1971). She presented children with short stories in which the main character encountered various situations. For example, the character would go to a birthday party, or get lost in the woods, or have a quarrel. The children listened to these simple stories and then chose from a selection of pictures the face that showed the character's likely emotional reaction. Even three- to four-year-olds were good at this task. They were able to identify situations that would lead to happiness and they were reasonably accurate for situations that would lead to sadness, or anger. Apparently, at this age, children can readily anticipate what emotion will be felt in various familiar situations.

Later work has shown that young children can also work in the opposite direction. If they are given the emotion, they can suggest a situation likely to cause it. Tom Trabasso and his colleagues gave three- to four-year-old children six different emotion words: *happy, excited, surprised, sad, angry* and *scared* (Trabasso, Stein and Johnson, 1981). For each emotion, the children were asked to make up a story to explain how the story character had come to feel that way. For example, they were told: 'One day, Jennifer got very, very angry. She was so angry that her mother and father could tell she was very angry. And all her friends could tell she was very angry. Why do you think Jennifer was so angry?' Across the six emotions, about three-quarters of the suggestions made by the children were appropriate.

Thus, three- and four-year-olds are good at figuring out which situations go with which emotions. They can work forwards from a given situation to predict ensuing emotion and they can work backwards from a given emotion to specify a plausible situational cause. Yet there is clearly nothing in these results to require the complicated mechanism that I have proposed. Children could simply learn such links from their everyday experience. For example, they feel sad when they lose a toy, and they feel happy when they get a present; they might simply note and remember these links.[7] The essence of this account is that the child remembers a two-part script. Given one part of the script – an emotion or a situation – the child can supply the other part. A good deal of recent research on children's understanding of emotion can be easily fitted into this formulation (Barden, Zelko, Duncan and Masters, 1980; Harris, 1985; Lewis, 1989).

Despite its inherent simplicity, this list would certainly help children understand other people's emotions. Suppose that a child only knows what has happened to another child, but cannot see the child's emotional reaction. For example, the child is listening to a story in which the protagonist is lost in the wood, or is given a present. The child should be able to anticipate the emotional reaction of the protagonist. Similarly, on learning that a story character or a playmate feels a particular emotion, the child should be able to think of likely causes. Most important of all, children could use such an empirical list to guide their behaviour toward other people: as we saw in the previous chapter, they will know what situations to create in order to provoke, amuse or comfort another person.

However, such a list is restricted to what children have previously experienced. Admittedly, children might supplement their knowledge by observing other people, by noticing what upsets their little brother or amuses their mother even if they themselves have a different emotional reaction. For example, Judy Dunn and Carol Kendrick quote the following comment by Bruce when he was not yet three years of age about his younger sibling, who was playing with a balloon: 'He going to pop it in a minute. And he'll cry . . . I like the pop' (Dunn and Kendrick, 1982). Yet, even with the addition of such astute observation of other people, the child would still be relying on past observation and such observation has a crucial limitation. It does not allow the child to appreciate how two people might react to the same situation with different emotions simply because of the way in which that situation fits or frustrates their particular desires. The more complex mechanism that I have proposed, on the other hand, would readily allow such an appreciation. If young children can project themselves into the mental world of another person by imagining what that individual wants, they should readily acknowledge that different people might bring different desires to a given situation, so that their emotional reactions will vary depending on how well situation and desire fit. Is there evidence that young children do take desires into account when they anticipate another person's emotion? If there is, it would show that young children are not simply operating with an empirically-derived list of emotion scripts.

Children certainly do mention desires when explaining someone's emotion. Nancy Stein and Linda Levine (1987) gave children stories in which a desire of the protagonist was identified at the outset, and a later event either fulfilled or blocked that desire. For example:

> Tina loves puppies and she wishes she had one. One day, Tina's friend comes over to Tina's house, and brings a puppy with her. When Tina's friend goes home, she forgets to bring her puppy with her. Tina calls up her friend on the telephone, and tells her friend that she will bring the puppy back in the morning. But today, Tina has a puppy to play with.

Three-year-olds certainly noticed whether the desire of the main character was met. They almost always said that he or she would be happy if the desire was met, and sad or angry if it was not. In explaining these judgements, they typically mentioned the outcome of the story – what the protagonist did or did not have – but with further probing, most children also referred back to what the protagonist liked or wanted. Here is a typical exchange:

Experimenter: Why do you think Tina feels happy?
Child: Because she's got a puppy.
Experimenter: Why does having a puppy make Tina feel happy?

Child:	Because her friend brought her one.
Experimenter:	Why did it make Tina happy that her friend brought her a puppy?
Child:	'Cause she likes puppies.

Thus, three-year-olds do refer to desires but it is not clear whether they systematically take them into account to help decide whether someone will be happy or not. After all, children might like puppies themselves, and simply use that knowledge to predict Tina's reaction.

We need to find out whether children can set aside their own desires and preferences. The critical test is to ask whether children understand that the same situation can provoke different emotions in different people depending on the desires that each individual brings to that situation. This is an important test because a positive answer would show that young children do not approach situations on a purely empirical basis, remembering how they or another person felt in that situation. Instead, they must understand how an emotion is born of the mental states that are brought to the situation.

Together with some colleagues, I carried out this test (Harris, Johnson, Hutton, Andrews and Cooke, 1989). The children listened to stories about animal characters who only liked certain types of food or drink. For example, they were introduced to a toy elephant, Ellie, and told either that Ellie liked only milk to drink and nothing else, or that she liked only Coke to drink and nothing else. In the next part of the story, a mischievous monkey called Mickey tricks Ellie by substituting the contents of one container for another. For example, Mickey might pour all the Coke out of a Coke can, replace it with milk and then offer the Coke can to Ellie. We asked children how Ellie would feel when she found out the real contents by taking a drink from the can.

Both four- and six-year-olds adjusted their prediction depending on what Ellie liked to drink. If she liked milk, they said that she would be happy to discover milk in the can. If, on the other hand, she liked Coke, they correctly predicted that she would be sad to find that the Coke had been removed and replaced by milk. Not only do preschool children mention a person's desires in post hoc explanations of their judgements about emotion, they take such desires into account in making their judgement in the first place. These results strongly suggest that children can imagine what another person might want and can simulate what the other person will feel by comparing the actual outcome with that desire. They have a mechanism for working out another person's emotion even when that emotion does not correspond to what they themselves would want or feel. They are not simply storing a list of emotion scripts, because such a list offers no way to predict that people will have different and even opposite emotions to the same situation depending on the desires that they bring to it.

Beliefs and emotions

The mechanism that I have described so far, complicated though it may appear, will lead children to make incorrect predictions, under certain circumstances. What ultimately determines a person's emotion is not the fit between desire and situation, but the fit between desire and apparent situation. For an illustration of this distinction, consider the following true story. A not particularly brave householder wakes up alone in a house and hears the sound of an intruder. He immediately feels afraid. He locks the bedroom door, and telephones the police. After an agonizing delay, the police arrive and ring the door bell. The householder emerges nervously from the bedroom, rushes downstairs and lets them in. The police search each room of the house. Having found no sign of an intruder, they come to the last remaining room. They open the door and find a disconsolate robin, unable to find its way out of the window that has been left ajar. The police are amused; the householder is relieved but embarrassed.

The story illustrates that it is someone's beliefs about a

situation that determine emotion, not the situation itself: the person was afraid of the apparent intruder, not the real robin. Moreover, even when those beliefs are objectively false, they still determine emotion just as forcibly and effectively as do true beliefs. The fear of an intruder was genuine (I can assure you) even though it was misplaced. How good are young children at figuring out a person's emotion in such circumstances? Earlier, we noted that children gradually become capable of conjuring up and explicitly marking a possible state of affairs that deviates from what they consider likely to happen (future hypothetical reference) or from what they know to have happened (past hypothetical reference). It is exactly this capacity for imagining a non-existent situation that the child needs in order to understand the way in which people's mistaken beliefs can cause emotional reactions. Just as before, the child must imagine or simulate the desires of the person. Then, he or she must conjure up a possible state of affairs which conflicts with known reality, and mark it as the world that the other person takes themselves to be in. The next step is to check whether this assumed state of affairs matches the person's desires.

Are young children capable of this type of imaginative understanding? Let us return to Mickey the monkey and Ellie the elephant. Recall that Mickey had tricked Ellie by removing the Coke from a Coke can, pouring milk into the can and then innocently offering her the Coke can with no explanation. We asked children how Ellie felt when she eventually discovered the actual contents. We also asked them how she felt *before* opening the container. Is she happy or sad when she comes back hot and thirsty after her walk and is presented by Mickey with a Coke can whose contents he has surreptitiously replaced? To answer this question correctly the children need to bear in mind not only what Ellie wants to drink – Coke or milk – but also what she mistakenly thinks is in the Coke can. If, the children concentrate exclusively on what Ellie prefers, and assume that she, like they themselves, knows the real contents, they will make an incorrect prediction. We found that four-year-olds typically did just that. The majority failed to take Ellie's mistaken beliefs into account. They claimed that Ellie would feel happy or sad according to whether the contents of the can, as yet invisible to her, were her favourite or not. Asked to explain their judgements, they referred to these hidden contents of the container ('It's milk'; 'Cos she likes milk' etc.). Six-year-olds, by contrast, were much more accurate. Most of them realized that before opening the container, Ellie would feel happy or sad depending on whether she liked the apparent contents of the can (i.e. Coke) as opposed to the milk hidden inside. They justified their predictions by referring to the apparent contents of the container ('Cos it's Coke'; 'Cos Ellie doesn't like Coke' etc.).

These results show that six-year-olds have an understanding of emotion that is far from egocentric. They watched the trick being played out, and knew full well what was inside the container. Nevertheless, they could work out what Ellie would feel given her mistaken belief about the contents. Such understanding requires that the child see the world from the point of view of another person. More generally, the results re-confirm that the child understands that someone's emotional state cannot be predicted from a list or dictionary specifying the emotions that go with particular situations. The child's understanding of emotion is one part of a much more general understanding of other people's psychological states. Specifically, in anticipating what emotion someone will feel children incorporate the key notions of desire and belief.

Empathy and imagination

I have argued that emotional contagion is not needed to gain insight into another person's feelings. Such contagion is no more informative than 'belief contagion' might be about another person's beliefs, or 'desire contagion' might be about another person's desires. Does this mean that empathy in the conventional sense of feeling along with another person rarely occurs? Such a conclusion is at variance with our everyday experience and it needs to be scrutinized very carefully. I think that empathy does occur, but it is not a precondition for understanding other people's emotion.

Consider what happens when we listen to friends telling us about some distressing experience that they have had. Our imagination is activated as we envisage the events that have befallen the friends. To the extent that we have a shared history with those friends or similar circumstances, their fate may be experienced as if it were our own. We respond as if their fate had actually befallen us and the emotions that would be aroused, were we in their place, are triggered, not in an 'as if' fashion, but in actuality. Such emotions are no mere pretence because they are often accompanied by the physiological signs of genuine emotion. Tears may swim in our eyes, or our heart may start to race.

When we watch an absorbing film or play, or read a novel, similar empathic processes can also occur. The setting is often sufficiently vivid that our imagination has very little constructive work to do. Moreover, works of drama or fiction focus on common or universal aspects of emotional experience, so that our identification with the fortune of the hero or heroine is assured. All that is needed for genuine emotion to be triggered is a temporary suspension of our disbelief in the fiction that has been created.

Sometimes, we may deliberately engage such an imaginative process. For example, a therapist will actively try to visualize the childhood or marital experiences of a client, and as a result, feel something equivalent to the pain or anger experienced by the client.[8] Indeed, we have found that six-year-olds can engage in such deliberately empathic processes (Meerum Terwogt, Schene and Harris, 1986). The children listened to a story in which the main character had to say goodbye to a best friend because the family was moving to a new town. They were asked to listen to the story in one of three ways: to feel along with the story character; to remain detached; or to follow their own preferences. These instructions appeared to be effective: children asked to identify with the character were more likely to remember or even elaborate on the sad episodes in the story. Moreover, in a later interview, some children could articulate the strategies that they had used to follow the instructions. They explained that they had managed to detach themselves from the fate of the story character by saying to themselves: 'it's only a story'; alternatively, they had engaged themselves in that same fate by pretending that the story events were really happening to them. These strategies were almost identical to those reported by adults in a similar experiment in which adults were given various instructions before watching a distressing film about accidents in the work-place (Koriat, Melkman, Averill and Lazarus, 1972).

Pulling together these various examples of empathy, we arrive at the following general formulation. Often, we can imagine the situation facing other people and the goals that they have. We can then imagine their ensuing emotional reaction without experiencing that emotion ourselves. Nevertheless, under certain circumstances, genuine emotion is triggered: when the other people's situation is vividly recreated or when the separation between them and ourselves is reduced, by dint of personal history or deliberate strategy, we cease simply to imagine the situation facing the other people. We start to experience it as a real situation. Our ensuing emotion will match theirs and it may have the physiological accompaniments of genuine emotion, such as tears or a pounding heart. Viewed in this way, empathic feelings do not reflect a more penetrating insight into the fate of another person. Instead, they reflect a stance that we take towards that fate: we can hold it at arm's length in the realm of the possible or the fictive, or we can allow it to come close and touch us as actual events do.

A theory of mind?

I have argued that children come to understand the links between beliefs, desires and emotions. To what extent are they operating with what has come to be called a 'theory of mind' (Astington, Harris and Olson, 1988)? A theory usually involves the postulation of unobservable entities whose interrelations can be shown to explain and predict observable events. For example, a theory of planetary motion might involve the postulation of gravity, and centripetal force, that permit the explanation and prediction of observable events such as the orbit of a planet. Similarly, it has been argued that the postulation of unobservables such as beliefs and desires can be used to explain and predict what people say, do and feel. Therefore, if children have recourse to such unobservables they should be credited with a theory of mind (Wellman, 1988). In some respects, I think that this characterization of children's understanding is appropriate and fruitful. Children do explain the behaviour of other people and of the characters that they invent in pretend play by reference to their beliefs and desires. Their understanding of other people is not confined to a piecemeal, empirical observation of various links between situations and behaviour. Finally, children understand that certain observables (such as whether someone will feel happy or sad) must be explained in terms of the relationship between states such as belief and desire. Recall that the children who correctly predicted Ellie's initial reaction to the monkey's trick needed to appreciate that she (falsely) believed her desire to have been fulfilled or frustrated. Ellie's reaction could not be anticipated by considering her beliefs or her desires in isolation from one another. In all these respects, children certainly act like theoreticians rather than mere empiricists.

However, there are ways in which the child's theory of mind is quite unlike a theory of planetary motion. Gravity is an unobservable, theoretical postulate. I do not think that we can say the same of beliefs and desires. As I have argued in this chapter, children have desires and beliefs, and they can report them. So far as they are concerned, there is nothing hidden or unobservable about their own mental states, whatever the opacity of other people's. Therefore, children do not invoke unobservable entities. They invoke mental states that they experience every waking day.[9] Second, children do not 'postulate' such states when they explain someone's behaviour. They simply imagine wanting or believing a particular state of affairs. This is not to deny, of course, that the imagination plays a role in the generation of such theoretical entities as gravity, but it does not play a role by projecting from our own personal experience. There is no sense in which we explain planetary motion by imagining ourselves to be a planet subjected to a given set of gravitational forces. In short, the psychological process by which a theory of mind is constructed bears little relation to the psychological process by which scientific theories about the non-psychological world are constructed. It is for that very reason, I suspect, that the child is a theoretician about the psychological realm long before he or she starts to construct theories in physics or biology.

Summary and conclusions

This chapter has travelled through some mixed terrain. It will be useful to point out once more the important landmarks. Although it is tempting to assume that the understanding of another person's emotion involves a kind of emotional resonance or contagion, there will be many circumstances in which this is not the case. Just as we can work out what another person perceives, or wants, or intends, without in any way sharing those perceptions or desires or intentions, so too we can understand what they might feel without necessarily experiencing a similar emotion.

How is such psychological understanding possible? By about two or three years of age, children can conjure up pretend or imaginary states of affairs and mark them explicitly as such. These imaginary states of affairs are not confused with reality. Moreover, at this same age children can conjure up pretend or imaginary psychological states, such as desires or beliefs, and project them on to their dolls and toy soldiers. The understanding of another person's emotion also depends critically on the ability to imagine such states. The child pretends to want or imagines wanting something that another person wants. If the child now examines the reality facing that other person, the child can anticipate what emotion will ensue when reality either satisfies or frustrates that desire. The child can use the outcome of that simulation to attribute to the other person the appropriate emotion, be it sadness or happiness.

Children can also imagine believing something that they know to be false. This type of imaginative projection is complex, since it is necessary to set aside known reality. Again, such a simulated belief will trigger an 'as if' version of the emotions that are normally associated with such beliefs, and these in turn can be attributed to someone holding such beliefs.

These postulates offer an explanation of how it is possible to appreciate and anticipate another person's emotion without experiencing that emotion. Nevertheless, such empathic reactions obviously do occur. According to my account, they occur when the imagined situation facing the other person, or the imagined beliefs and desires that the person has, are no longer marked as imagined but take on the potency of reality.

Finally, children can be credited with a theory-like understanding of the mind. They explain and predict people's behaviour and emotion by considering the relationships that hold between concepts such as beliefs and desires. They do not merely detect empirical associations between situations and responses. To invoke such concepts, however, the child need not postulate unobservable entities. Young children have beliefs and desires, and they can report them. Their understanding of psychology is based upon their own experience, rather than on deduction from a set of theoretical postulates.

NOTES

1 Hoffman (1981) does argue for the importance of emotional contagion. He makes two related claims. First, he argues that very young children who observe another child in distress will often react with distress themselves. Second, he suggests that such emotional contagion combined with an increasing ability to distinguish self from other will teach children to seek comfort for the other person, just as they seek comfort for themselves. Thus, Hoffman implies that contagious responding is prevalent in the early months and instructive for later developments in the second year, since it is converted into sympathetic and active concern. However, given that during the second year emotional contagion declines and active efforts to help the other person in distress become more common, one could equally plausibly argue that the tendency to offer comfort competes with emotional contagion and is in no way fuelled by it.

2 As Gordon (1987) notes, there are important similarities between his ideas and those of Leslie (1987), particularly in their emphasis on pretending. Nevertheless, they differ in their analysis of the role of pretending. Whereas Leslie argues that a computational mechanism (a 'decoupler') underlies both pretending and the attribution of mental representations, Gordon claims that pretending is directly implicated in making such attributions. Hence, for Leslie (but not for Gordon) a deficit in pretending need not impede attribution. Conversely, for Gordon but not for Leslie, aids to pretending could directly improve attribution.

3 Pretending to hold a false belief is difficult because it requires that the child conjure up a belief that he or she knows to conflict with reality and such false beliefs are typically experienced only in retrospect when, for example, the child discovers that a previously entertained belief is false. There is emerging evidence that children understand that people can entertain desires that do not match reality earlier than they understand that people can entertain beliefs that do not match reality (Bartsch and Wellman, 1989; Harris, Johnson, Hutton and Andrews, 1987; Perner, Leekam and Wimmer, 1987; Yuill, 1984). If children understand the mental states of others by projecting their own mental states on to other people, this difference between beliefs and desires is readily explicable. Children will have considerable experience of wanting something that does not match current reality. They will also have some experience of having believed something that turns out not to match reality. However, these two experiences are different subjectively. Although it is quite common to experience a desire that is *currently* known to be at variance with reality, it is not common to experience a belief that is *currently* known to be at variance with reality. We usually update our beliefs.

Thus, we acknowledge only that our past beliefs were false but not our current beliefs. In attributing false beliefs to someone, therefore, children will have to conjure up their own *past* false beliefs, and at the same time acknowledge that, without knowledge of the true current state of affairs, someone will maintain such a false belief.

4 Caution is needed when using children's spontaneous utterances as evidence for their self-awareness. Children could, in principle, use mental state terms without intending to refer to mental states. For example, 'I wanna . . .' might be an unanalysed formula that is produced to mark a request; 'I know' might be used to emphasize an assertion; 'I'm sad' might be a way of expressing sadness rather than reporting it. It is reassuring, therefore, that similar findings emerge when more stringent criteria are adopted to define a mental state reference. For example, in their longitudinal study of a single child (A.K.), Shatz, Wellman and Silber (1983) excluded 'conversational' uses such as 'Know what?' Using these criteria, they locate the onset of mental state reference somewhat later than Bretherton and her colleagues. Nevertheless, they also found that references to the mental states of the self preceded references to the mental states of others by about three months. Admittedly, this precedence was not replicated in a cross-sectional study but the children were observed for only 20–30 minutes every two months, so that developmental trends could be much less easily discerned.

5 Alternative interpretations of the linguistic priority of self-referenced statements are available. Beeghly, Bretherton and Mervis (1986) report a similar pattern of change for mothers' speech to their children. References to perceptual and volitional states are common in mothers' speech to infants aged 13 and 20 months, whereas references to cognitive states are quite rare until about 28 months. Similarly, references to the child predominate at 13 and 20 months, whereas references to other people, and other objects (during pretend play) are quite rare until 28 months. Since these shifts in focus are found in both the children's and the mother's speech, it could be that the child's speech influences that of the mother, or vice versa; it is also possible that some third factor (e.g. the ease with which mental states of a certain type or belonging to a particular person can be reliably identified) influences both child and mother alike.

6 It is important to note that the ages given for the attribution of make-believe sensations, emotions and thoughts should not be taken as rigid indices of the earliest age at which the capacity for imaginative projection emerges. The ease with which children engage in pretence depends upon several factors, including the similarity between a prop and the object for which it substitutes. For example, children will treat a doll as a substitute person more readily than they will treat a block of wood as a substitute person (Rubin, Fein and Vandenberg, 1983). Similarly, it is likely that children can imagine a mental state belonging to a creature like

themselves (i.e. another person) more readily than they can imagine a mental state belonging to an animal or an inanimate object such as a doll. Thus, although pretend play provides clear and convincing evidence of the child's capacity to imagine particular mental states, it does not necessarily indicate the earliest availability of that capacity.

7 A similar point concerning Borke's results was made by Chandler and Greenspan (1972).

8 Arietta Slade drew my attention to the importance of empathy in clinical practice, and led me to think more carefully about the conditions that elicit it.

9 Carl Johnson convinced me of the need to take seriously children's awareness of their mental states. This approach avoids various problems, but it leaves others unresolved. Especially difficult is the question of how exactly the child comes to think of his or her own mental states in terms of desires, beliefs, and so forth. Is experience structured into different categories from the outset (cf. Johnson, 1988)? Does the community offer the child a way of talking, a gloss, that provides instruction in how to conceptualize mental states? Finally, is there some hitherto uncharted conjunction between the innate structure of experience and linguistic instruction? We need much more study of the child's earliest expressions of desire and belief before we can begin to answer these questions, although a start has been made (Bretherton and Beeghly, 1982; Shatz, Wellman and Silber, 1983).

4

Pride, shame and guilt

If a boy has bred and raised a bird by himself, and he shows it to one of his friends, then he feels proud.

Ten-year-old boy living in eastern Nepal

In the last chapter, I argued that young children of four and five years of age begin to understand simple emotions like happiness and sadness in terms of the mental states – the beliefs and desires – that lead to those emotions. This argument implies that children do not understand an emotional state simply by focusing on the way that the emotion is expressed, nor by noting, in a rote fashion, the diverse situations that provoke the emotion. Rather, they identify the mental perspective that someone adopts with respect to those various situations.

In this chapter, I extend this analysis to more complex emotions such as pride, shame and guilt. I shall argue that four- and five-year-old children see people chiefly as agents who pursue their goals, and feel happy or sad depending on whether those goals appear to be realized. Older children, by contrast, gradually appreciate that people's emotional lives are not only regulated by the consequences of their actions, but also by an awareness of the emotions that other people will express towards those actions and their consequences. This wider perspective brings the issues of responsibility and normative standards into view because approval and disapproval from other people depends on whether a child was responsible for an outcome and whether that outcome meets a particular standard.

What do children know about the situations that provoke more complex emotions such as pride and guilt? We questioned Dutch and English children ranging from 5 to 14 years using a set of 20 different emotion terms (Harris, Olthof, Meerum Terwogt and Hardman, 1987). Because we wanted to test children across a wide age range, we needed to find a task that was understandable for young children but still challenging for older children. The children were presented with different emotion terms and asked to tell us about the situations that would elicit each emotion. The emotion terms were chosen to include 'basic' emotion terms, such as *happy* and *sad* but also terms like *guilty*, *disappointed*, *relieved* and *proud*, which have no obvious facial expression associated with them.

As we had hoped, the children readily understood the task. Depending on their age, they told us about situations that would plausibly elicit several or indeed most of the emotion terms that we presented. To check whether children suggested situations that were distinctively associated with a particular emotion, or loosely associated with several emotions, adult judges were shown each of the children's responses and asked to decide which of the 20 emotion terms the child had been responding to. For example, faced with a response such as 'getting a bicycle' the judges had to decide whether this was a response to *proud* or *happy* or *grateful*, etc. This criterion was quite stringent because it required that children not only describe a situation that was plausible, but one that was distinctively associated with the particular emotion term. Its stringency, however, established that children were able to individuate the emotions in terms of the situations that would provoke them.

The youngest children, who were five years old, from both the Netherlands and Britain, were able to suggest distinctive situations chiefly for emotions having a recognizable facial display: *afraid, happy, sad and angry*. Children in both countries also proposed appropriate situations for *shy*, which does not have a particular facial expression associated with it. On the other hand, shyness is often expressed through a distinct posture and demeanour.

By seven years of age, the picture in both groups had

changed considerably. In addition to the earlier set of terms, children now offered appropriate and recognizable situations for several emotions with no obvious expressive display: *proud, jealous, grateful, worried, guilty* and *excited.* This list was even longer at 10 and 14 years, and included terms such as *relieved* and *disappointed.*

We concluded that children may start off by establishing the situational elicitors for emotions that have a distinctive facial display or behavioural expression, but they are not confined to that set for long. Even using the stringent criterion that we adopted, seven-year-olds in both the Netherlands and Britain had moved beyond that basic set of terms to discover and describe situations that would elicit more complicated emotions such as guilt, pride and jealousy.

The lives that children lead in Britain and the Netherlands, and the languages that they speak, do not differ dramatically. To find out whether this same pattern would be found among children living in a quite different culture with a radically different language, we carried out a study of Nepalese children. The children lived in Pangma, a remote Himalayan village. They were all native speakers of Lohorung, a language of Tibeto-Burman descent, and belonged to the Rai tribe, who live in and around the Arun valley in eastern Nepal. Although schooling is valued by the Lohorung Rai, family tasks, including child-care, planting, harvesting and herding, often prevent children going to school.

The children in the village had rarely encountered any foreigners before. The village is quite remote, so that trekking parties do not pass through it; the only Westerners living in the region were two medical workers in a market town to the east, at least two days' walk away. All interchange among neighbouring villages must be carried out on foot and the nearest air-strip is one day's walk away. The wider world enters the village only occasionally by means of one or two radio sets (Hardman, 1981).

Rather than seeking to translate the emotion terms that we had used in Europe, we asked adults in the village to supply us with a list of 16 emotion terms commonly used in Lohorung. Not surprisingly, the list covered some of the basic emotion concepts found in English and Dutch (*afraid, happy, angry,* etc.) but, as we had hoped, it also included emotions for which there is no distinctive expression (*proud, jealous, relieved,* etc.).

We interviewed two different age groups, one with an average age of eight years, the other with an average age of 13 years. The younger group had about one and a half years of education on average and the older group about four years. We talked to the children informally in a variety of locations: in their own home, in a hut temporarily lent to the experimenters, and sitting beside the village footpaths. The interview was carried out in Lohorung but as soon as the child made a reply, this was translated into English and written down.

The procedure for analysing the responses was the same as that for the first study, and the results were remarkably similar. Distinct situations were proposed for 11 of the 16 emotions by the younger group, and for 14 of the 16 emotions by the older group, and in each age group appropriate situations were supplied for situations having no obvious facial expression.

The children's replies offered a poignant and vivid picture of the concerns of their lives in Pangma. Certain preoccupations appeared again and again. The burdens and anxieties of agricultural labour were one refrain; the pleasure associated with certain special foods or treats in an otherwise bland diet of rice or maize and lentils was a second; the proximity of serious illness, poverty and death was a third. By comparison, the European children interviewed in the first study inhabited a more protected world of toys, pets and school.

Summarizing across the two studies, the one carried out in Europe and the other in Nepal, a clear picture emerges. In quite disparate cultures, children start off by sorting out the situations that will elicit a set of basic or core emotions that can be readily associated with a particular facial expression or mode of behaviour. Yet even when we employ a stringent criterion for situational knowledge, children move beyond this restricted set by seven or eight years of age. They can describe the particular situations that would elicit emotions having no distinct facial or behavioural expression. Of course, jealousy, pride and guilt are associated with some type of expressive display. The important point, for our purpose, is that the display cannot help the child to identify the distinctive situational determinants of those emotions, since the display overlaps with those that accompany so-called basic emotions. Whatever is distinctive about these emotions is closely connected to the type of situation that elicits them. Accordingly, we need to look closely at the development of children's understanding of those eliciting conditions.

In line with the account developed in the last chapter, I shall argue that understanding such emotions depends on the ability to imagine the mental states of someone in a given situation. To focus the discussion, let us consider the examples of pride, shame and guilt. These emotions are interesting because they are intuitively more complex than emotions such as sadness and happiness. We typically feel pride when we believe that we have been responsible, directly or indirectly, for bringing about some outcome that meets or surpasses a normative standard. For example, we feel proud if we score a goal, pass an examination or make a generous donation. On the other hand, we feel shame when we believe that we allow or bring about some outcome that falls short of a normative standard and guilt if it falls short of a moral standard. So, we feel shame if we score an own goal, and guilt if we cheat in an examination or fail to make a donation.

These emotions do not turn simply on whether we believe that we have attained or lost some desirable outcome, as in the case of happiness and sadness. Rather, they turn on two additional notions. First, the outcome must be something that we think we are responsible for bringing about; and second, the outcome must be something that is not simply desirable to us, but falls within the purview of norms or standards, including moral standards.

In the next section, we shall see that although young children can describe situations that would be associated with pride, shame and guilt, their sensitivity to the crucial features of those situations has yet to become more refined. At around five to six years of age, children attribute these emotions without necessarily taking personal responsibility and normative standards into account. Between the ages of about five and ten years, however, they become increasingly sensitive to the importance of each.

Taking personal responsibility into account

Sandra Graham and Bernie Weiner (1986) argue that when we attribute a complex emotion such as gratitude or pride to someone, we engage in a two-stage analysis. In the first stage, we evaluate the situation that faces the person in terms of outcomes, essentially seeking an answer to the question: is this a desirable outcome or not? Even three- and four-year-olds can manage this kind of analysis, as we saw in the last chapter. In the second stage, a causal analysis is carried out that provides an answer to the question: why has this outcome occurred? Depending on the particular conclusion that is reached, a different emotion will be appropriate. For example, if a desirable outcome has been reached with the help of another person, then *gratitude* is appropriate, but if that same outcome has been deliberately blocked by another person, then *anger* is appropriate. Graham and Weiner argue that there are two broad classes of emotion: emotions that simply require an appraisal of the outcome and more complex emotions that require an appraisal not only of the outcome but also of the cause of the outcome.[1] Pride and guilt, for example, are felt when a desirable or undesirable outcome has occurred and the person also believes that he or she is responsible for it, or could have prevented it.

Are children sensitive to these causal considerations? Sandra Graham and her colleagues looked at this issue (Graham,

Doubleday and Guarino, 1984). Children ranging from six to 12 years were asked to describe a past episode when they had felt guilty, and to rate the extent to which they felt personally responsible for what had happened. This question was phrased to make it understandable to the youngest children: they were asked to point to a scale to indicate how much the cause of the emotion was something that 'you made happen, something you couldn't stop from happening, or partly something you made happen and partly something you couldn't stop from happening'.

The most interesting finding was that children's sensitivity to the role of personal responsibility changed markedly with age, especially between six and nine years. The six-year-olds described episodes that caused them to feel guilty even though they claimed to have little control over the outcome. For example: 'I felt guilty when my brother and I had boxing gloves on and I hit him too hard . . . sometimes I don't know my own strength'; or 'I felt guilty when I did the ceremony wrong at my grandfather's funeral . . . I forgot how to do it.' The older children confined their guilty feelings to outcomes that were more obviously within their control: 'I felt guilty when I didn't turn in my homework because I was too lazy to do it'; or 'I felt guilty when the new girl failed the initiation test into the neighbourhood club because we asked questions we knew she couldn't answer.'

There are two quite different ways of interpreting this age-change. First, younger children might find it harder than older children to decide whether a particular outcome could have been prevented; they might assume that an involuntary outcome such as forgetting what to say at a ceremony is their own fault. A second possibility is that young children do know whether they are responsible but simply do not appreciate the relevance of responsibility to guilt. In a follow-up study, Sandra Graham (1988) examined these two possibilities. She presented children with two different versions of the same story. In one version, the accident could scarcely have been prevented: the main character causes a bicycle accident by trying not to collide with a small child who wanders into the road. In another version, the accident could obviously have been prevented: the character causes an accident while trying to perform a trick on a bicycle in a crowded section of the park. Children were asked to make two separate judgements: how readily the protagonist could have prevented the accident and how guilty he or she would feel.

The five- and six-year-olds distinguished adequately between the unavoidable and the crash that could have been prevented. On the other hand, they were likely to judge that the protagonist would feel almost equally guilty after both. The implication of these results is that when they attribute guilt, young children focus on outcomes, ignoring the cause of the outcome even though they can figure out whether someone is to blame for it or not.

If this analysis is correct, it ought to apply to pride as well. Recall that an appropriate conception of pride also turns on an analysis of personal responsibility: it is appropriate to feel proud if something linked to you, such as your effort or ability, has brought about an approved outcome, but not if some external factor such as an intervention by another person is responsible. Do young children ignore this consideration in their diagnosis of pride, and restrict their attention to the nature of the outcome itself, whatever its cause? In a test of this question, Sandra Graham (1988) again presented two versions of a story to children in which the same outcome was caused in two different ways. In one story, a high score was obtained through effort and in a second story it was obtained because the task was very easy. The youngest group aged five-six years again accurately distinguished the causal factors involved, judging that an easy task was an external factor rather than an internal factor. Nevertheless, they went on to claim that the story character would be quite proud whatever the cause.

Other studies tell the same story. One group of researchers asked children to think back to a time when they had felt various emotions and to describe what happened (Seidner,

Stipek, and Feshbach, 1988). Even the youngest group aged five years were more likely to describe episodes that involved their own efforts in the case of pride as compared with happiness, but they still often mentioned outcomes that were clearly beyond their control: 'I felt proud when my uncle got married'; or 'I felt proud when my grandma and grandpa came to visit.' It seems unlikely that five-year-olds think they cause such events; instead it seems much more plausible that their concept of pride is still quite fuzzy, and overlaps, at least in part, with happiness. This conclusion also fits the results obtained by Ross Thompson (1989). He told children stories involving various types of causal sequence, including those in which the hero or heroine achieved success through his or her own efforts and could feel proud. The youngest group who were seven years of age were quite likely to decide how the character felt simply in terms of the outcome. For example, after a hard-won success, they would judge that the story character was happy rather than proud, and explain their judgement simply in terms of the successful outcome, rather than the effort that had gone into achieving it.

Thus, whether we look at a negative emotion such as guilt or a positive emotion such as pride, we find a parallel age-change: younger children neglect the personal responsibility of the protagonist in deciding how he or she feels, even though they can diagnose that responsibility accurately. By contrast, older children do acknowledge its relevance. Notice that the younger children do not necessarily deny that someone who is responsible for a bad outcome will feel guilty or that someone who has earned success will feel pride. Rather, in focusing too narrowly on the outcome to the neglect of its cause, they attribute pride and guilt to those who are not responsible for an outcome, and mere happiness or sadness to those who are responsible.

The role of standards

Emotions like pride and guilt turn on an analysis of two dimensions: personal responsibility and conformity to normative standards. Young children often disregard the role of personal responsibility in assessing these emotions, it seems. Do they also disregard norms and standards? This is an interesting question because moral dilemmas often involve a conflict between doing what one wants and violating a normative standard. If young children focus simply on desires and outcomes – and they certainly can take desires and outcomes into account, as we saw in the last chapter – they should decide that someone who does what they want will feel happy even if it involves a moral breach. Qualms of conscience over having violated a normative standard should not enter the picture.

Imagine a boy who deliberately hits or steals from another child. If the boy acts deliberately, he presumably gets what he wants; he succeeds in upsetting the other child or in making off with the stolen goods. If young children neglect normative standards about hitting and stealing when they assess how someone feels, and focus instead on desires and outcomes, they should decide that the boy will be happy rather than sad because he got what he wanted, despite his moral breach. On the other hand, if children acknowledge the role of such standards, they should expect the boy to feel sad or unhappy when he fails to live up to them.

In a striking series of experiments, Gertrud Nunner-Winkler and Beate Sodian (1988) tested these predictions. Children ranging from four- to eight-years listened to various stories in which the main character deliberately stole, lied, or attacked another child. Consistently, the younger group of four- and five-year-olds claimed that the character would be happy about his or her misdeed. They backed up their judgement by referring to the outcome of the story, for example the fact that the protagonist had managed to hurt the other child or run off with the stolen goods. By contrast, older children, around eight years of age, claimed that the character would feel sad or bad. In explaining these emotions, the older children rarely mentioned the likelihood of punishment. Rather their explanations were morally oriented: they referred to the character's misdeed, to the fact that he or she had been nasty, or to the likelihood that the character would have a bad conscience about doing something that violated a moral rule. They also implied that feeling bad following a misdeed was not just a likely consequence of wrong doing; it was prescribed, because a child who stole and felt sad was not so bad as a child who stole and felt happy.[2]

One possible explanation for this age change is that four- and five-year-olds do not know that it is wrong to hurt another child or steal something, whereas eight-year-olds do know these moral rules. Recall from chapter 2, however, that preschool children are quite sophisticated in thinking about such rules. They certainly judge that it would be wrong to hit or steal. Indeed, they judge that it would be wrong to hit or steal even if there were no rule forbidding such actions. They also offer a very plausible explanation of why such actions are wrong; they point to the harm or distress that the victim suffers. Indeed, when asked whether hitting or stealing was wrong, the younger children readily agreed that it was wrong to do such things. Moreover, they claimed that the protagonist would feel sad or upset if he or she accidentally hurt someone, for example in a bicycle crash.

Thus, younger children have two difficulties. They ignore the relevance of responsibility in the attribution of pride, shame and guilt. Second, they ignore the relevance of normative standards. These two problems do not arise because they do not know about responsibility or normative standards. They can make accurate diagnoses with respect to each. They know whether someone did something deliberately or by accident. Similarly, they know the normative standards that have been violated. Their difficulty is in seeing the relevance of those two considerations to their emotional life. Older children, by contrast, see both considerations as relevant. They appreciate that someone may experience distress if they deliberately flout a moral rule, even if they get what they want by doing do.

If the preceding analysis is correct, the emotional universe of the four- or five-year-old turns on a different axis from that of the seven- or eight-year-old. The younger child typically sees people as agents who set out to get what they want; if they succeed, they are happy and if not, they are sad. The older child sees people as agents who should conform to a normative or moral standard; if they manage to do so, they may feel proud but if they deliberately ignore or defy that standard, they are likely to feel guilty or ashamed.

How does the older child come to understand that people's emotional lives are regulated in this fashion? I shall argue that the child has to switch from seeing people simply as agents to seeing them as observers of their own agency, observers who assess their responsibility in matching up to normative standards. There are two preconditions for this switch. First, the child must acknowledge that people's emotional reactions to what they have done are influenced by other people's emotional reactions, particularly their approval and disapproval. Second, the child requires the imaginative capacity to grasp such interlocking mental states. Let us begin by examining the child's awareness of the emotional impact of an audience.

The role of an audience

One of the first writers to consider the role of an audience in our emotional lives was C. H. Cooley. Cooley was a contemporary of the developmental psychologist Baldwin, and it is from Baldwin that he borrowed and developed the notion of the 'looking glass self'. He identified three components of this reflected self: the imagination of our appearance in the eyes of another person; the imagination of that person's evaluation of our appearance; and an ensuing sense of pride or shame. Cooley encapsulated these notions in the following statement: 'The thing that moves us to pride and shame is not the merely mechanical reflection of ourselves, but an imputed sentiment, the imagined effect of this reflection upon another's mind' (1902, p. 153). At first, Cooley argued, pride and shame depend on the close proximity of that other mind and its expressed emotion. In the course of development, the child will experience pride and shame with greater autonomy. The proximity of an audience is no longer critical.

These ideas are intriguing because they show how we might build on the argument that I presented in the last chapter. There, I claimed that young children can understand another person's emotion by imagining the situation that confronts that person and the desires that he or she brings to it, so that an 'as if' emotion is generated. By extending that analysis, we can see how the child will eventually come to both experience and understand a new set of emotions, including pride and guilt. We begin by thinking about how children first come to experience these emotions.

To take a concrete example, a child completes a puzzle; the child's parent responds with approval; this approval, in its turn, elicits pleasure in the child (Reissland, 1988b). The child will be keen to repeat the activity, and will do so boldly. Eventually, the child may start to aim at certain accomplishments not just for the pleasure of mastery, but precisely in order to gain parental approval. He or she starts to anticipate the approval that an accomplishment will earn, for example, by alerting the parents to some new feat that he or she is about to perform. Gradually, children start to enjoy not just the actual receipt of approval but its anticipation. For example, having won a prize at school, they ruminate about what will happen at home and imagine the praise that this success will earn from their parents. As a result of this imaginative anticipation, children savour the pleasure – or pride, as we may call it – that such approval usually arouses.

A similar analysis can be put forward for guilt. A child commits a transgression and, seeing the disapproval that it arouses in his or her mother, experiences distress in response to the mother's emotion. This distress may gradually start to accompany the performance of the action: it may be carried out in an apprehensive or bashful fashion. Eventually, the child anticipates ahead of time the disapproval that the transgression will produce. This anticipation arouses the emotion that disapproval usually provokes, even before the child's mother knows about the deed.

An *understanding* of pride and guilt, as opposed to the capacity for *experiencing* these emotions carries this imaginative projection one step further. Children must be able to envisage the circumstances under which the emotions will be aroused in another person. To do this, they must be able to diagnose the emotion that will be aroused in another child if that child has done something and imagines the approval or disapproval of some important person such as the child's father or mother. The child who starts to understand pride and guilt is effectively saying: 'I can imagine how Jack will feel when he imagines how his mother will feel.'

Susan Harter and Nancy Whitesell (1989) show that children's understanding of pride and shame is indeed linked to a recognition of the impact of an audience. They first interviewed children aged 4 to 11, about their experiences of pride and shame. The youngest children appreciated that pride was a good feeling and shame a bad feeling, but they could not provide very compelling examples of either. Six- and seven-year-olds, on the other hand, could provide examples but they often attributed the emotion to their parents rather than to themselves: 'Mom would be proud of me if I cleaned my room'; 'Dad was really ashamed of me when I broke the window.' By the age of eight years, children were able to produce convincing examples of how they themselves might feel ashamed or proud: 'I was really ashamed that I broke my friend's bike and didn't tell him'; 'I dived off the high diving board.'

The role of an audience was examined more closely in a related study (Harter, Wright and Bresnick, 1987). Children were told stories involving incidents likely to provoke either pride (performing a flip on a gymnastic bar), or shame (taking coins from a jar in the parents' bedroom). In one version, the parents saw the child carrying out the act; in the other version, the parents were not there and did not see what the child did.

A three-stage developmental sequence emerged. Five-year-olds claimed that they would feel happy after the gymnastic feat and scared (of being caught) after stealing the money but they did not mention feelings of pride or shame. At the next stage, between the ages of six and seven, children did refer to feelings of pride and shame, but only if the parents had seen the action in question. If the parents were elsewhere at the time, they denied that they would feel either emotion.

At stage 3, which emerged at around eight years of age, children acknowledged that pride and shame could arise without an actual audience, and they were explicit that the object of the emotion would be the self: 'I would feel proud (or ashamed) *of myself*.' Note that even at this stage an audience is not entirely dispensed with. It is simply that the child operates within the framework of a new audience. Two distinct roles for the self are envisaged: observer and agent. The self-as-observer watches and judges the actions of the self-as-agent.

Indeed, even at stage 3, the child does not fully replace the parent as judge. This was especially clear in the story about stealing. Asked if they would confess later, most of the oldest group, aged eight years and upward, said yes and gave an explicit rationale; a confession, they explained, would relieve the feeling of shame that would otherwise weigh on their mind. These older children have a vivid image of themselves as agents who may or may not live up to moral standards. If they transgress those standards, they predict that their thoughts will remain in the grip of a negative emotion, unless remedial action can be taken.[3] Very often, the self alone lacks authority to forgive the transgression and put an end to the emotion; the child must seek out the final arbiter, the parent, for whom he or she has been a substitute, and seek reassurance that the deed was not so bad after all, or alternatively hand over the burden of disapproval to the parent, thereby relieving the self.[4]

Understanding social emotions

We now have the seeds of an overall explanation for the various changes that we see in young children's understanding of the social emotions. To sum up the argument so far, children do not initially acknowledge the relevance of personal responsibility and normative standards to the attribution of pride, shame or guilt. Their neglect of these two factors is probably not coincidental. To perceive the relevance of each factor, they must see themselves and other people not as agents who may or may not attain their desires, and feel happy or sad as a result, but as social beings who voluntarily try to live up to certain norms or standards, and feel pride, or shame or guilt, depending on whether they succeed or fail in doing so.

What brings about this shift? My guess is that it depends on the child's increasing awareness that a person's feelings about his or her actions are governed not just by the outcome of those actions but also by an anticipation of the approval or disapproval that other people will express towards actions that meet or fall short of a normative standard. If the emotional reactions of other people are ignored, it is only the outcome that is important in determining the emotion, rather than its manner of attainment or its conformity with social norms or standards. However, when other people's approval and disapproval are kept in mind, the importance of normative standards and responsibility is immediately highlighted. Approval from other people depends critically on whether the child manages to live up to various social standards. Approval will be given if the child does meet those standards, especially if it is through his or her own efforts. Conversely, approval will be withheld if the child fails to meet such standards, especially if the child was capable of doing so. To the extent that the child steps momentarily outside his or her role as agent and views an outcome from the perspective of a neutral bystander, the harm or benefit to other people that an action has produced comes into focus.

On this account, we should expect that children's understanding of the social emotions will depend, in part, on their parents' behaviour. When parents consistently underline a breach of moral standards by emphasizing to the child the harm that he or she has done, the child will be more likely to anticipate guilt after a transgression and expect others to experience the same feeling. A good deal of research on the impact of parental disciplinary techniques points to exactly this link (Hoffman, 1970). For example, parents who use reasoning or induction, as opposed to more punitive or coercive methods, are likely to have children who both experience and anticipate guilt (Hoffman and Saltzstein, 1967). Such children are likely to come to their parents unbidden to 'confess' a wrongdoing, and they are also likely to predict that a story character will feel guilty following a transgression.

Eventually, children come to envisage such emotions arising without an actual audience, and in the absence therefore of any approval or disapproval from another person. That understanding rests, however, on an intermediate stage in which children grasp that these emotions arise as a response to the emotions engendered in a real audience: pride is the pleasure that would arise in the context of real rather than imagined approval; shame or guilt is the pain that would arise in the context of real rather than imagined disapproval. The implication of this argument is that children's capacity to take other people's emotional reactions into account makes children increasingly aware of themselves as agents who are expected to live up to certain norms or standards. Hence, they start to view people not simply as agents, but as more neutral bystanders or observers, who in lieu of a disapproving caretaker, judge their own actions.

This analysis also allows us to resolve an apparent conflict in recent theories of moral judgement. The work of Elliot

Turiel and Judith Smetana, which was discussed in chapter 2, shows that even preschool children have strong intuitions about what counts as a moral rule; they realize that aggression and theft are wrong, whether or not there are rules proscribing them. They realize that violation of such rules causes distress and harm to the victim. Yet, the monumental research of Kohlberg and his associates shows that when children are asked what someone should do, even at 10 years of age or more, they often emphasize the instrumental benefits or the approval that a course of action will produce rather than its moral integrity (Colby, Kohlberg, Gibbs and Lieberman, 1983). One interpretation of this conflict is that young children can only voice their moral intuitions if they are asked very simple questions. Asked to justify a course of action in their own words, they offer a rationale (e.g. adult approval or the avoidance of punishment) that masks their true insight into the basis for moral rules (Shweder, Turiel and Much, 1981).

I suspect that the discrepancy is attributable not to the complexity of the questions but to their thrust. Turiel (1983) and Smetana (1981) have asked what actions are wrong, whereas Kohlberg has asked what someone should do (cf. Nunner-Winkler and Sodian, 1988). To an adult ear, these questions are inextricably related. Having worked out what is wrong, one should not do it. Yet the two questions may be very different for young children. They may know a good deal about what is wrong without assuming that such knowledge has much impact on one's course of action. From their own experience, they have noticed that what does have an impact is the emotional state that one will attain as a result of an action. The four- and five-year-old has learned that people are happy if they get what they want; hence, they will do what they want. The seven- and eight-year-old may have noticed that people are happy if they receive approval; hence, they will do what gains approval even if it is at the expense of doing what they want. It may take several more years to work out that people can gain satisfaction if they do what they judge to be right; hence, they may do what is right even if it is not what they want, and even if it gains them no approval. These modes of thought coincide quite well with the three main stages of the Kohlberg system.

The interlocking of mental states

We have now fitted together three concurrent age-changes in the child's understanding of the social emotions of pride, shame and guilt: the acknowledgement of the role of personal responsibility; the recognition of the importance of normative standards; and the recognition of the role of an audience or observer. If this is correct, it raises a further question. Children are sensitive to the approval and disapproval of their parents long before the age of seven- or eight-years. Why then do they take so long to understand the appropriate attribution of the social emotions that are contingent upon approval and disapproval? To answer this question, we need to examine children's understanding of the mind in other domains. Their difficulties in understanding socially interlocking mental states, and the social acts that presuppose such interlocking, extend beyond the narrow domain of emotion.

Consider a deliberate act of deception, such as a lie. To understand that Jill is lying to Jack, children must be able to appreciate that she wants to influence his beliefs. Her lie implies that Jill *wants* Jack to *believe* something that she does not believe. Therefore, an observer who understands the interaction between Jack and Jill must understand that the intention behind Jill's utterance is directed at achieving a particular mental state in Jack. This analysis helps to clarify the difference between lying and joking (Perner, 1988). If Jill lies, she wants Jack to believe something that she does not believe, but if she makes an ironic remark, she may make a false statement, but she does not want Jack to believe it. To understand fully the force of another person's utterance, children must be able to appreciate what desires the speaker has about the ensuing beliefs of the listener.

This kind of understanding of the way in which one person's mental state is directed at another person's mental state is unlikely to emerge before children are about six years of age (Harris and Gross, 1988; Perner, 1988). For example, children below the age of six years have difficulties in understanding how the emotion that one person expresses depends upon what that person wants onlookers to believe about his or her emotional state (see chapter 6).

If pride and guilt are inherently social emotions as Cooley argued, an observer who is trying to understand these emotions in another person must also be able to cope with such interlocking mental states. This can be spelled out explicitly in the following way. The audience feels happy that the child has met a particular standard (e.g. performed an athletic feat), or angry that the child has violated some standard (e.g. stolen something). In turn, the child feels pleased that the audience approves of his or her feat; alternatively, the child feels upset that the audience disapproves. An observer who wishes to understand the child's emotional reaction must appreciate that the child *is pleased* that the audience *is happy* that a standard was met; alternatively, the observer must appreciate that the child *is upset* that the audience *is angry* that a standard was violated. Viewed in this way, it is clear that an observer must understand that what the child is pleased or upset about is not so much the achievement or misdemeanour, but rather another emotional reaction, namely the reaction of the audience. Just as an understanding of lying requires that an observer understand how the mental state of the liar (his or her desire) is directed at the mental state of the listener (his or her beliefs), so an understanding of the social emotions requires that an observer understand how the mental state of the protagonist (his or her emotion) is directed at the mental state of the audience (its expression of approbation or disapprobation).

Note that this analysis is still pertinent to the older child who appreciates that pride and guilt can arise in the absence of an actual audience. The audience is not eliminated; rather it is replaced by the child's alter ego who continues to serve as an approving or disapproving audience. As Harter and her colleagues point out, the emergence of this alternative audience is reflected in children's form of words; at about eight years of age they begin to speak explicitly of feeling proud or ashamed *of themselves*, whereas younger subjects talk about the other people who will be proud or ashamed of them.

Finally, it is worth emphasizing that the emotions of pride and guilt, like the simpler emotions of sadness and happiness, can obviously be understood by an observer who does not experience those emotions at the time. The children who work out whether the protagonist will feel proud or ashamed in the stories used by Susan Harter and her colleagues obviously do not need to feel pride or guilt in order to make an appropriate emotional attribution. What I assume they do is to imagine that they had performed the relevant feat or transgression, just like the protagonist in the story, so that they trigger an appropriate 'as if' emotion. In this respect, the mechanism of imaginative projection described in chapter 3 with respect to the emotions of happiness and sadness can be extended to more complex emotions.

The social construction of emotion?

I have deliberately focused on pride, shame and guilt because, as we have seen, they are intimately linked to social norms. Many writers, particularly those who have been influenced by social anthropology, claim that emotions in general have this close connection to social norms (cf. Harré, 1987). Indeed, because of that connection, it has sometimes been argued – against the Darwinian emphasis on a universal set of biologically-based emotions – that emotions are culturally variable, social constructions. I shall argue that these two approaches need to be integrated rather than set in opposition to one another.

Anthropologists often deny that children spontaneously feel

a set of universal emotions. Instead, during development children are taught how to appraise particular situations according to local standards or beliefs, and they are also taught what emotion to feel in the light of that appraisal. Catherine Lutz (1987) illustrates these points by means of an anecdote from her field-work on the island of Ifaluk in the Western Pacific. Seated outside of the house of a sick villager whom she has come to visit, she chats to the woman seated next to her. A four-year-old girl approaches, does a little dance, and makes a silly face. Lutz smiles at her antics but the woman reprimands her, saying: 'Don't smile at her she'll think that you're not *song* [i.e. justifiably angry].' Further ethnographic analysis provides an interpretation for the woman's remark. On Ifaluk, children's happiness or excitement as shown in the girl's antics is expected to lead to misbehaviour. The prospect of such misbehaviour ought to be fended off with a display of *song*, rather than condoned with a smile. A display of justifiable anger will arouse *metagu* (i.e. fear or anxiety) in the child. This episode, analysed in terms of the folk theory of emotion employed on Ifaluk, illustrates how efforts are made to create an appropriate emotional response in the child: *song* is used to prompt the child to regard an uninhibited display of excitement as a misdemeanour, and to feel the appropriate emotion, namely *metagu*, when that misdemeanour is committed.

The analysis made by Catherine Lutz fits readily into the approach that I have described. She suggests that *metagu* (like guilt and shame) will be frequently experienced in response to the actual or anticipated anger of another person following a rule violation. Here, we see again the way in which complex or social emotions depend upon a social interlocking of actor and observer. Of course, it may be that what counts as a rule violation on Ifaluk would not be regarded as such in the West. However, that simply means that the occasions for feeling the emotion of *metagu* have no Western counterpart. It does not mean, ipso facto, that the psychological processes by which it is experienced and understood have no counterpart.

In other respects, however, my emphasis differs from those

who stress the social construction of emotion. In their analyses, children acquire the script for any particular emotion from their culture. Once they have acquired the script, children feel and express the emotion appropriately. However, I have tried to show that the emergence of the emotions of pride and shame, and the eventual understanding of those emotions, cannot be completely derived from a culturally prescribed script. It begins with an understanding of basic emotions such as happiness, sadness and anger. Moreover, children do not need to appreciate social norms in order to experience these basic emotions and to attribute them to other people.

Thus, children do not begin their emotional lives by learning a script from their culture. They are born with the capacity to experience basic emotions of sadness, anger and joy when desirable goals are lost or blocked or achieved. They also come to understand that other people may experience those emotions. That understanding is gradually incorporated into a more complex script that specifies not just how the child will feel, nor how an adult will feel, but how the child will feel in relation to the emotional state of the adult.

Indeed, the roles of actor and observer may continue to feed off one another, in a recursive fashion. Observing another's shame, the child may feel concern, embarrassment or contempt, and particular cultures may orient the child in one direction versus another. Again, the understanding of one emotion constitutes a precondition for experiencing another. More generally, changes in the child's understanding will beget new emotions and new social roles. In contrast to the social constructivists, therefore, I would emphasize the process of imaginative construction that the child engages in both to experience and to understand emotion. For this process to be set in motion, the child must first appreciate the operations of basic emotions, whose script is likely to have a universal base. Although there may indeed be emotions in one culture that have no obvious equivalents in another, the existence of such emotions does not disprove, rather it presupposes the existence of a basic set, on whose foundations they are constructed.

Summary and conclusions

Between the ages of approximately four and ten years, children begin to understand the conditions under which pride, shame and guilt are experienced. During this period, their appreciation of the life of the emotions undergoes a major shift. They cease to view people as agents pursuing their desires, and see them much more as social beings, whose actions are judged either by others or by the self. To explain this shift, I have argued that children become increasingly alert to the fact that the emotional state of one person is influenced by the emotional state of another. For example, people feel pride when they have done something that will elicit approval, and they feel shame when they have done something that will elicit disapproval. Initially, children assume that these evaluations will be supplied by other people, but gradually children appreciate that they can also be supplied by the self.

Approval and disapproval are meted out if a person is responsible for an action that meets, surpasses or falls short of a normative standard. Accordingly, to the extent that children understand that a person is sensitive to approval and disapproval, they will take issues of responsibility and standards into account.

This approach shows that the emotions of pride, shame and guilt are intimately linked to social norms. However, they are not simply social constructions. The emergence of these emotions builds on the experience and understanding of basic emotions such as anger and joy.

NOTES

1 Graham and Weiner (1986) do not stress the point, but it should be emphasized that the understanding of another person's emotion will depend critically on the ease with which one can analyse his or her appraisal of both the outcome and its cause, whether or not one concurs with that appraisal. Just as we noted in the last chapter that the

attribution of happiness and sadness depends on an analysis of the other person's beliefs and desires concerning any given outcome, so the attribution of gratitude or anger to another person will similarly depend on a correct analysis of the way in which that person appraises the cause of a given outcome, whether or not the appraisal is accurate.

2 The findings of Nunner-Winkler and Sodian (1988) do not stand in isolation. Very similar findings have been reported in earlier studies (Barden, Zelko, Duncan and Masters, 1980; Thompson and Hoffman, 1980).

3 I have concentrated on one form of remedial action - namely confession. There are, of course, others such as reparation to the victim. Graham (1988) found that when children between 5 and 11 years were asked to predict how much reparation a child who had damaged a bicycle would make to the owner of the bicycle, older children tied their prediction to whether or not the child felt guilty about the damage, and they expected the degree of guilt to depend on the child's degree of responsibility. Younger children, by contrast, predicted that the child would make reparation, irrespective of the degree of guilt, and irrespective of the degree of responsibility. Here again, we see older children viewing people as moral agents making amends for a transgression that they feel guilty about, whereas younger children see people as attempting to repair damage.

4 More evidence for the child's emerging concept of the mind as a seat for persistent and painful rumination is presented in chapter 7, when children's strategies for dealing with homesickness are discussed. It is interesting to note that even in adulthood, many people continue to seek out a parental figure to help relieve feelings of guilt. In confession, the adult seeks a parental figure who disapproves but offers forgiveness. In therapy, the adult seeks a parental figure who withholds disapproval, and gradually encourages the client to do likewise.

5

Mixed feelings

Interviewer: *'The other day, I was talking to two children. One said that you could feel happy and sad, both at the same time. The other child said that was silly: you couldn't feel happy and sad at the same time. Who was right do you think? Can you feel happy and sad at the same time or not?'*
Six-year-old child: *'No, because you haven't got two heads – you haven't got enough brains.'*

I have argued that children initially learn about the situations that provoke basic emotions like happiness or anger, and then begin to understand the situations that provoke more complex emotions like pride and guilt. In doing so, a simplifying assumption has been made: that any given situation elicits a single emotion. Although this may often be the case, it is not always true. When we are about to start some new venture, we often feel a mixture of apprehension and excitement. Conversely, when an opportunity slips through our fingers, we might feel disappointment tinged with relief. These cases of mixed emotions are intriguing because they involve ambivalence: a combination of positive and negative emotion. Indeed, when we consider our relationships with other people, feelings of ambivalence are almost inevitable at certain times.

As we shall see in this chapter, the explicit recognition of ambivalence is difficult for children. It takes several years before they can put such feelings into words, even though their behaviour shows that ambivalent feelings are quite common from an early age. For this reason, it is important to distinguish between the behavioural expression of ambivalence and its conscious recognition. The behavioural expression of ambivalence can be seen even among one-year-olds, whereas its conscious acknowledgement is rare before seven or eight years of age.

Ambivalence in behaviour

There are two well-documented examples of ambivalence in the preschool years. The first was discovered by Mary Ainsworth and her colleagues in their pioneering studies of mother–child attachment (1978). They observed one-year-old children experiencing a series of short separations from their mothers. A minority of these children displayed an overtly ambivalent reaction to their mother when they were eventually reunited with her. These ambivalent babies did not obviously differ from other babies in terms of their initial approach to the mother on being reunited with her: to varying degrees, they went towards her and tried to maintain contact with her. They did differ, however, in their resistance to contact with the mother: they actively resisted being picked up by her or cuddled. They seemed to vacillate between seeking out contact with her and then resisting that contact when it was offered.

A series of follow-up studies has confirmed the existence of the ambivalent pattern in other samples of children. For example, Joseph Campos and his colleagues (1983) reviewed five different American studies of one-year-olds and concluded that about one in six babies showed the resistant or ambivalent pattern at 12 months. Moreover, almost half of these children continued to behave in the same fashion when they were re-tested six to seven months later (Campos, Barrett, Lamb, Goldsmith and Stenberg, 1983).

There is considerable controversy about the origins of such ambivalence. Following Mary Ainsworth, most writers on attachment have attributed it to inconsistent handling by the mother, but cross-cultural studies throw some doubt on whether maternal handling is the only factor involved. For example, the proportion of ambivalent or resistant babies varies quite markedly from culture to culture. In Sweden, only about one baby in 25 showed the ambivalent pattern (Lamb, Hwang, Frodi, and Frodi, 1982). By contrast, in Japan this proportion rose to more than one baby in four (Miyake, Chen and Campos, 1985). Whatever the exact origin of this pattern of behaviour, we can conclude that ambivalent emotional reactions toward the mother are not uncommon at 12 and 18 months.

Further examples of ambivalence in early childhood come from the observations of siblings made by Charlotte Bühler (Bühler, 1937) and more recently by Judy Dunn. Older siblings often vacillate between tenderness and hostility in their approach to a younger sibling. For example, Laura said to her younger brother: 'All right, baby,' as she caressed him. A moment later, she turned to her mother and said: 'Smack him.' Fay behaved in much the same way toward her younger sister: 'Baby. Baby,' she said as she stroked her, and then: 'Monster. Monster.' Her mother remonstrated: 'She's not a monster,' but Fay remained unconvinced: 'Monster,' she insisted (Dunn, 1984).

Conceptualizing positive and negative emotions

Given such ambivalent comments and behaviour, one might think that young children would readily link the same situation or the same person to both positive and negative feelings. Yet children dichotomize those situations that elicit positive feelings and those that elicit negative feelings. The split emerges whether they are asked to say what situation would provoke a particular emotion or to say what emotion would be provoked by a particular situation (Stein and Levine, 1987; Trabasso, Stein and Johnson, 1981). This conceptual schism between positive and negative emotions turns out to be widespread. When we presented Dutch, English and Nepalese children with a set of emotion terms and asked them to think of situations that would be likely to provoke each emotion, there was very little overlap in the situations that they suggested for positive as opposed to negative emotions (Harris, Olthof, Meerum Terwogt and Hardman, 1987).

Catherine Lutz observed a similar phenomenon when

carrying out her field-work among the Ifaluk, a Malayo-Polynesian community that lives on a small coral atoll in the Western Pacific. She asked members of the community to sort emotion words into groups depending on their perceived similarity. Two distinct clusters of terms emerged, one associated with positive emotions and the other with negative emotions (Lutz, 1982).

Although these cultures are enormously diverse, ranging from European urban communities to tiny farming hamlets in the Himalayan mountains to fishing communities in the Pacific Ocean, a recurrent pattern emerges. Emotions may be grouped together – for example the same situation might be mentioned for both pride and happiness, or fear and guilt, but such groupings rarely cross the dividing line between positive and negative emotions. This division between positive and negative terms is ubiquitous and also stable: it is apparent when we test small children at the age of three to four years, and it is still found among adults.

Recognizing ambivalence: basic findings

So far, we have looked at two aspects of emotional development: the emotions that children express, and the emotions that they consider to go together. Children in the first years of life express ambivalent feelings. Their willingness to comfort and soothe a sibling can be rapidly replaced by aggression or teasing. Their demands to be held and comforted by their mother can alternate with resistance and rejection. At the conceptual level, however, they rarely describe the same situation as provoking positive and negative feelings. Instead, we see a pervasive split between these two clusters of emotion.

What happens if the child is explicitly asked whether the same situation or the same person can cause both positive and negative feelings? On the one hand, we might expect children to admit to such a possibility because they express ambivalence in their behaviour and spontaneous remarks. On the other hand, we might expect them to deny it, given that they dichotomize situations, conceiving of some as provoking only positive feelings and others as provoking only negative feelings.

Susan Harter was the first person to look systematically at this issue. She noticed that many of the children she saw in clinical practice had great difficulty in admitting to mixed feelings, particularly towards a relative or caretaker (Harter, 1977). Provoked by this observation, she initiated a study of the ability of normal children to acknowledge such feelings (Harter, 1983; Harter and Buddin, 1987). Her technique was to ask children to describe situations that would provoke each of several emotions, including the basic emotions of happiness, anger, sadness and fear. Children were also asked to describe situations that would provoke two emotions in succession, and two emotions at the same time.

She found that the child develops through several stages. Very young children, aged three to six years, are not able to conceive of two emotions being provoked either successively or simultaneously. They can readily describe situations that will elicit one of the basic emotions, but deny that it is possible to provoke two. At around six to eight years children begin to describe situations that will elicit two emotions, but with one emotion following the other: 'I'd feel happy that the present I was getting might be something I liked and then mad if it was something I didn't like'; or 'I'd feel excited about getting on the roller coaster but scared once it got going'; or 'If you were in a haunted house you'd be scared but then you'd be happy after you got out of it.' These same children continue to doubt that it is possible to experience two feelings at the same time. Only at about seven or eight years of age do they start to describe situations that could cause two simultaneous emotions. At first, they describe situations that would be likely to evoke two feelings of the same valence – two positive feelings or two negative feelings. They describe either a single incident – for example, 'If your brother hit you, you would be both mad and sad'; or two distinct incidents that might occur at the same time – for example, 'I'd be mad if she took one of my rings and sad if she broke one of my pictures.'

The most difficult task is to integrate two opposite feelings. Harter and her colleagues found that children begin to produce appropriate examples at about ten years of age. Initially, they describe situations that involve two separate but concurrent situations: 'I was sitting in school feeling worried about all of the responsibilities of a new pet, but I was happy that I got straight A's on my report card.' Roughly one year later, at 11 years of age, they described a single episode with two intertwined aspects: 'I was happy that I got a present but mad that it wasn't what I wanted.'

Taken together, the studies illustrate a fascinating developmental sequence. Initially, children deny that a given situation will provoke more than one feeling. At an intermediate stage, they can suggest situations that would provoke two feelings, but one after the other. Finally, at a third stage, they suggest situations that would provoke two feelings at once. This third stage can itself be broken down into various sub-stages: initially, children describe situations that would provoke two feelings of the same valence both positive or both negative; only later do they describe situations that would provoke two feelings of a different valence. Most difficult of all is the acknowledgement that a single episode or target can elicit such ambivalence. Note that it is exactly the latter type of ambivalence that very young children express to members of their family. In sum, although there is evidence from observational studies that toddlers and pre-school children express mixed feelings towards a single target such as their mother, brother or sister, such ambivalence is not consciously and explicitly acknowledged for many years.

Recognizing ambivalence: further evidence

Although the results of Harter and her colleagues are very intriguing, the children were always asked to invent or remember situations in which mixed feelings would be possible. Arguably, they do recognize mixed feelings but find it difficult to recollect situations when they have experienced them. Perhaps Harter's findings simply reflect children's improving ability to remember or construct illustrative situations, rather than any developing insight into their existence as such.

On the other hand, if children really do find it difficult to recognize ambivalent feelings they should continue to do so even if all difficulties of memory and invention are removed. For example, if they are told about ambivalent situations rather than asked to remember or invent them they should still not recognize that mixed or opposing feelings would be provoked. This was the procedure adopted by Mark Meerum Terwogt and his colleagues in a study carried out in the Netherlands (Meerum Terwogt, Koops, Oosterhoff and Olthof, 1986). Children listened to short stories in which the main character encountered a situation likely to elicit mixed feelings, and they were then asked to say how the character would feel. For example, one story described a child at the circus who was asked by a clown to come out of her seat to help the clown in the ring. The younger children of approximately seven years tended to focus on one feeling only. They might say that the girl would be excited to help the clown. The older children, in contrast, often said that the girl would be excited to help the clown, but at the same time nervous about stepping into the ring in front of so many people. The overall pattern was clear: older children recognized the existence of more than one emotional reaction to the same episode, especially when those multiple reactions involved a mixture of positive and negative feelings.

Nadja Reissland (1985) asked children to offer examples of ambivalence from their own experience, and also to analyse the feelings of a story character. As one might expect from the results described so far, children performed in a similar fashion on both tasks. Children below the age of seven and a half years typically produced non-simultaneous examples from their own lives, and they identified only a single emotion for the story character. By contrast, most of the older children were able both to produce their own examples of ambivalence, and to analyse correctly the feelings of the story character. Therefore, even when difficulties of invention or memory are circumvented by presenting ambivalent situations, younger children still find it difficult to acknowledge mixed feelings, just as Harter and her colleagues would predict.

Before turning to an explanation of why children's understanding of ambivalence develops so slowly, we may consider one further issue. Younger children might differ from older children not so much in terms of their ability to recognize mixed feelings, as in terms of the way that they view such complicated situations. Consider the example of the circus clown once again. Perhaps younger children simply do not think of the situation as anxiety-inducing, so that it is not a question of their failing to acknowledge mixed feelings. They simply appraise such a situation rather differently from older children.

To check this possibility, we gave children stories that contained two separable events, a positive event likely to elicit happiness and a negative event likely to elicit anger, or sadness or fear (Harris, 1983; Experiment 2). One of the stories went as follows: 'Late one night, there is a bark outside the door. It's Lassie, your dog. She has been lost all day and she has come home, but she has cut her ear in a fight.'

Lassie's homecoming has two conflicting components. She has been lost so that her homecoming is a happy event but she has also cut her ear so that her homecoming is, at least in part, a sad event. Children listened to each story in one of two ways. They either heard a single story with each of the conflicting events included, as in the story above. Alternatively, they listened to two separate versions: one contained the negative event and the other contained the positive event. For example, the negative version story did not mention that Lassie had now come home after being lost. It only described her cut ear: 'Late one night, there is a bark outside the door. It's Lassie, your dog. She has cut her ear in a fight.' Similarly, the positive version did not mention that Lassie had hurt her ear. It only described her happy homecoming. 'Late one night, there is a bark outside the door. It's Lassie, your dog. She has been lost all day and she has come home.'

The results were quite straightforward. Both six- and ten-year-olds said that the story character would feel happy in response to positive events (for example, Lassie coming home after being lost) and sad, angry or afraid in response to negative events (for example, Lassie's cut ear). When these two events were integrated into a single story, however, the two age groups gave different replies. The six-year-olds almost always focused on only one of the two events, some claiming that the story character would be sad, and some claiming that the story character would be happy, but not both. The older children were much more likely – about three times as likely, in fact – to say that the story character would feel a mixture of positive and negative emotion.

We also asked children to tell the story in their own words. Their memory for the stories turned out to be surprisingly good. Younger and older children alike typically remembered each of the relevant emotionally charged components, whether they were presented in isolation, as in the truncated versions, or in combination, as in the more complex integrated stories. The contrast in the younger chiidren between their blinkered assessment of the story character's feelings and their comprehensive recall of the story was striking. A child would claim that on opening the door to Lassie the story character would feel only happiness and not sadness. The same child went on a moment later to recall both critical events in the story, to remember, for example, not just that Lassie had come home, but also that she had returned with a cut ear.

Apparently, younger children were not forgetting or simplifying the mixed emotion stories: they understood and remembered both events, and they admitted that one would elicit positive feelings and the other negative feelings when they considered them in isolation. Yet when the two events were connected together in a unified story, they focused on one emotion to the exclusion of any other.

Taken together the findings of these various studies all converge on the same conclusion. Until about eight to ten years of age children have difficulty in recognizing the existence of two concurrent emotions, particularly when those feelings are in conflict with one another, one being positive and the other being negative, and particularly when those feelings have been aroused by one situation or one person. The difficulty arises whether children are asked to recall such situations from their own past, to invent appropriate situations or to analyse the feelings of a character in a story. Moreover, the problem does not lie in any inability to appreciate that a situation may contain two conflicting components. As soon as the components are presented in isolation, even six-year-olds can identify one component as positive and the other as negative. Their difficulty in recognizing ambivalence only arises when the two components are re-integrated.

We do not know, of course, exactly how younger children think about such dual-faceted situations, but it may be useful to liken their difficulties to those that we encounter as adults in dealing with ambiguous perceptual figures. Consider, for example, the well-known ambiguous figure of the duck-rabbit. At first sight, we may see this exclusively as a duck and disregard its potential rabbit-like appearance (or vice versa). Young children appear to interpret emotionally ambiguous situations in much the same way. As soon as they focus on one emotionally-charged component, the other disappears from sight. If they now shift their focus to the second, the first disappears from sight.

Explanations

The results reported so far are dramatic. We have evidence of an enormous lag between children's behaviour and their conscious report. As early as the second year, toddlers express ambivalence in their behaviour, particularly when dealing with family members such as mothers, and brothers and sisters. On the other hand, children explicitly recognize the existence of mixed feelings only at about eight to ten years.

How should this gap be explained? One possibility is that it is due to the obvious difference between facing an emotionally-charged experience and thinking about hypothetical or past experiences. Children might identify ambivalent feelings when they are encountering a complicated two-factor situation, but not when they are interviewed about some hypothetical or past situation. Maybe it is difficult to imagine experiencing ambivalence in a situation that one is not now facing but easy to recognize it if one is experiencing it. If this argument is correct, it should be possible to reduce or eliminate the gap between what children express and what they admit, simply by questioning them about what they feel in a real situation, rather than what they might feel in an imagined situation. The available evidence does not support this plausible expectation. Mark Lipian, a paediatrician with an interest in the psychological aspects of children's illness, talked to children about their feelings surrounding illness. Some of the children were ill at the time and were interviewed in hospital. Others, who were healthy, were interviewed in school and they were asked to think back to the time that they had last been ill. The children who were ill showed no greater recognition of mixed feelings (Harris and Lipian, 1989; Lipian, 1985). The typical pattern of development was found when ten-year-olds were compared with six-year-olds. The older children said that being ill made them feel miserable or upset, but had its positive side in terms of missing school and getting special treats, but younger children rarely identified such mixed reactions. If anything, the children who were not actually experiencing illness and asked to think back to the last time that they had been ill were more likely to say that they could experience mixed feelings about being ill.

A further piece of evidence comes from Harter's original observations, which were made in clinical settings (Harter, 1977). She noticed that several of the children in her clinical practice had difficulty in recognizing that they felt ambivalent towards particular family members. The children oscillated between anger and affection towards these people but denied that they felt both emotions. In sum, there is no indication that young children are more able to identify mixed feelings when they are actually experiencing them. The problem seems to lie in the way that they understand their feelings – or the situation causing those feelings – not in the immediacy of the feelings themselves.

Why are mixed feelings so hard to understand? One possibility is that children give what they take to be sensible, internally consistent responses to the questions that are put to them by the interviewer. We have already seen that children, even from three years of age, make a sharp distinction between the situations that provoke negative emotions and those that provoke positive emotions. It would not be surprising, therefore, if they came to think of emotions like *happy* and *sad*, or *loving* and *angry*, as mutually exclusive opposites. There is certainly evidence that children of this age can respond in an oppositional fashion to pairs of words such as *big* and *little*, or *tall* and *short* (Harris, Morris and Meerum Terwogt, 1986). Similarly, they might be reluctant to describe a person, including themselves, as both *happy* and *sad*, just as they avoid describing the same toy or brick as *big* and *little*. We obtained some tentative support for this argument (Harris, 1983). When six- and ten-year-olds were explicitly asked whether a person could be happy and sad at the same time, most six-year-olds claimed that this was impossible, and they sometimes went on to emphasize the apparent contradiction between feeling happy and sad at the same time: 'Because they don't go together'; 'Well, because they're the opposite of each other; it's either good or it's bad.' A similar insistence on logical or semantic incompatibility was found in a study of children entering a boarding school, to be described in more detail in chapter 7 (Harris and Guz, 1986). For example, 'No, 'cos if you're excited, you're happy and if you're worried, you're sad.' 'Because if you're unhappy, it means that you're not excited.'

However, although such scholastic justifications were common, there were also many other quite different justifications: 'No, because you can't make your face go down and up'; or 'Because you can't think two ways.' Susan Harter reports equally graphic denials: 'There is no way you could have two feelings at the same time since you only have one mind!' 'You'd have to be two different people to have two feelings at the very same time.' 'You can't make your mouth go up and down at the same time!' (Harter and Buddin, 1987). The children's justifications are quite varied, so that they are probably giving post hoc explanations of their initial denial, explanations that do not necessarily lead them to that denial in the first place. All in all, the variety of justifications produced by the children make it unlikely that they are simply striving for what they regard as logical consistency.[1]

The explanation that I favour builds on two of the key points that have already emerged. First, there seems little doubt that young children express ambivalence. This implies that, at some level, they can appraise people or situations in terms of both positive and negative features. In order to admit that certain situations arouse mixed feelings, children need to interpret more carefully the emotional reactions that they already express. To explain why they take so long to engage in accurate scrutiny, we need to turn to the second point that has emerged: a major stumbling block lies in children's conception of the way that emotions are linked to situations. Recall that children progress through a series of stages in acknowledging ambivalence. Following their blanket denial of any such possibility, they begin to allow that two successive situations can arouse first one feeling and then another; still later they admit that two concurrent situations can elicit mixed feelings; and, finally, they admit that a single target – a particular person or situation – is sufficient. Each of these stages in the recognition of mixed feelings involves a change in the child's conceptualization of the causal links between situations and emotion.

Note that development might have taken a quite different

route; children might have found certain emotions or certain combinations of emotion to be a particular stumbling block. For example, they might have found it especially hard to identify feelings of sadness and happiness, but easier to admit to simultaneous feelings of anxiety and excitement. The available research, however, does not offer much support for such a suggestion. It is children's assessment of the way in which situations cause emotion that appears to be changing, rather than their conceptualization of the emotions that ensue.

Granted these two points, how exactly does the child's scrutiny of the link between situation and emotion come to change? We may speculate that upon encountering an emotionally-charged situation the following sequence occurs: first, the child engages in an initial, global appraisal of the situation; that appraisal leads to the arousal of emotion, be it positive, negative or both; following the arousal of emotion the child becomes aware of his or her emotionally-aroused state – there may be various subjective, physiological and behavioural signs that signal emotion – and seeks some explanation by looking for an appropriate, emotionally-charged event that has just taken place.

Hence, there are two systems in the mind of the child: the initial appraisal system and the explanatory system. These two systems operate quite differently. Initial appraisal operates in an exhaustive fashion, and can include both positive and negative elements of the situation so that a mixture of positive and negative emotion may be triggered and expressed. The search for an explanation, however, is not exhaustive; the child scans what has happened most recently – or rather what remains vivid in memory from the recent past – and identifies events that are similar to those that have in the past led to emotion. The child then regards such events as causes of any current emotionally-aroused state and these links between emotion and situation are stored away in memory.

These assumptions allow us to offer an explanation for the two findings that have been established: first, the huge lag between the expression of ambivalence and its conscious recognition; and second, the progressive re-conceptualization of the link between situation and emotion. The process of initial appraisal leads to the child's expression of emotion. We may assume that this process is available even in infancy, and it leads to the ambivalence that babies and toddlers express in their behaviour. The subsequently activated explanatory system which undergoes important changes during development gives rise to the child's knowledge and understanding of the circumstances in which particular emotions are felt. The actual expression of emotion can be ambivalent because the appraisal system scans the current situation in an exhaustive fashion. The explanatory system, by contrast, is non-exhaustive. It concentrates on the detection and storage of recurrent links between particular situations and particular emotions, and it does this by focusing on an emotion that is currently being experienced and linking it to a recent event that is vivid in the child's memory. The immediately preceding situation is only examined selectively and non-exhaustively. Therefore, young children may express ambivalence without being consciously aware that they feel ambivalent.

We now need to explain how, during development, the explanatory system comes to re-conceptualize the links between situation and emotion so that the existence of ambivalence is gradually recognized. If children link their current emotion to the most recent and vivid event, they will inevitably conclude that positive and negative emotions typically have different causes. This follows from the fact that positive emotions are usually preceded by positive events, and negative emotions are usually preceded by negative events. Having established these typical linkages, children will assert that it is impossible to experience mixed feelings. Since they tie emotion to its most immediate and plausible cause, and since the causes of positive and negative emotions rarely overlap, they will find it difficult to conceive of a situation that would elicit both. Even when they express mixed or conflicting emotions in their behaviour, they will still seek to explain their emotionally aroused state by focusing narrowly on a single recent event, insisting that they feel positive or negative feelings rather than both at the same time.

Nevertheless, in their everyday experience, children will come to note that links between particular situations and particular emotions can themselves be joined into longer chains. For example, in seeking an explanation of their current happiness, they might look back at what has just happened and note that some lost object has been restored; looking further back, they may also recall that before the restoration, they felt sad about what they had lost. The chaining together of such links between situation and emotion should lead children to admit that although mixed feelings cannot be experienced concurrently, they can be experienced successively.

We now come to a crucial step. How can children's experience ever instruct them that positive and negative feelings can be felt alongside one another, especially if they obstinately focus on one recent event that is salient in consciousness or at best two successive events that provoke first one feeling and then another? There is an important bridge between successive and simultaneous feelings. Sometimes children will experience two consecutive events but the emotions may not be consecutive. An earlier feeling can often persist, so that a later event simply arouses another emotion alongside the first emotion rather than displacing it. For example, the child loses a favourite toy; this lost toy is never found but the child is given something in compensation that does not quite match the original. To the extent that the child remembers and misses the original object, sadness will persist, and endure alongside the pleasure that is taken in the new object.

These circumstances or, more generally, any circumstance in which an earlier emotion is sustained so that it endures alongside a later conflicting emotion, ought to be especially instructive according to the assumptions that we have made. First, children will express mixed feelings, or more likely a vacillation from one feeling state to the other. They should then search their memory of the immediate past for events that plausibly explain their emotionally-aroused state. This search should lead child to waver between two equally vivid events, one that happened more recently, and an earlier event that continues to live on in the child's memory. For example, the child might think about the gift that has just been received, only to be immediately reminded of the lost toy that the gift was supposed to compensate for. The child's attention will be drawn to two plausible and separate links between recent events and current emotion. Such experiences should prompt children to realize that successive events can engender two feelings that are experienced separately in an oscillatory fashion, if not concurrently.

There are several pieces of evidence that provide some support for this emphasis on successive events that generate parallel feelings. First, as we shall discuss in chapter 7, children rapidly come to understand that an emotion does not disappear abruptly, but can persist beyond the precipitating situation (Harris, Guz, Lipian and Man-Shu, 1985). Second, six- and seven-year-olds are prepared to admit that two concurrent feelings can be aroused in a staggered fashion by two distinct successive events, even though they doubt that such feelings can be aroused by concurrent events. For example, we told children stories about a character who first had a quarrel on the way home from school but was then given an unexpected present on arriving home (Harris, 1983). Even six-year-olds appreciated that the story character's feelings would not be exclusively governed by the gift; they realized that the character would feel a mixture of happiness about the gift and distress about the earlier quarrel. Similar results were found by Sally Donaldson and Michael Westerman (1986). Again, children listened to stories in which a happy event followed a sad event. For example, the story character's pet kitten was lost and replaced by another kitten. Seven- and eight-year-olds often spontaneously said that the story character would experience two feelings; for example: 'kinda happy and kinda sad because the new kitten would remind him of Snowball [the lost kitten].'[2]

Note that the recognition of ambivalence in these two studies is precocious relative to the norms provided by Susan Harter and her colleagues but the stories contain two consecutive episodes, and they involve feelings that persist from the first episode to the second. This is an easy situation to analyse according to the account just described, precisely because the two events are each vividly and separately represented in memory and each comes to mind as a distinct but plausible explanation for the current emotional state.

In line with this analysis, further probing by Donaldson and Westerman showed that although seven- and eight-year-olds claim that the both feelings can be experienced, they deny that the feelings commingle. They either think of them as alternating over time:

Interviewer: Do the sad feelings mix together with the happy ones or stay separate?
Child: Stay separate.
Interviewer: When Bill is happy do the sad feelings go away?
Child: Yes.

Alternatively, they envisage a curious corporeal fission:

Interviewer: So, does that mean he feels both happy and sad?
Child: Yeah.
Interviewer: How does that work?
Child: Some part of his body is happy and some part of his body is sad.

Such segregation would be expected if the child finds it easier to focus on one situation–emotion link at a time rather than engaging in a comprehensive interpretation of the mix of feelings that is engendered.

Having realized that two consecutive events can arouse

feelings that are concurrent, the child is now prepared for the final step: the recognition that two concurrent events or even a single situation with two components can arouse ambivalent feelings. The child can highlight his or her ambivalence by mentally focusing first on one and then on the other plausible link between situation and current emotion. Such a phenomenal vacillation – repeated often enough – should gradually persuade the child that events that co-occur in reality and not just events that are held concurrently in memory can elicit ambivalent feelings. This insight should be easier if two separable events are involved, since the child can more readily identify each causal link and already appreciates that two events separated in time can elicit ambivalence. It should be harder when the events are intertwined with one another, involving, for example, the same person or a single event with two opposing implications, just as Susan Harter and her colleagues observed.

Once such intertwined causation is understood, we might expect the child finally to admit that the emotions themselves commingle. Sally Donaldson and Michael Westerman observed exactly this developmental shift. Unlike the younger children, most 10- and 11-year-olds recognized that two feelings could coexist at the same time and interact with one another. For example, sadness over the loss of Snowball might temper happiness when the new kitten arrived; indeed, the vacillation between the two feelings could be puzzling:

Child: Well, maybe when she first opened the door [and sees the new kitten] she'd be really, really happy but then she'd be in between – she'd be glad to have a new kitten but sad a little too.
Interviewer: What's that feel like inside?
Child: Well, you don't know how you feel really, you're not really sure.
Interviewer: . . . Is it confusing?
Child: Yes.

Conclusions

Research on children's understanding of mixed feelings has produced a surprisingly orderly picture. Children are quite slow to admit to ambivalence, even though they express it from an early age. The gap between understanding and expression suggests that the child's emotional life must operate at two distinct levels. On the one hand, the child engages in a thorough analysis at some automatic or semi-conscious level that leads to the overt expression of ambivalence in behaviour. By contrast, the child's retrospective and conscious analysis of the links between situation and emotion is, at least in its initial stages, non-exhaustive. Having noticed that situations typically elicit either positive or negative feelings, children start off by denying that mixed feelings are possible. Gradually, they reconceptualize the links that exist between situation and emotion. Their phenomenal experience of shifting feelings gradually intrudes and breaks down their insistence that the two types of feeling are quite separate.

If this interpretation is correct, it shows that we can properly speak of the child gaining insight into his or her emotional life. The recognition of ambivalence is not simply the adoption by the child of a more sophisticated, but equivocal folk theory, that is promulgated by adults or the community at large. It is a genuine case of the child turning round on his or her own schemata, and gaining new insight as a result.

NOTES

1 A study by Gnepp, McKee and Domanic (1987) provides further ammunition against the proposal that younger children are striving for what they take to be logical consistency. The children were asked whether certain emotionally equivocal situations (e.g. being asked to sing in front of an audience) might provoke *either* a positive *or* a negative

emotion in the same person, with no implication that *both* emotions be felt at the same time. The youngest children (five-year-olds) were likely to claim that only one emotion would be felt, whereas older children (eight-year-olds) recognized that either might be felt. Since there is nothing logically inconsistent about claiming that an event might be positive *or* negative, the younger children's focus on only one alternative again reveals a non-exhaustive analysis of the situation, rather than logical nicety.

2 I am grateful to Michael Westerman for supplying an unpublished coding manual from which these quotations are taken.

6

Hiding emotion

'She didn't want the other children to know that she's sad that she fell over.'

Six-year-old explaining emotional restraint.

The Chewong are a small aboriginal group of hunter-gatherers and shifting cultivators in the tropical rain forest of peninsular Malaysia. Signe Howell, a social anthropologist who lived with them for more than a year, describes their remarkable restraint as follows:

> The Chewong [do not] employ a wide range of bodily and facial expressions. They rarely use gestures of any kind and their faces register little change as they speak or listen. The outsider is constantly struck by their restrained behaviour even at meetings and partings, and the fact that they never seem to 'lose control'. (Howell, 1981)

The Chewong have a variety of explicit rules regarding the display of emotion. For example, *Punen* stipulates that one must not 'speak badly'. Bad speech can consist in talking about a forthcoming pleasurable event. A hunter who has successfully killed a monkey should not express his pleasure at the prospect of eating the delicacy that night. Similarly, no emotion should be expressed after an accident such as falling over or losing one's possessions. Another rule, the rule of *Pantang*, even prohibits the display of pleasure or grief at major life events such as birth, marriage and death. The Chewong claim that failure to obey these rules and various others concerned with sharing food, and laughing at or teasing particular animals – can provoke misfortune, be it an illness or an attack from a tiger.

Michelle Rosaldo, another social anthropologist, describes the quite different culture of the Ilongot in northern Luzon in the Philippines. The Ilongot are a tribe of hunters and shifting cultivators who, at least before the mid-sixties, engaged in the practice of head-hunting. Various pressures, including the efforts of the government and missionary zeal, have meant that they have abandoned the practice. Nevertheless, based on field-work in the late sixties and in 1974, Rosaldo (1980) constructed an ethnography of their traditional way of life and placed the practice of head-hunting in its wider social context.

One of the key ideas that emerges from her ethnography is that the Ilongot have a distinctive concept of the role of anger or more generally of passion in men's lives. The Ilongot think of *liget*, roughly translated as energy/anger/passion, as a positive virtue, a force that is especially potent in young men, and is readily stirred by slight insults and by real or imagined grievances. This energy can rouse men to kill, not simply as an act of vengeance, but as a means of emotional expression and as a means of emulating the feats of their fathers and elders. By such acts, they achieve a sense of pride and potency. The elders of the tribe deliberately fostered the expression of *liget* among the young men by volunteering their skills and experience in the planning and execution of a head-hunting raid.

The Ilongot believe that emotion requires cultivation. They do not see passion as a natural capacity of the infant; rather, it is cultivated in the course of social experience. They also acknowledge that tolerance and forbearance are crucial within the immediate social circle of the extended family if daily life is not to be constantly disrupted. They insist that children and especially adults must display *adug* (tolerance). Local insults are dealt with by resignation, by allowing time for passions to dissipate, and for the insults to be forgotten. Youths are reckoned to lack the knowledge and restraint to show such forbearance and so rebellious, thoughtless acts of irritation from them are accepted and even expected. The mature adult is thought to combine passion (*liget*) and knowledge (*beya*) in ways that permit a planned concentration of energy, or a gradual diffusion of that energy where it is appropriate.

The contrast between the Chewong and the Ilongot illustrates how cultural practices regulate the expression of emotion. These practices do not mean that the otherwise spontaneous display of emotion by the young child is gradually inhibited or suppressed during development. The Ilongot positively encourage the exhibition of *liget* among their young men. Even among the Chewong, it would be wrong to say that all emotional display is discouraged; timorous children who exhibit a respectful hesitation are praised by adult Chewong. It is only boisterousness and disrespect that are criticized. Thus, cultural practices encourage the suppression of certain emotions and the display of others; which particular emotional themes are amplified or stifled will vary from culture to culture.

What is the impact of such rules for display or suppression on members of a given culture? One possibility is that they alter, not just what is outwardly expressed, but what is inwardly felt: the experience of emotion moves into line with the expression that is cultivated. An alternative possibility is that such prescriptions influence the outward display of emotion, leaving private experience untouched. In this chapter, I shall explore evidence for this second possibility. I shall argue that even if our culture does sometimes teach us what to feel, as seems likely, it also sometimes teaches us what emotion to display without at the same time transforming our emotional experience. As a result, there is an important distinction to be made between people's apparent emotion and their actual emotion. Children themselves come to make that distinction quite systematically and they make it at approximately the same age in different parts of the world. Before presenting the evidence for that claim we will take a closer look at the use of display rules by adults.

Experimental studies

Cross-cultural variation in the use of display rules for emotion has rarely been studied in the laboratory, but Paul Ekman and his associates have shown that it can be done (Ekman, 1973). They presented Japanese and American adults with two films, a neutral travelogue, and a disturbing film about sinus surgery. As they watched the films their facial expressions were filmed and subsequently analysed. Not surprisingly, the two films provoked different reactions. The surgical film elicited more surprised, disgusted, sad and even angry facial expressions, whereas the travelogue provoked more happy expressions. The Japanese and the Americans responded in much the same way to the two films – negatively to the surgical film and positively to the travelogue. Detailed analysis showed that the frequency with which six basic emotions were expressed was very similar in the two groups.

At first glance, this similarity between the two cultures is surprising. I have just argued that cultures are selective in the way that they encourage their members to express some emotions rather than others. Why then did no differences emerge, especially given the common observation that the Japanese are more reticent in expressing negative emotion? Ekman and his colleagues had taken the precaution of showing the two films in semi-darkness. Under these circumstances, the normal culture-specific rules governing the display of emotion seem to have been suspended. Apparently, both the Japanese and the Americans felt no need to suppress their spontaneous expressions of emotion when they could watch unobserved and their expressions were therefore similar.

Differences between the Japanese and the Americans did emerge when they were subsequently interviewed about the films by a member of their own culture. The Japanese tended to conceal the discomfort and distress that they had displayed when watching the film. Instead, they maintained a smiling or positive expression even when describing the surgical film. In contrast, the Americans were less likely to hide the feelings they had experienced. In effect, their facial expressions were more likely to resemble the negative reactions they had spontaneously shown when they watched the films. This study shows how cultural display rules can regulate the overt display of emotion – especially in a public situation – without altering the private experience.

People may attempt to conceal their emotions, but how far can they do so successfully? Paul Ekman and Wallace Friesen (1974) found that partial but not complete success is usually achieved. They chose to study student nurses because it is sometimes part of their job to conceal their anxiety from patients and relatives. The nurses saw a distressing film that included pictures of amputations and the treatment of severe burns. Afterwards, they were asked to attempt to mislead an interviewer into thinking that they had seen a pleasant film.

Judges who were given samples of both honest and deceptive behaviour by the nurses were quite poor at deciding which was which. They did best if they were first familiarized with the nurse's normal behaviour and then shown film of her deceptive bodily movements rather than her face. The nurses were better able to monitor their facial expressions than their posture and limb movements, so that although their face was often misleading, their bodily movements gave them away. The nurses themselves provided support for this selectivity. When they talked afterwards about their efforts at deception, they were especially likely to mention efforts to control their facial expression rather than their posture or limb movements.

The development of display rules

When and how do children start to follow display rules, especially facial display rules, when they express their feelings? In a pioneering study, Carolyn Saarni observed the extent to which children attempt to hide their feelings of disappointment. She asked children ranging from six to ten years of age to help her by looking through a textbook, solving a problem in it, and then giving their evaluation of the textbook (Saarni, 1984). When they had done this, they were thanked and given an attractive present. Later, they were asked to do the same thing again but this time they were unexpectedly given a drab-looking toy, such as a plastic key on a ring. Their behaviour during the unwrapping of the gift, and immediately afterwards, was filmed for both sessions.

In the first session, when the children were given an attractive toy, positive reactions – a broad smile and an enthusiastic 'thank you' were common among boys and girls alike. In the second session, when the children were presumably disappointed, most of them avoided expressing it overtly. Admittedly, the youngest group of boys often remained unsmiling, but the other children typically produced so-called transitional expressions. They looked as if they were attempting to suppress their disappointment but without being able to substitute a fully positive reaction. They offered a slight smile and mumbled their thanks.

Pamela Cole followed up these findings by looking at still younger children, a group of three-to four-year-old girls (Cole, 1986; Study 2). She too observed children's reactions to being given a disappointing gift but she made two important changes to the procedure. She made sure that the gift would definitely prove disappointing. The children were asked to rank-order a set of toys in terms of how much they liked them, and the gift that they eventually received was the toy that they liked least. She also compared the girls' reactions to disappointment in two different situations. In one situation, the interviewer was present as the child opened the gift. In the other, the interviewer withdrew so that the child opened her present alone.

This comparison is informative because although the gift, and presumably the degree of disappointment, is the same in each situation, the motivation to hide disappointment is likely to be more acute when the interviewer remains present and can watch the child's reaction. It is possible to compare the child's spontaneous or natural reaction with the reaction that is expressed when a display rule is being applied, just as Paul Ekman and Wallace Friesen had done in their study of Japanese and American adults. Behaviour in the two situations proved to be noticeably different. The girls openly expressed their disappointment when the interviewer was not there to watch, but concealed it with a half-smile if she remained present. This neat study provides the strongest evidence we have so far that children can monitor their emotional expressions from a very early age. It is likely that such monitoring occurs in all sorts of situations and becomes increasingly potent.

Understanding display rules

If children are beginning to conceal their emotions from other people at three or four years of age, do they do this consciously and deliberately or do they do it automatically 'without thinking'? To answer this question, we will need to be more precise about the contrast between deliberate and automatic concealment. We might argue that children know what impact their facial expressions can have on other people, so they deliberately substitute a more innocuous or positive expression in order to give a misleading impression of what they actually feel. We might also argue that such an interpretation is far too elaborate. Young children could not possibly engage in anything as complicated as a deliberate strategy for concealing their emotion from other people. What they have learned is a rule of politeness. They have been told, perhaps repeatedly, that when they are given a present they should smile and say 'thank you', irrespective of how they feel about it. They may have been praised for acting in this polite fashion, and reprimanded for not doing so. The application of this rule will be carried out more or less successfully, depending on the extent to which it is disrupted by any spontaneous expression of disappointment. According to this account, young children are scarcely aware that they have displayed an emotion that does not correspond to what they feel, much less do they appreciate its potentially misleading impact on other people.[1] They have simply learned to produce a particular expression on cue.

After they had received their disappointing gift, the children in Pamela Cole's study were interviewed to find out whether they did have any explicit understanding of display rules. They were asked whether the adult who was present when they opened their gift knew how they felt about it. None of the children pointed out that she would not know because they had not let their disappointment show on their face. The implication is that young children are not aware that they reveal their feelings by their facial expression nor conversely that they can conceal them with a misleading display.[2] Effectively, they cannot distinguish between their real emotion and their apparent emotion.

Our results confirm this conclusion. We have found that children understand the difference between real emotion and expressed emotion only at around five or six years of age rather than three or four years, that is to say *after* they have begun to put display rules into practice. We devised stories in which either a sad or a happy event befell the main character. In each story, we explicitly attributed to this character a reason for hiding what he or she felt. Having listened to the stories, we could ask children two key questions: what emotion does the story character *really* feel? – and what emotion *appears* on the character's face? A typical story went as follows: 'Diana is playing a game with her friend. At the end of the game Diana wins and her friend loses. Diana tries to hide how she feels because otherwise her friend won't play any more.'

Note that although the story explicitly describes a situation that should make Diana happy (i.e. winning) and also a reason for concealing that emotion, neither her real emotion nor the emotion that she might display are named. This meant that in order to answer our questions, children could not simply parrot what we had told them; they had to work out the character's real emotion and apparent emotion and keep them distinct.

We also devised stories in which the story character really felt upset but tried to look cheerful. Here is an example: 'David wants to go outside, but he has a tummy ache. He knows that if he tells his Mum that he has a tummy ache his Mum will say that he can't go out. He tries to hide the way he feels so that his Mum will let him go outside.'

Six-year-olds and ten-year-olds were quick to see the point of the different stories. They realized that in some of them the character would really feel sad but try to look happy, whereas in others the character would really feel happy but try to look sad (Harris, Donnelly, Guz and Pitt-Watson, 1986). At this age, therefore, they appreciate that emotion is not necessarily visible on a person's face: the real emotion may be quite opposite to the emotion that is displayed.

We will come back in a moment to discuss in more detail what children of this age understand about the difference between real and apparent emotion. For the moment, we may ask about younger children. Recall that the children in the study carried out by Pamela Cole were three or four years of age. They managed to conceal their disappointment to some extent but they did not explicitly distinguish between their actual feelings and their overt expression. We have now carried out several studies, in different parts of the world, and the results show that three- and four-year-olds do have great difficulty in making that distinction.

Our first study was carried out in Britain. To give the younger children as much help as possible to show what they knew, various safeguards were built in to ensure that they understood and remembered the stories (1986; Experiment 2). These safeguards were effective because the four-year-olds succeeded in answering two preliminary but critical questions about the event that provoked the story character's real feelings, and the reason for hiding those feelings.

When we asked them to say what the story character's real

and expressed feelings would be, they had much more difficulty. They were good at judging what the main characters – David and Diana – would really feel, but they were likely to go wrong when it came to saying what feelings they would show on their face.

Our second study, this time carried out in the USA, produced similar results (Gross and Harris, 1988). As before, six-year-olds successfully distinguished between how the story characters would feel and how they would look. The four-year-olds, on the other hand, despite their grasp of the essentials of the story, could not work out what misleading facial expression the story character might adopt. After these two studies, we suspected that we were facing a conceptual limitation in the four-year-olds. Their difficulties appeared to stem from the admittedly tricky requirement that they work out how appearances could be used to mislead. However, as a last effort, we carried out one further study in Japan.

Recall that Paul Ekman and Wallace Friesen found clear differences between Americans and Japanese when they described an unpleasant experience. The Japanese were more likely to adopt a bland or positive facial expression even though they were asked to describe a disturbing film that included footage of various surgical procedures, during which they had actually looked distressed, anxious or disgusted. In Japan, training to adopt such display rules starts early in life. Joy Hendry, a social anthropologist who was working in Japan, went along with her son to his kindergarten to study the school and the way that Japanese practices compare with those in the West (Hendry, 1984; 1986).

She observed that children are taught to keep their emotional impulses in check, particularly with regard to younger children: when a dispute over toys occurs, older children are encouraged to give in to younger children as a way of showing their greater maturity. When a quarrel breaks out, the instigator is expected to apologize, and the injured party is expected to accept an apology when it is offered. Crying is discouraged, even if it has been caused by a physical injury, and children who persist in crying may be singled out by teachers and teased or ostracized by the other children. In general, young children are taught that they should be *nakayoku*: they should stay on good terms with one another and play harmoniously within the group.

This pressure on the child to exercise control over the display of emotion is accompanied by explicit attention to the way that others might feel. The child is encouraged to imagine how the victim of its antisocial behaviour feels as a result. Moreover, the distinction between real and apparent emotion is verbally marked for the young Japanese child. There are various Japanese words that can be readily used to refer to the inner self – the world of private thoughts and feelings, as opposed to the 'face' shown to the world.

Finally, there is good evidence that pressure on children to exercise control over the display of their feelings is exerted earlier than in the West. Robert Hess and his colleagues asked Japanese and American mothers at what age they expected their children to master various developmental tasks: some tasks fell into the domain of emotion-management, others fell into the domain of self-assertion and others were more concerned with the child's intellectual development. Although Japanese and American mothers had similar expectations about the overall rate at which their children would develop, they had different expectations in specific domains. Japanese mothers expected their children to control their emotions one or even two years earlier than did American mothers. Conversely, American mothers expected their children to stand up for themselves and their rights a good deal earlier than Japanese mothers (Hess, Kashiwagi, Azuma, Price and Dickson, 1980).

For all these reasons – the early pressure on emotional control, the signalling of other people's hurt feelings, and the explicit marking of the difference between inner and outer – we expected that the young Japanese child might find it easier to conceptualize the distinction between real and apparent emotion.

Accordingly, we repeated our earlier study in a preschool in Hiroshima (Gardner, Harris, Ohmoto and Hamazaki, 1988), making only a few minor changes. Specifically, on the advice of our Japanese colleagues, we altered the setting of the stories to a preschool to make them more suitable for Japanese children. As before, four- and six-year-old children were tested. The results were quite straightforward. Although both age groups judged that the main characters – Hiroshi and Yoshiko – would really feel an emotion that was more intense than the one they expressed, this distinction was again made much more systematically by the six-year-olds than the four-year-olds. The age change that we found in Japan was very similar to the one that we had found in Britain and the USA.

If we put these findings together with those described earlier concerning the display rules that children actually adopt, we arrive at the following picture. At about three or four years of age, children can hide their feelings of disappointment to some degree. They may not be completely successful in misleading an onlooker, but the emotion that they display is recognizably more positive than the uninhibited expression of disappointment that they show when they are alone. Nevertheless, when children of this age are interviewed about the distinction between real and apparent emotion, they have little insight into the distinction. They are usually able to work out what someone would really feel in a given situation – for example, if they have just fallen over, won a game or received a present. What they find difficult is to appreciate that the expressed emotion can differ from the actual emotion. By six years of age, this distinction is firmly grasped. Children systematically distinguish the outward expression of emotion from the experience of emotion. Moreover, they arrive at this distinction at about the same age whether they are growing up in the West, or within an Oriental culture.

This conclusion implies that when three- and four-year-olds begin to put display rules into practice, they do so with little conscious and explicit appreciation of the gap between real and apparent emotion that is thereby created, and little appreciation of the potentially misleading effect that such displays can have on an onlooker. Only after they have started to follow display rules do they appreciate these subtleties. We may now return to the issue we set aside earlier: what exactly have six-year-olds discovered about the distinction between real and apparent emotion?

Real, apparent and attributed emotion

To find out more about how six-year-olds conceptualize the difference between real and apparent emotion, we looked closely at the way that they answered questions about the reasons for one as compared with the other (Harris and Gross, 1988). They usually explained the story character's real emotion in a straightforward way by referring back to the situation that had caused the emotion. Their explanations of the character's apparent emotion were more complex. They focused on the character's reasons for concealment and in doing so they often produced replies in which one statement was successively embedded in another. Consider the following story: 'Diana falls over and hurts herself. She knows that the other children will laugh if she shows how she feels. So she tries to hide how she feels.'

One child who claimed that Diana would look happy explained her choice as follows: 'She didn't want the other children to know that she's sad that she fell over.' In this justification, there are several embedded clauses. The clause 'that she fell over' is embedded within the longer phrase 'she's sad that she fell over'; this clause is itself embedded in the still longer phrase 'the other children to know that she's sad that she fell over', and so on. We found that such complex justifications were quite common. Almost 50 per cent of the six-year-olds produced either a three-clause embedding ('She didn't *want* her sister to *know* that she *hided* her toy') or a four-clause embedding ('She didn't *want* her friend to *know* that she really *feels* happy that she *won*').

These embedded sentences illustrate that six-year-olds can readily articulate the *recursive* structure of display rules: a particular mental state of mine (e.g. my feelings) can be the object of one of your mental states (e.g. your thoughts), but that mental state of yours can, in its turn, be the object of a mental state of mine (my desire to conceal my emotion). Thus, I may not *want* you to *know* how I *feel*.

That recursive ability should enable six-year-olds to appreciate the function and likely effect of display rules – to grasp that the discrepancy between real and apparent emotion is intended to create a false impression that will lead other people to regard the outward appearance as the real emotion. To check this prediction, we used stories similar to those we had used before but we asked the children three questions instead of two (Gross and Harris, 1988). As before, we asked about the character's real feelings, and about the character's apparent or expressed feelings. We also asked a new question about the misleading impact of the character's facial expression. For example, 'How do the other children think that Diana feels?' The six-year-olds proved to be quite systematic in their replies to all three questions. Not only did they appreciate that the character's expression would belie his or her actual feelings, they also realized that other people would be misled and think that the character's expressed feelings showed what he or she really felt.

This insight requires considerable conceptual sophistication. It requires the ability to work simultaneously with two different views of what is going on: a view of the actual state of affairs, and also of the state of affairs that is apparent to an onlooker. In the real state of affairs, the character's real feelings are correctly diagnosed and marked as genuine. Things look quite different to the mistaken onlooker: from his or her perspective, it is the apparent feelings of the character that are diagnosed as being genuine. To understand display rules, therefore, children have to understand these two different points of view, and also the intended relationship between them. They need to understand that the protagonist has deliberately created conditions that will result in two different perspectives. It is not surprising, therefore, that four-year-olds have a conceptual difficulty in understanding that intent, and the resultant discrepancy between real and apparent emotion.

Notice that four-year-olds do realize that one can deliberately produce a fake or pretend expression. Even in the second and third year of life, they produce various pretend emotions in their play (Bretherton, Fritz, Zahn-Waxler and Ridgeway, 1986) and there is no indication that they are confused when others join in their pretence. The understanding of pretence or mimicry, however, is less complicated than the understanding of deceptive display rules. Pretence or mimicry is carried out as part of a game or piece of make-believe. It is not intended to mislead anyone. Display rules can and do mislead, and it is precisely their deceptive intent and impact that six-year-olds articulate and diagnose.

Understanding privacy

The discovery that emotions can be concealed is very important. It offers the child a barricade between the private world of experience known only to the self, and the public world in which behaviour and facial expression are visible to others. How does the child come to realize that the potential for such privacy exists? At first glance, it seems easy to answer this question. Surely, the child gets better at reading the signs of emotion in other people and spotting, for example, that something is not completely genuine about their smile. According to this argument, the child becomes a more subtle or acute observer of emotion, one who is able to distinguish the genuine from the fake.

The available evidence shows that this argument, plausible though it appears, will not work. Young children and indeed adults are poor at distinguishing between genuine and fake displays of emotion. Paul Ekman (in press) points out that it is possible to make the distinction in his laboratory but he and his colleagues observe the signs of emotion through the equivalent of a microscope. Each muscle movement recorded on film is minutely analysed with the help of repeated slow-motion viewing. In everyday life, neither adults nor children have the opportunity for such painstaking analysis. Not surprisingly, when children are asked to distinguish between genuine displays of emotion and fake displays, they can rarely tell the difference (DePaulo and Jordan, 1982).[3]

I think children's understanding of the potential privacy of their emotional experience is a cognitive discovery, not a refinement of their observational skills. It is a cognitive discovery that comes about in an unusual and intriguing fashion. Let us consider once again the three- or four-year-old child who successfully applies a display rule. Consistent with the analysis described in the last chapter, the child will seek some explanation for his or her emotional state, and think about what has just happened. If the child has just been given a drab gift that falls short of expectation, then that episode will be taken as a plausible explanation for any current negative feeling.

Other people, however, will engage in a different process of interpretation. They will notice the child's smile, possibly overlook its half-heartedness, and react as if the child were pleased with the gift. Thus, even if the child's adoption of a display rule was not intended to mislead, it can have a misleading impact. These experiences should provide a setting in which the child can gradually discover that other people can be misled about what he or she actually feels. To make that discovery, of course, it will not be enough for the child to be confronted by a person who has been misled. The child will have to be able to make sense of what has happened: keep in mind the actual emotion, imagine the emotion that is apparent to the onlooker, and keep those representations distinct. Still, such encounters seem much more plausible candidates for teaching children about the privacy of their own mental life than any putative improvement in observational accuracy.

If this argument is correct, it illustrates an important point about the way in which children come to understand emotional states. In order to explain the development of that understanding we may be tempted to think that the child adopts what philosophers call a first-person perspective. From this perspective, the child would slowly make sense of his or her own emotional states by a process of introspection, ignoring any action or behaviour that might be discrepant. The other perspective that the child might adopt is the third-person perspective: the view that an observer has of other people's emotion, as it is revealed through their actions and expression. If the child adopts this perspective exclusively, it appears that he or she must become an expert at detecting misleading signs of those states – yet that expertise is never acquired. If my argument is correct, the child's understanding of emotion cannot be based on either perspective in isolation. It must be based on a consideration of both. On the one hand, adopting a first-person perspective, the child needs to be aware of his or her feelings. On the other hand, by taking into account the perspective of an observer, the child must come to appreciate that those feelings may not be apparent to an observer. An adequate understanding of emotion, and its potential privacy, requires a coordinated understanding of both points of view.

The function of display rules

It seems likely that a stable cognitive timetable governs children's initial realization that real and apparent emotion may differ. On the other hand, we have found that children differ considerably from one another in their understanding of the function of display rules (Adlam-Hill and Harris, 1988; Taylor and Harris, 1984).

In our first study, we talked to emotionally disturbed boys attending a special school. Such schools admit children with a wide assortment of emotional problems. Some suffer from anxiety or depression, but many have temper tantrums, or behave in an uncooperative or inconsiderate way. We compared boys ranging from 7 to 11 years attending such a school with boys of the same age range attending ordinary day schools. During the interview, we asked the boys to imagine various situations and to say how they would feel and look. For example, one situation concerned a disappointing gift from a well-meaning, favourite relative. This hypothetical situation was similar to the situation created by Carolyn Saarni and Pamela Cole except that we introduced a relative rather than an unfamiliar adult. The boys were asked how they would look on their face after discovering that they did not like the gift, and to explain why they would look that way.

A clear difference emerged between the two groups. About three-quarters of the normal boys mentioned the possibility of hiding their disappointment, whereas just over a third of the disturbed boys did so. In our next study, we used a broader variety of situations, again comparing emotionally disturbed boys and normal boys. Although they were attending different schools, the boys in the two groups were similar in other respects: they were all about nine years old, they were equated for verbal intelligence, and they came from similar family backgrounds.

As before, we found a marked difference between the two groups. The normal boys were again more likely to suggest that their real feelings and their expressed feelings would not correspond. Because we had included more situations in this study, we were able to check whether the difference was especially obvious for certain situations and not others. Consider again the case of the disappointing gift. Hiding disappointment in this situation serves to avoid hurting the feelings of the person who has given the gift. Sometimes, however, a display rule can be adopted for more egocentric reasons. For example, we asked the boys to imagine being a page-boy when their aunt gets married, and having to walk past everyone in the church wearing an embarrassing red velvet suit with a lace collar. In this situation, it might be helpful to look cheerful, however uncomfortable one felt, in order to minimize one's discomfiture in front of other people. When we looked at the various situations, it turned out that the emotionally disturbed boys were just as likely as the normal boys to volunteer a display rule in situations that called for the protection of their own feelings. Only when other people's feelings were at stake did they differ from the normal group.

The distinction between protecting the self as compared with protecting the feelings of another person also proved to be critical when we asked the boys to explain their reasons for adopting a display rule. The two groups were equally likely to explain that it was possible to avoid being reprimanded or being conspicuous if you hid your feelings. The normal boys, on the other hand, were much more likely to mention the thoughts or feelings of other people; they either said explicitly that other people would be less upset if you hid your feelings, or they pointed out that other people would be saved from knowing your feelings – and by implication would be less upset – if you could hide them.

Why should the groups differ in this way? One plausible explanation is that emotionally disturbed children have less insight into the causes of emotion in other people. They know how to hide their feelings – after all, they explain how to do so in order to protect themselves – but they are less attuned to the emotional dialogue that takes place between people, whereby the expression of emotion by one person arouses thoughts and hence feelings in another. Insight into that dialogue carries the recursive structure of display rules one step deeper than that described earlier. The child who adopts a display rule to protect another person's feelings is not just saying : I do not *want* you to *know* how I *feel* but is anticipating the emotional repercussions of that knowledge and effectively saying: I do not *want* you to be *saddened* by *knowing* how I *feel.*

Summary and conclusions

Cultures teach their members to express certain emotions and to suppress others. Experimental evidence shows that at least some of the variation between cultures is attributable to differences in the display rules that govern the expression of emotion. Members of different cultures express different emotions in public even when the emotions that they express when they are alone are very similar. The existence of such display rules means that real and apparent emotion may not coincide.

Children seem to move through two different stages in their adoption and understanding of display rules. At first, at around three and four years of age, they learn to mask their true feelings under certain circumstances, but they appear to do this in a semi-automatic fashion, perhaps under pressure from adults to appear polite or well-behaved. At this age, they show little explicit appreciation of the potential discrepancy between real and expressed emotion and they do not understand that the deliberate display of emotion can be used to mislead other people, and not just to conform to adult expectations about acceptable behaviour. By six years of age, an understanding of the deceptive impact of display rules is well in place. It is attained by this age in diverse cultures – in Britain, Japan and the United States. It is also clearly articulated by six-year-olds in the shape of complex, embedded justifications in which they shuttle back and forth between the mental state of the protagonist and the mental state of onlookers.

Armed with that insight, children are in a position to realize that display rules can serve different functions. They can help to protect the self from other people's laughter or anger. They can also help to protect other people from knowledge that would distress them.

An appreciation that one person's feelings need not be communicated to another constitutes an appreciation of the potential privacy of the individual's emotional world. That appreciation might emerge following a more refined and expert scrutiny of other people's expressive behaviour. This argument seems unlikely because such expertise is rarely attained. Even adults find it difficult to distinguish between genuine and deceptive displays of emotion. A more likely explanation is that when children follow display rules, they discover that other people may not know what they feel. If this argument is correct, privacy is recognized as a property of the self before it is attributed to others.

NOTES

1 The study of deceit in children and in non-human primates has recently become a lively and interesting research issue. When deceit is carried out deliberately, it may imply an ability to gauge the way in which another person (or animal) gathers information and draws conclusions. Hence, the capacity for deliberate deceit can reveal an ability to assess and also to act upon the mental states of others (Byrne and Whiten, 1988; Whiten and Byrne, 1988). In children, there is good evidence that even two- and three-year olds can engage in deliberate deceit. For example, they deliberately remove clues that might tell another person where to look for an object, and they even supply clues that point in another direction instead (Chandler, 1988). They also pretend to be tired or to need a nappy-change if they anticipate that their pretence might help them to obtain an object that they have been refused (Dunn, 1988). However, deliberate deceit can be carried out with different goals. Low-level deceit can be aimed simply at bringing about an action by another person (e.g. search in a given place or the offer of a particular object) by the creation of a context in which the other person would normally engage in the desired action. Higher-level deceit can be aimed at another person's beliefs and only indirectly at his or her ensuing action. For example, a child who wants to keep an object hidden from another child might deliberately point in the wrong direction. This might be an example of low-level deceit – the creation of a context in which the other child will search in the wrong place. Alternatively, it might be a case of higher-level deceit – a gesture intended to lead the other child to think that the object is in another place, so that as a result he or she will search in the wrong place. Observation of a single deceptive act may not reveal whether it is intended to influence another person's behaviour directly (i.e. low-level deceit) or to achieve the same end by influencing the person's beliefs (i.e. higher-level deceit).

2 Readers who are concerned either with the children's welfare or with methodological nicety will be reassured that after the interview the children were given an opportunity to trade in their disappointing gift and choose something different. Every child did so, underlining the fact that whatever pleasure they might have expressed on their face upon

opening the gift, and however inarticulate they might have been about the difference between what they felt and what they expressed, they were disappointed and remained so for some time afterwards. Their actual feelings did not move into line with their facial expression.

3 Again, my argument should not be taken to imply that young children cannot identify make-believe or pretend emotions (Bretherton, Fritz, Zahn-Waxler and Ridgeway, 1986; see also chapter 3). For example, some two-year-olds enjoy games with their mother in which the child pretends to smack the mother, who in turn 'cries' and is comforted by the child. It seems highly likely that when they play these games, children know that their mother's display is mere pretence. However, the mother's display is often exaggerated and it is produced in a context that is already marked as playful. Diagnosing these displays as pretence is considerably easier than diagnosing deliberately misleading displays as fake. The latter are not produced within a clearly marked pretend context, and they usually lack the exaggerated hamming that is found in imaginative play.

7

The control of emotion

'Work hard and play on the field.' ['How does that cheer you up?']
'Well you're doing something all the time – if you're doing something you don't really notice that you're homesick.' ['How is it that you don't notice?']
'Well, your brain just gets locked into what you're doing and you just don't notice really.'
(Interview with an eight-year-old boy newly arrived at a boarding school).

The Chewong – the small group of hunter-gatherers and shifting cultivators described in the last chapter – constantly impressed Signe Howell with their emotional restraint. 'They never seem to lose control,' she commented. Do the Chewong enthuse and grieve just as intensely as us beneath their outward restraint or does their control lead to an inner moderation? It has sometimes been implied in psychology that a sharp distinction between our subjective emotional state and its outward display is misguided since it is our outward state that tells us what we are feeling. William James, for example, one of the first psychologists to ask how we know what we are feeling, argued that the emotional behaviour that we display provides us with an important cue in deciding how we feel. The implication is that if we could successfully display a restrained demeanour, we would judge ourselves to feel calm.

Although outward restraint might sometimes be used to blunt our subjective experience, it seems crucial to maintain the distinction between the outward expression of emotion and the emotion itself. One piece of evidence is our everyday social experience. We are often aware of feeling more upset, disappointed or impatient than we reveal. The detectable and insistent gap between the emotional restraint that we may convey to others and the distress that we privately feel shows that no matter how guarded our expression of emotion, it does not subdue our subjective experience. Young children also make this distinction between expression and experience. Recall from the last chapter that they distinguish between the way that someone might look on their face and the way that someone might really feel; they realize that the facial expression will provide a misleading rather than a correct indication of the way that the person feels.[1]

Mindful of the distinction between outward display and experience, adults typically adopt different coping strategies depending on what they seek to change. As we saw in the last chapter, display rules are directed simply at keeping up appearances, particularly the appearance of the face. Other strategies are intended to change the emotion that is felt. Coping strategies of this second type may be further subdivided. Sometimes we seek to change the situation that led to the emotion in the first place: we make reparations of various sorts. Sometimes, however, particularly if the situation is inevitable or unalterable, we direct our efforts not at the external factors giving rise to our feelings but at the ensuing emotional process. That process has a cognitive starting point: it is triggered by the way in which we think about the situation that is affecting us. Hence, we may try to short-circuit the process by making use of cognitive strategies. We attempt to change the way that we think about the situation, by re-evaluating it, by focusing our attention only on certain aspects, or by not thinking about it. These coping techniques turn out to be quite effective among adults.[2] Indeed, when adults are in a situation over which they have little control, for example when they face dental or surgical procedures, cognitive avoidance or 'blunting' may be a more effective coping strategy than a vigilant monitoring of the situation (Miller and Green, 1985).

Two basic questions immediately arise if we ask about children's insight into these techniques for coping with the experience of emotion. First, do they grasp the distinction between changing the outward expression of emotion and changing the experience? Second, do they appreciate that their emotional state can be changed by intrapsychic or cognitive strategies as well as those aimed at the environment itself?

In our first investigation of this issue, we attempted to obtain a broad cross-sectional view of children's understanding. We talked to children aged 6, 11 and 15 years about several different aspects of emotion, including the strategic control of emotion (Harris, Olthof and Meerum Terwogt, 1981). To check whether children could distinguish between changing the *display* as distinct from the *experience* of emotion, we introduced several paired questions. The following pair illustrates our questions about sadness. First, we asked about control of the outward display: 'Imagine that you've been on vacation and now you're back home again. You're unhappy because the vacation is over. Could you pretend to be happy?' We then asked about control of the experience: 'Of course, it would be better if you were *really* happy. Could you do anything to make sure that you were *really* happy?' In answering the first question about the display of emotion, children in all three age groups often claimed that it was possible to display a pretend emotion by acting out the appropriate verbal, behavioural or facial reactions. In answering the second question about the experience of emotion, such answers were rare even in the youngest group. Children focused instead on changing the situation: 'Then you should call up your friends and play with them.' Alternatively, they recommended changing the mental processes normally caused by the situation: 'You mustn't think of it any more, otherwise you'll get sad again.'

These replies fit well with the conclusions we reached in the last chapter. Even six-year-old children realize that outward expression and emotional state need not coincide, and in keeping with that differentiation, they grasp that their emotional state cannot be altered merely by changing their outward behaviour or expression. To change their emotional state, they focus on changing the immediate situation or the thought processes associated with the emotion.

Although the distinction between expression and experience is established by six years of age, children suggest different strategies for changing that experience as they get older. All three age groups proposed changing the situation, but only the two older groups mentioned the more mentalistic technique of re-directing their thoughts with any frequency. This pattern has re-emerged in our later research. In a study of how children cope with illness, mentioned in chapter 5, Mark Lipian asked 6-, 10-, and 15-year-old healthy children about how they felt when they were ill and whether they could do anything to change those feelings (Harris and Lipian, 1989; Lipian, 1985).

Some six-year-olds were quite pessimistic. They denied that it was possible to do anything. Yet even those six-year-olds who thought that there was something that they could do formulated their suggestions differently from the older groups. The most popular strategy was to change the immediate situation by engaging in some activity or game; no further mentalistic explanation in terms of distraction or forgetting was offered even with further prompting. The link between activity and change of emotion was seen as immediate and direct. Here is a typical exchange:

Interviewer:	Say you were ill, and you felt sad. Is there anything you could do to *change* the way you felt, to change that feeling of sadness?
Child:	Try and be happy.
Interviewer:	How?
Child:	By playing about.
Interviewer:	What would that do?
Child:	Get happy – make me feel happy.

Only very occasionally did the younger children attempt to provide any intervening cognitive process by way of explanation. Here is a rare attempt from a 6-year-old girl:

Child:	You could go and play outside and try to forget about it.
Interviewer:	What would happen then?

Child: I'd feel a bit happy.
Interviewer: How would you try to forget? – What would you do?
Child: I don't know. . .just. . .I don't know how, just try and forget it.

The ten-year-olds, by contrast, were more alert to the role of cognitive processes. They divided their proposals between two strategies – the straightforward game or activity strategy just mentioned, accompanied by no cognitive explanation, and a strategy that was more obviously cognitive or mentalistic. They explained how an activity could 'take your mind off' the negative emotion.

Here is a response from a 10-year-old boy:

Child: Well I could stop thinking about the pain or what's gonna happen and get my favourite toy out or my favourite thing.
Interviewer: And what would that do?
Child: It would make me not think of being sad and it would cheer me up.

And another that is equally typical:

Child: Well, if you read quite a lot.
Interviewer: What would that do?
Child: Well it'd probably boost my morale a little - reading something; it'd get me away from feeling very sad, and get me into the book.
Interviewer: Anything else?
Child: Well, anything to get me away really – watch the telly or cards with my dad. . .
Interviewer: Get you away?
Child: Yeah, you know, distract me – so I don't think about it all the time.

Among the 15-year-olds, the strategy of cognitive distraction was almost ubiquitous. For example:

Child:	Well anything that occupied my mind fully.
Interviewer:	Such as?
Child:	Reading, doing a crossword – just keeping my mind on things I enjoy. Cheerier prospects than being ill!'

And finally a response that is more idiosyncratic but makes the same point:

Child:	Well, I always find a book – I'm always the one with the vivid imagination. . .and sometimes, you know, I just forget that I'm ill altogether. I think that in many ways feelings have to do with imagination – if you just forget that you're miserable you don't feel miserable at all, and I just try and forget all about it, and do things to occupy my mind, get me away from it.

These results confirmed the age-change that had been apparent in our earlier investigation. Young children are likely to mention the creation of a new situation or an enjoyable distraction. Older children are more likely to mention cognitive strategies. If they do refer to distracting or pleasurable activities, they indicate the cognitive process that makes them effective. Mark Lipian's results document this developmental change especially clearly since his interview was quite probing. In particular, he was able to distinguish between those children - typically six-year-olds – who mentioned activities, and could offer no mentalistic explanation even with further prompting, and those children – typically ten- or fifteen-year-olds – who mentioned activities but could go on to explain their cognitive impact.[3]

How do children learn to use distraction to cheer themselves up, and how do they come to focus on the mental processes that sustain emotion? I would suggest that children are not simply borrowing ideas or explanations from other people.

During development, they are also capable of making discoveries about the causal regularities inherent in their emotional experience, and using those discoveries to change their emotional state deliberately.

To make this autodidactic process clearer, we need to spell out the type of experiences that would be instructive. There are two recurrent experiences that seem plausible candidates. First, the intensity of an emotion varies depending on the events that succeed it: a sad experience may be less distressing if it is immediately followed by something positive. Second, once an emotion has been generated its intensity usually dissipates with the passage of time. Thus, when later events provide a distraction or when time passes, the original emotionally-charged situation loses some of its potency. These changes in the intensity of felt emotion are usually accompanied by cognitive changes. Thoughts about the event become less intense as attention is taken up by later events or as the original event recedes in time. Children could discover from such experiences that the suppression of thoughts associated with the original emotionally-charged event provides emotional relief. We look now at evidence for these insights.

Distraction from emotion

What do children know about the way in which successive episodes influence a person's emotional state? We considered one aspect of this issue in chapter 5, when we asked whether children appreciate that an earlier emotion may endure and persist alongside a later-aroused emotion. Here, we ask whether children also appreciate that a later emotion can moderate one that was aroused earlier.

To investigate this issue, we told six- and ten-year-old children stories in which a distressing experience was followed by a happy one (Harris, 1983; Experiment 3). For example, the story character might have a quarrel with some school friends on the way home, but unexpectedly receive a gift on arriving home. Younger and older children alike realized that if a later positive event did offset the quarrel, the character would cheer up, whereas he or she would remain sad if nothing positive occurred. They also realized that the subsequent event might not banish all distress – the protagonist would feel unalloyed happiness about the unexpected gift only if the journey home had been uneventful. Apparently, even by six years of age, children realize that situations that take place after an upsetting emotionally-charged event can mitigate the earlier emotion but may not abolish it altogether.

This insight provides an obvious basis for the self-control of emotion: when sad feelings are aroused, they can be moderated by deliberately engaging in an activity that is normally associated with feeling happy. Rather than simply accepting the course of events, the child needs to take matters into his or her own hands and create a situation that is known to be enjoyable. Having learned that changes in circumstance are associated with marked changes in emotion, even when the change in circumstances is quite unconnected to the original distress, they can put this discovery to use in an opportunistic fashion to change current mood deliberately.

Dissipation of emotion

Children not only propose the use of enjoyable activities as a way of cheering themselves up, they also increasingly elaborate on the way that thoughts and feelings interact. In particular, they indicate that doing something else will cheer you up because it makes you stop thinking about or forget your sadness. One obvious way that children might discover this link between thoughts and feelings is by noticing that as time passes, they cease to think about an event that has upset them and they also gradually feel more positive. Do children understand this link between thought and emotion?

To explore these questions, we told children stories about a character who encounters some emotionally-charged situation, and asked them how that character felt immediately after the situation had arisen – and at various points in time thereafter. For example, the character might lose a fight with the school bully just before school started in the morning. We asked how the character felt immediately after losing, at various points during the day, and the following morning (Harris, 1983; Harris, Guz, Lipian and Man-Shu, 1985; Taylor and Harris, 1983).

We found that children appreciate from a very young age – even at four years – that an emotional reaction is initially intense and gradually wanes in strength. It makes no difference whether the emotion is positive or negative – in each case, children judge that it wanes over time. Moreover, they make the same claim if they are asked about experiences from their own past. Finally, when we carried out a similar study in China, we found that children living in Shanghai made judgements that were virtually identical to those that children produced in the West. The implication is that the gradual waning of intense emotion is a universal of human experience, and young children everywhere rapidly discover that regularity.

If children appreciate that emotion declines in strength as time passes, they may also grasp that the intensity of an emotion depends on whether one continues to think about the event that precipitated it. We asked children how a story character would feel if he or she woke up and started thinking about an emotionally-charged event that happened the day before, or alternatively forgot about it. Ten- and six-year-olds were remarkably consistent in their judgements: they claimed that if the earlier event had been a happy one, the story character would be happier thinking about it rather than forgetting it. Conversely, if the earlier event had been sad, they made the opposite judgement: the story character would be happier forgetting about it rather than remembering it (Harris, Guz and Lipian, 1985; Harris, Guz, Lipian and Man-Shu, 1985). Thus in response to explicit questioning, children show some appreciation of the link between cognition and emotion by six years of age.

If children understand that emotion wanes over time and also that forgetting about an event reduces its emotional impact, do they put these two regularities together? Do they appreciate that emotion usually declines in intensity because one gradually stops thinking so much about the precipitating event? To answer this question, we asked children to explain how a story character could be very happy or sad at first (after an emotionally-charged event) but feel less happy or sad later.

The children's replies could be divided into two broad categories: those that referred to situational factors and those that referred to mental factors. Situational replies described some change in the original emotionally-charged situation. For example, after listening to a story about a pet dog that died, children might explain that eventually the story character would be given another dog, or, more fancifully, the original dog would 'get better'. Occasionally, they introduced some quite different situation that had not been mentioned or implied by the interviewer – the story character would go out to play, or do something else – but the bulk of their replies involved restoration, either partial or total, of the original loss. The other category of reply included a reference to the cognitive processes of the story character. Children described how the story character would forget about, stop thinking about, or get used to the original situation. Unlike situational replies, these answers carried the implication that the original situation remained unaltered. For example, in explaining reactions to a bicycle being stolen, children claimed that the story character would eventually feel less sad: 'Because he forgets it's stolen' or, more actively, 'Because she wanted to forget it. She just didn't want to think about it any more.' When we compared the replies of different age groups, we found that children shift during development. Four-year-olds concentrate on situational explanations and ten-year-olds concentrate on mentalistic explanations (Harris, Guz and Lipian, 1985; Harris, Guz, Lipian and Man-shu, 1985).

Pulling together these various pieces of evidence, the

following developmental pattern emerges: By four years of age, children have repeatedly experienced how intense emotion, be it positive or negative, wanes over time. They take note of that regular decline in intensity, they report it for their own experience, and they project it on to other people, including story characters. By six years of age, children have also noticed an additional regularity: emotion is less intense if one stops thinking about the event that led to the emotion. Eventually children being to see the connection between these two regularities: emotion wanes in intensity over time *because* one gradually stops thinking about the event that precipitated the emotion. Judging by their explanations of the time-course of emotion, they become increasingly aware of this causal connection between four and ten years of age. Younger children often concentrate on adventitious changes in the situation facing someone after an emotionally-charged event, whereas older children attend more to the mental changes that ensue.

These discoveries provide, in their turn, a technique for coping with emotion. As with distraction, the child needs deliberately to set in motion a process that normally occurs unintentionally. The child can attempt to accelerate the waning process that would normally occur by deliberately forgetting about an emotionally-charged event or by not thinking about it.

Entering a British boarding school

In the interviews described earlier, we found that older children do not shift to an exclusively cognitive strategy. Although they do sometimes recommend simply ceasing to think about the emotionally-charged event or trying to forget about it, they do not abandon the use of distracting activities. Rather, they put the two strategies together (Harris, Olthof and Meerum Terwogt, 1981; Lipian, 1985). On the one hand, they suggest that it is important to engage in some absorbing or pleasurable activity. On the other hand, they are able to give a rationale for this suggestion in terms of the link between thought and feeling. They spell out the way that concentration on the distracting activity allows one, temporarily at least, to stop thinking about whatever it is that is making one worried or sad.

In a further study of children's understanding of control strategies, we obtained some striking descriptions of this strategy of cognitive suppression through distraction. The descriptions are particularly interesting because they were made by children talking about an emotionally-charged experience of their own rather than answering questions about a story character facing some hypothetical dilemma. The children had newly arrived at a boarding school and they were questioned about their feelings of homesickness. Before describing the results, it is useful to give some background information to the study.

Boarding schools have been praised and criticized for the educational advantages they supposedly offer. The teachers are usually well qualified, the material facilities of the school are often superior to those found in state-maintained schools; lessons, games, private study and religious worship are regulated by routine and by explicitly stated aspirations. Because the schools cater to a minority, comment and research has chiefly been directed at the social privileges that they can confer.

However, the emotional impact of being sent to a boarding school is also worthy of study. The practice of sending children away from home to an institution that may be hundreds of miles away, within whose confines they eat, sleep, work, play and worship, supervised and taught by adults predominantly of the same sex as themselves, who as likely as not spent their own childhood in such institutions, is not common in the world's cultures. It would not be surprising if it called for various coping strategies, especially upon arrival.

We interviewed two groups of boys, eight-year-olds and 13-year-olds, soon after their arrival at a new boarding school

(Harris and Guz, 1986). The eight-year-olds had just arrived at preparatory boarding schools. For almost all of them, it was their first experience of boarding. The 13-year-olds had just arrived at public boarding schools. For most of them it was not their first experience of boarding because they had previously attended a preparatory boarding school. Nevertheless, like the eight-year-olds, they were in strange new environment, separated from their parents, with few familiar faces.

We talked to half the boys in each age group in their first or second week at the new school, whereas we talked to the other half in their fifth or sixth week. We divided the boys in this way because conversations with the headmasters and housemasters suggested that boys show the most obvious signs of homesickness, distress and anxiety in the first couple of weeks at the school. Thereafter, the majority, outwardly at least, settle into the school. Irrespective of when they were interviewed, the boys were asked to focus on their first week or two at the school, and to tell us about their emotional reactions and those of the other boys during those two weeks. Effectively, then, we interviewed half the boys about their current emotional reactions to the new school; we interviewed the other half about their emotional reactions in the recent past. In the event, few differences emerged between the two groups and I shall concentrate on the themes that emerged in both.

The boys were interviewed about several of the issues that have been explored in previous chapters: Was it possible to have mixed feelings about the school? How long would their initial emotional reactions last? We will concentrate here on the boys' answers on two issues: Could feelings of anxiety or distress be concealed from the other boys? And could feelings of homesickness be changed?

As might be expected from the results discussed so far, the boys' replies on these two issues differed. Asked whether it was possible to hide their feelings, the most common answer was to agree that it was possible to act cheerfully even if you really didn't feel cheerful. An eight-year-old put it as follows:

'If you smile and act cheerful, it doesn't show that you're actually afraid and worried really.' Another eight-year-old added a social dimension; 'Well, you'd have to act cheerfully and try and make friends with everybody.' The older boys also underlined the difference between actual feelings and outward appearance although their answers were sometimes more cautious: 'You can hide your feelings easily by day, if they're not too bad, when everyone's watching you, by joining in and by smiling and getting on with other people. But at night when no one is watching you, you can go back to being normal. If you're upset, you're just upset.' 'It is possible but it's quite difficult if you smile all the time. Normally, you can see through a false smile.'

In answer to questions about changing emotion, none of the boys ever spontaneously recommended simply displaying a cheerful appearance, and even if they were explicitly asked whether it might be helpful to smile, the most frequent reply was a reiteration of the fundamental distinction between outward display and actual emotion. One eight-year-old explained: 'You keep your thoughts. Smiling doesn't make you lose your thoughts.' Another pointed out: 'I still feel sad – 'cos it's not doing anything to stop me from thinking about mother and father.' Again, the older boys made the same basic point, albeit in a more articulate fashion: 'Well, it's just an action. I don't see how an opposite action can help. I don't think that smiling which is a movement of your mouth can help things in your mind.' Or 'Because that's just moving your muscles; it isn't moving anything inside.' Even boys who conceded that simply smiling might cheer you up often hedged their conclusion or introduced other considerations. For example, one younger boy said: 'It helps a tiny bit but I don't think that much. It helps 'cos smiling makes other people think you're in a good mood.' An older boy acknowledged that smiling might help, while at the same time distinguishing appearance from reality: 'Yes, it seems to. If you seem more happy, then you feel more happy inside. If you smile, you tell yourself you're more happy and you believe it and you start acting happy.'

Given that the boys were generally sceptical about the value of simply acting cheerfully, what strategies did they advise for homesickness? They often recommended trying to change the situation that was causing the feeling of homesickness. For example, they suggested calling home, writing a letter or making friends. More often, however, they proposed various forms of distraction – playing with the other boys, playing sports or watching a film. The following reply from an eight-year-old conveys the flavour of such replies: 'If there was a film on that night you could go and watch it and distract yourself, or you could go swimming or play a game of marbles or something.' As in the studies described earlier, the boys were often capable, particularly when prompted, of explaining how such distractions helped. Their explanations were usually couched in terms of cognitive suppression: an absorbing activity could prevent you from thinking about your home or your homesickness. One eight-year-old put it as follows: 'Well, if you were in the dorms, you could read a book; if the lights were out you could try and get to sleep; if you were in the middle of a lesson just occupy yourself. [*Interviewer:* 'What does that do?'] Well, once you get started and you're really doing it, then you forget about being homesick and don't really think of it.' Another suggested: 'I would try and forget all about it or try and get my mind off it with going to play with my friends . . . or getting stuck into work or something like that.' Another suggested: 'Take more part in things. [*Interviewer:* 'How does that help?'] Well, it takes your mind off it, and stops you thinking about home.'

These answers capture the thrust of many replies. The boys appeared to be working with the implicit assumption that consciousness has a limited capacity: by occupying it with one type of mental content, other more painful contents are denied access. As one eight-year-old explained: thinking about other things than home helps '. . . 'cos it takes your mind off feeling sad. It occupies your mind. I don't think you can think two things at once.'

The replies of the 13-year-olds pursued the same theme: 'Do

something active so you forget about it – like playing table tennis or joining some society or playing squash. As long as you're doing something, you won't think about it – you'll be doing something else.' '. . . I'd try and pack as much into the day as possible so that I wouldn't have time to think about people back home.' '. . . Just try and play something so that hopefully you'll need your whole mind to do that.'

Some replies were noteworthy because they contained both positive and negative advice. They included an exhortation to keep busy, but they also warned of the danger or futility of thinking about home or making contact with home. 'I wouldn't try and cheer myself up. I'd try and get my mind off it. I wouldn't write letters. I'd probably go and do something active or do something with somebody.' 'The only thing you can do is try to forget, try to enjoy yourself. If you want you can be really miserable for the first two weeks by thinking of home. You can do that but I've boarded for so long now that I know there's no point in doing that. It's best to get on with it . . . Just get into the rota of things, all the sports and activities. Just enjoy them.'

The boys' belief in the limited capacity of consciousness emerged in another set of questions. We asked them about the effect of emotion on concentration. Specifically, in connection with doing some extra school work (learning French vocabulary) we asked: 'Say you were feeling worried about starting at this new school, do you think that feeling worried makes it easier or harder to concentrate or doesn't it make any difference?' The majority claimed that anxiety would distract them. Here are some typical explanations from eight-year-olds: ''Cos if you're worried, you think about things, other things, like I'm missing my mother and stuff and you wouldn't really concentrate with your prep.' 'Because you're thinking about other things when you're supposed to be thinking about stuff and it's difficult to think of two things at the same time.' 'Well, you wouldn't concentrate properly; you'd be thinking about home all the time.'

The 13-year-olds came to similar conclusions: 'If you were

thinking about something that was worrying you, you might keep thinking about that and forget things.' 'It definitely makes it harder. If you're worried when you're trying to learn the French words, you'll just think back and remember how worried you are. You can feel that you're worried and it just affects your concentration, and you can't think, so you don't learn very well.'

Superficially, there is a contradiction in the boys' answers to our two sets of questions. When we asked them how they would cheer themselves up if they were feeling homesick, they suggested that absorption in an activity would prevent painful thoughts. Conversely, when we asked them about studying, they suggested that painful thoughts would prevent them from studying.

Despite the apparent contradiction, the boys are probably correct: when activities and painful thoughts compete with one another, there will be different outcomes. Sometimes, the activity will pre-empt attention and sometimes the painful thoughts will do so. When the task is one that is imposed rather than self-selected, and when there is very little external input to keep track of, concentration may wander and return to worrying or distressing topics. Extra study – or prep as it is called – usually has to be done sitting in the classroom with the other boys, maintaining silence for 45 minutes or more. It is an imposed activity where there is little external input. By contrast, when the boys talked about activities that would offer emotional relief, they often mentioned vigorous leisure activities like squash, table tennis, or football, games that they find both enjoyable and absorbing. Nevertheless, one or two boys claimed that even studying would alleviate homesickness: 'Working takes your mind off homesickness. You just put your mind on the prep,' claimed one eight-year-old. More tentatively, a 13-year-old suggested: 'You'd try and avoid thinking about your sadness by working even harder but I don't know if it would work.' Another recollected that when he had first arrived at the school 'when I felt a bit homesick, I started doing mathematical problems.'

How have boys discovered the anaesthetic qualities of distracting activities such as games, sports, films and even studying? Two possible sources of knowledge seem likely. On the one hand, the boys might work it out for themselves. Having some insight into the limited capacity of consciousness, they might infer that a distraction or blocking strategy would be effective, try it out, and become convinced of its utility.

A second possibility is that the boys do not make the discovery for themselves. The teachers in boarding schools might tell their pupils more or less explicitly that if they keep themselves busy they will stop feeling homesick. Two pieces of evidence suggest that this might happen. On the one hand, Shirley Fisher and her colleagues found that teachers in boarding schools suggest that it is best to keep the boys busy because they have 'less time to think' (Fisher, Frazer and Murray, 1986). Teachers might therefore explicitly recommend such a strategy to their pupils. Second, in seeking permission to interview boys at boarding school, we met with several refusals. These refusals were justified on the grounds that discussion with the boys ran the danger of stirring up their feelings during what was acknowledged to be a testing time. The assumption was that it was better for the boys not to talk about their feelings. It is no great step from this assumption to the conclusion that the boys are better off if they have no opportunity to think about their feelings, in which case an explicit recommendation to them to keep themselves occupied might be deemed appropriate.

My guess is that neither of these two alternative explanations of the boys' insight tells the whole story. A more plausible explanation is that use of the cognitive suppression depends on a contribution both from the boys and from the institution. The institution provides an organized schedule that governs most waking hours. It includes a large number of collective activities such as lessons, games, worship, extra study (prep) and meetings. Such a rota of activity allows only a limited amount of free time. One of the leading characters in a play by

William Boyd (1985) freely based on the author's own experience at boarding school, puts it as follows:

> If you've led a public life for ten years, if everything you do, washing, eating, sleeping, everything is done in the company of other people for ten years . . . then it's going to be extremely hard to learn how to be private again when you leave . . . When you're there, it's twenty-four hours a day. A completely public life, shared by everyone. Everybody knows everything about you. You can't hide anything.

Engaged in this round of public activity, the boys are likely to discover that it offers a respite from their feelings of sadness or homesickness, and that during those moments when they are left to their own devices, when there is no activity to occupy their thoughts, then their feelings of distress come to the surface. As one 13-year-old put it: 'During the daytime there is [a way to cheer yourself up], because there are so many things to think about and so many other things to do – so that you wouldn't have time to think about it [feeling homesick]. At nighttime, you get a lot more upset because you start thinking about home.'[4] It seems likely that the boys monitor such fluctuations in the intensity of their feeling. After all, as we saw earlier in this chapter, even four-year-olds are aware that feelings can vary in intensity. Such monitoring would, over a short period of time, encourage them to adopt the suppression strategy deliberately, rather than to be its passive beneficiaries. It would encourage them during periods of leisure or free time to keep themselves busy, rather than give themselves over to solitude or silence. In summary, the suppression or distraction strategy probably flourishes as a result of two preconditions: on the one hand, the boys have enough self-awareness – certainly by eight years of age – to gauge changes in the intensity of their feelings of homesickness and to diagnose their causes; second, the highly organized culture of the boarding school provides its members with many opportunities for discovering the analgesic of distraction.

The distraction strategy has several features in common with the classical Freudian defence mechanism of repression. It presupposes that the capacity of consciousness is limited and that certain contents can be prevented from appearing there. This inevitably raises the question of how it is that 13-year-olds and even eight-year-olds can have so much insight into their mental processes. There are two points to be made here. First, there is an important difference between the way in which the boys at boarding school formulate the distraction strategy, and the way that the defence mechanism of repression is conceived within classical psychoanalytic theory. Repression is assumed to re-channel a supposedly constant supply of psychic energy, whereas the boys speak only of the cognitive suppression of particular mental contents. Second – and this difference is related to the first – the boys' knowledge is restricted to their conscious experience. They notice from personal observation that when they are absorbed in an activity, they do not think about home, and they feel less homesick; conversely, when they are alone or unoccupied, their thoughts return to home and they feel worse. Their formulation of the distraction strategy is entirely consistent with this description.

The Freudian account of the defence mechanisms, by contrast, is not simply concerned with the conscious results of defence, namely the anaesthetization of feeling. It is also concerned is with the unconscious sequelae of failing to allow psychic energy into consciousness: the panoply of symptoms, be it hostility, or hysteria or involuntary error, that results from such re-channelling. The boys never adopt such a hydraulic model of the mind; they postulate no unconscious machinery; and they foresee no side-effects of the blocking strategy other than what they seek to achieve, a cessation of conscious thoughts about home, and a consequent diminution of their distress. In short, the boys' articulation of their defensive processes is restricted to a description of what occurs above the threshold of consciousness; they do not, like the analysts, seek to penetrate into the unconscious. From our data, there is no indication that they ever postulate such a mental domain at all.

Does that mean that the conceptualization that the boys offer of their mental processes is too pat and simplistic? Do they simply succeed in anaesthetizing the pain that they feel when they separate from their family and friends, while failing to acknowledge the emotional scars that will necessarily remain? From our data, we cannot answer this question. What does seem possible, at least for some boys, is that the avoidant strategy that they describe could become a generalized strategy for dealing with painful emotion. Rather than communicating their distress to their parent or to someone to whom they become attached in the school, they learn how to keep themselves occupied and uncommunicative at times when other boys would seek comfort.

It is striking to note that the strategy of keeping busy, and avoiding thoughts about and even communication with parents, proposed by some of the boys, is a perfect cognitive analogue of the behavioural strategy that can be observed in a minority of one-year-old infants following separation from a parent. Upon reunion, such infants do not move toward the parent, and they make few bids for attention. Instead, they avoid the parent by busying themselves with the physical environment (Ainsworth, Blehar, Waters and Wall, 1978). Attachment theorists argue that when parents are not consistently available to reassure their child, avoidance can become elaborated into a stable strategy for coping with distress. Likewise, boarding schools may have a long-term impact on the emotional lives of their pupils not simply because they oblige young children to undergo a painful and sustained separation from their parents but because – for better or worse – they foster in some children a particular style of coping whereby distress – particularly the distress of separation - is actively suppressed from consciousness rather than confided.[5]

Summary and conclusions

In this chapter, we have examined two distinct but related aspects of children's understanding of the strategic control of emotion. From an early age, children distinguish between the outer signs of emotion and the experience of emotion. Armed with that distinction, they can grasp two different types of strategic control: control of the outward expression of emotion, and control of the experience. The insight that the outward display of emotion can be deliberately changed so that it misleads onlookers about one's true emotion is available to six-year-olds.

To control the experience of emotion, it is not sufficient to 'put on a happy face'. Children suggest more active strategies. The most popular strategy among younger children is to switch situations – to move into or create a situation that is more enjoyable. Such a technique seems to follow quite readily from their recognition that a later, positive event can mitigate an earlier negative emotion. Older children do not abandon this basic technique. Rather they refine it, and identify the critical causal mechanism. They increasingly appreciate that emotion wanes in intensity because one gradually ceases to think about the events that generated the emotion in the first place. They also start to describe how moving into another situation or engaging in an alternative activity can block an earlier emotion by suppressing the thoughts that maintain that emotion. They make the assumption, albeit implicitly, that consciousness has a limited capacity. Therefore, mental absorption in an alternative activity is sufficient to prevent other, more painful thoughts from returning to consciousness. More generally, children become aware that the limited capacity of consciousness is both a burden and a boon; they realize that painful feelings may prevent concentration, but concentration can block out painful feelings.

NOTES

1 There are experimental studies testing the claim that the adoption of a particular facial expression can change a person's emotional state. For example, an important and suggestive study was carried out by Laird, Wagenar, Halal and Szegda (1982). Their immediate concern was with the link between emotion and memory but their results are pertinent to the impact of display rules. Subjects were asked to move selected muscles so that eventually their face composed a particular facial expression, be it an expression of happiness, fear, sadness or anger without their realizing it. Some subjects claimed to feel the emotion that they were unwittingly expressing, and their performance in a recall task was consistent with such a shift of mood; they were better able to recall material congruent with the professed mood. Laird and his colleagues concluded that, for these subjects, the unwitting adoption of a particular facial expression was enough to shift their mood, and this in turn biased their recall. We should be cautious, however, in extrapolating from these results. First, the bias occurred only for some subjects. Second, it occurred in the absence of any emotionally charged situation. Putting on a happy face may do little to bias our mood if we remain in a sad situation. Moreover, reviews of similar studies indicate that such shifts of emotional state are modest when they occur (Matsumo, 1987) and may be diffuse rather than discrete (Winton, 1986).

2 Richard Lazarus (1975) has pioneered the study of these coping strategies among adults and has emphasized the distinction between so-called direct strategies, aimed at the environment and intrapsychic strategies aimed at the emotional process itself.

3 The age-change that we observed has subsequently been observed by other investigators. Band and Weisz (1988) asked 6-, 9- and 12-year-old children to recall a variety of stressful episodes and to explain what they had done 'to help or make things better'. As compared with younger children, the older children were more likely to mention strategies directed at the emotion itself (including not thinking about the stressful situation or re-evaluating it). This age-change was especially noticeable when children were asked about an unavoidable situation (getting an injection from the doctor). Similarly, Altshuler and Ruble (1988) and Tolmie (1988) found that when children ranging from 4 to 11 years were questioned about coping strategies, the strategy of cognitive avoidance was mentioned more often by older children. Specifically, older children were much more likely to suggest either thinking about something else or avoiding thoughts of the stressful situation.

4 Fisher, Frazer and Murray (1986) found in a diary study of children at boarding school that over 70 per cent of episodes of homesickness were

associated with periods of mental and physical passivity, even though such periods are likely to form a relatively small proportion of the school day.

5 Mary Main and her colleagues have identified this 'dismissive' or 'detached' pattern among some adults when they describe their family relationships (Main and Goldwyn, 1985).

8

The experience of emotion

In this chapter, we consider children who are undergoing an emotionally charged experience, and ask how they make sense of their emotional reactions. Until now, I have often described children who have been interviewed on the sidelines, at some distance from real life. They have been asked about a story character facing a hypothetical event, or they have been asked to recollect their own past experiences. It would be unwise to assume that children's understanding in these circumstances is exactly equivalent to the understanding that will be displayed when they encounter an emotionally charged situation.

One investigation of this issue was described in the previous chapter. Entry into a new boarding school is clearly an emotionally-charged event. The children are separated from parents and friends at home, and they face an unfamiliar environment. Recall that half the boys interviewed in the boarding school had only arrived one or two weeks earlier, although the remainder had been there for five or six weeks and were presumably more accustomed to the school. We wondered whether the replies given by the two groups might be influenced by their immediate circumstances, particularly in the case of the group who had been there only one or two weeks and who might as a result be more distressed or more homesick. When we compared the two groups, however, there was no evidence that the recent experience of separation, or the anxiety provoked by a strange and somewhat challenging environment either constricted or enlarged the boys' insight into their emotional reactions or the means to cope with them. Irrespective of the timing of the interview, the boys mostly gave replies that were consonant with their age. The obvious conclusion to draw from this study is that the child's conceptualization of emotion is largely governed by the child's age and associated cognitive ability. It does not fluctuate markedly when the child enters an emotionally-charged environment. This is an encouraging conclusion from a theoretical point of view. It implies that the child's construal of emotion is fairly stable, and can be predicted from knowledge of the child's cognitive status, whatever his or her emotional circumstances might be.

However, we have found in other research that this theoretically simple and attractive solution is untenable. The child's understanding of emotion is not always a simple function of age or cognitive development; it can vary, depending on the child's circumstances. We draw this conclusion from a study carried out by Mark Lipian with a group of hospitalized children and a group of healthy children (Harris and Lipian, 1989; Lipian, 1985). The hospitalized children were composed of two age groups, six- and ten-year-olds. They were suffering from a variety of acute conditions, each of them severe enough to warrant hospitalization but none of them life-threatening. Complaints included a broken elbow, respiratory distress, suspected endocrine disorder, suspected appendicitis, an ingrown toenail, accidental ingestion of anti-depressant medication, multiple burns, and so forth. There was no attempt to select children with any specific medical condition.

On the second or third day of their stay in hospital, the children were interviewed about their emotional reactions to being ill. Children who had undergone an operation were interviewed one or two days after surgery. None of the children were either heavily sedated or in severe pain at the time of the interview.

The interview covered many of the topics that have been discussed in previous chapters: ambivalent feelings; strategies for hiding emotion; and strategies for changing emotion. One or two new issues of special relevance to illness were also raised. Thus, the children were questioned about psychosomatic causality, particularly the extent to which recovery might or might not depend on remaining cheerful and in good spirits.

For the purpose of comparison, two groups of healthy children, a six-year-old and a ten-year-old group were also interviewed about their emotional reactions to being ill.[1] These healthy children were interviewed in school. They were asked to think back to the last time they had been ill and then, like the hospitalized children, they were asked various questions about their emotional reactions to being ill.

It is important to stress that the hospitalized and healthy children were comparable intellectually and socially. They came from the same range of backgrounds, and their teachers rated their educational achievements as being similar. On the other hand, the situation facing the two groups obviously differed sharply. The hospitalized children were temporarily away from home; they were in a strange and somewhat frightening environment; they were ill and often miserable. The healthy children were living at home; they were interviewed in the familiar environment of the school; they were not ill and they were not noticeably unhappy. These various differences between the two groups will come into focus when we consider the ways in which they responded to the interview.

Mixed feelings

Several questions examined the children's ideas about the coexistence and interaction of particular emotions. Some questions focused on the situation of illness itself. A second set focused on a situation entirely removed from illness: children were asked to imagine a day at the fair and to report on how they would feel during and after the outing. Finally, a third set of questions combined the first situation with the second, to create a complex and emotionally ambiguous setting: children were asked to imagine a day when they were ill but went to the fair all the same, and to report once more on how they would feel both during and after the outing.

Not surprisingly, only a handful of children spontaneously mentioned having experienced positive as well as negative feelings in reaction to being ill. The majority mentioned exclusively negative feelings. They frequently said that they were sad, unhappy or upset. Other negative feelings that were sometimes mentioned included feeling scared, cross and bored.

In a follow-up question, the children were probed further about whether mixed feelings were possible as a reaction to illness. They were asked if being ill could ever make you feel an emotion opposite in valence to the emotion that they had just mentioned. For example, a child who claimed to feel sad at being ill was asked if being ill could ever make you feel cheerful, and to explain how. In response to this question, a pattern appeared that was to be repeated many times throughout the interview: the hospitalized children – particularly the ten-year-olds – gave answers that were less complex, more appropriate for younger children, than did the healthy children with whom they were being compared. Among the healthy children there was a familiar and clear developmental trend. Approximately a quarter of the healthy six-year-olds agreed that you could feel both happy and sad about being ill, but this proportion increased to about three-quarters of the healthy ten-year-olds. In explaining such mixed emotions, the healthy children usually referred to some compensating feature of being ill or in hospital. For example, one ten-year-old boy explained: 'Yeah . . . when you're in hospital sometimes they have all the games and you're ill but you're playing and it makes you feel happy.' This developmental trend was much less obvious among the hospitalized children. Although a quarter of the six-year-olds agreed that mixed feelings were possible, the proportion increased to less than a half among the ten-year-olds.

There is one obvious interpretation of these results. We may not be observing a genuine difference in conceptualization between the two groups, but simply a different interpretation of the question. The hospitalized group would presumably have referred the question to their own current illness, which was, after all, severe enough to bring them into hospital. By contrast, the healthy children might have been thinking of something much less severe – their last cold or bout of influenza. This difference might explain why the hospitalized children were less willing to admit to positive as well as negative feelings about being ill.

A later question is especially significant in this connection. Recall that children were asked about going to the fair despite being ill. For this question, children were explicitly probed about the impact of a specific illness, rather than left to imagine an illness of varying degrees of severity. Having said that if they went to the fair when they were ill, they would feel a negative emotion – 'sad', 'fed up', 'disappointed', and so forth, the interviewer interjected: 'Well, say it was just a little illness – a cold or a little sore throat. What feelings would you have at the fair then?'

The same pattern still emerged despite this interjection. Among the healthy children, about one-third of the six-year-olds and almost three-quarters of the ten-year-olds acknowledged that they would experience mixed feelings. This developmental trend was eliminated among the hospitalized children. Only a handful of children in each age group (4 per cent of six-year-olds and 16 per cent of ten-year-olds) admitted to the possibility of mixed feelings.

In summary, the children's willingness to conceive of mixed feelings in the face of illness depended on their status. The children in hospital doubted that their negative reaction might be tempered in any way by positive feelings, whereas the healthy children, particularly the ten-year-olds, were more sanguine.

Coping strategies

Several questions were posed about the possibility of hiding or even changing feelings, particularly the feelings of sadness or distress that many children had acknowledged at the beginning of the interview. With respect to changing emotion, the following question was asked: 'Say you were ill and you felt sad [or whatever feeling the child had mentioned initially]. Is there anything you could do to *change* the way you felt, to change that feeling of being sad?'

Among the healthy children, there was a clear-cut age change. Although many six-year-olds – more than half – denied that anything could be done, the ten-year-olds were much more optimistic: almost all of them claimed that there was something you could do to cheer yourself up. They recommended the distraction strategy described in the previous chapter; they either proposed some enjoyable activity with no further elaboration of how it might be effective, or they proposed such an activity, together with an explanation of the way that it would stop one thinking about the illness and the distress that went with it.

Among the hospitalized children, there was little developmental change: over half the children in each age group reached the gloomy conclusion that there was nothing to be done. Moreover, they reached that conclusion despite probing from the interviewer. Here are a couple of examples. The first is taken from an interview with a ten-year-old girl, and the second from a ten-year-old boy; the girl was about to undergo an appendectomy and the boy had undergone the operation two days earlier.

Interviewer: . . . Is there anything you could do to *change* the way you felt?
Girl: Not really.
Interviewer: Anything you can ever try to do to change the feeling you have?
Girl: No.
Interviewer: If you feel a certain way, it's just there to stay, and it's impossible to do anything to change it?
Girl: Just impossible, yes.

Interviewer: . . . Is there anything you could do to *change* the way you felt?
Boy: No, not really.
Interviewer: If you're scared or sad, that's just the way you feel and there's nothing you can do about it?
Boy: Pretty much, yeah.
Interviewer: Anything you might try?
Boy: Not really, no.

Those hospitalized children who did agree that it was possible to do something to change their feelings were asked to explain what they could do. Here, their answers reflected the usual age-change. Among the six-year-olds, the most popular strategy was to resort to activities normally associated with positive emotion. They either suggested using 'props' (toys and games), or engaging in boisterous physical activities (running about, jumping, and so forth). They rarely justified these proposals with any mentalistic explanation, even with prompting. For example, a six-year-old girl, hospitalized with suspected appendicitis:

Girl: I could get someone to play with me.
Interviewer: What would that do?
Girl: Make me feel more cheerful.
Interviewer: How?
Girl: Because I could play with them – a game.
Interviewer: What if you were all by yourself.
Girl: I could play with my spinning-top.
Interviewer: What's that do?
Girl: I'm happier.
Interviewer: How come.
Girl: 'Cos it's good fun my spinning-top.
Interviewer: Anything else you could try?
Girl: No.

Some ten-year-olds in hospital also proposed a game or activity with no explanation of any intervening mental component. Just as often, however, they suggested strategies in which the mentalistic component was spelled out more clearly. Instead of simply mentioning an enjoyable activity, they explained its distracting effect.

For example, a ten-year-old girl, hospitalized with a suspected bone-infection in her hip:

Girl: You could do something – play a game or read something.
Interviewer: What would that do?
Girl: Well, it would take your mind off what you were thinking.
Interviewer: And that would cheer you up?
Girl: Yeah.
Interviewer: What do you mean: 'take your mind off'?
Girl: Well, you know – stop thinking about the pain or what's going to happen next.

In the same vein, children occasionally recommended thinking about happy events or ideas. A boy with acute asthma had this suggestion:

Boy: Just think about something else – about what you get for Christmas and make yourself happy.
Interviewer: Would that work?
Boy: Sometimes it does.

Summing up, we find that children recommend techniques for coping with illness that are similar to those they recommend for coping with homesickness in the boarding school: they seek to distract themselves from their distress by engaging in other activities or other thoughts. Moreover, whether we look at the children in hospital or the healthy children interviewed in their school, development proceeds in the same way: six-year-olds focus on enjoyable activities with little explanation of how they work beyond an insistence that they will cheer you up, whereas ten-year-olds are more likely to allude to the importance of forgetting about your illness and your distress and substituting more positive thoughts.

Despite this overall similarity in strategy content, the hospitalized children are more pessimistic about such strategies than their healthy peers. They are much more likely to reject the suggestion that it is possible to set about cheering oneself up. This altered conception of emotion is particularly obvious among the ten-year-olds, echoing the findings for mixed feelings. The customary difference between six- and ten-year-olds is partially eliminated among the hospitalized children because the older children often reach conclusions that are characteristic of younger children.

Hiding negative feelings

The children were asked several questions about their strategies for hiding as well as changing their feelings. The initial question was fairly open-ended: 'Say you were with your mother or father, and you were ill. Could it ever happen that your mother or father didn't know you felt sad [or whatever feeling had been voiced at the outset]?' Among the healthy children, there was a sharp age-change: fewer than half the six-year-olds but almost all the ten-year-olds argued that such a misleading display was feasible. By contrast, the familiar pattern of slippage reappeared among the hospitalized children. A handful of six-year-olds and only about a third of the ten-year-olds pointed out that one could hide one's feelings by acting or talking in a manner that did not correspond with one's real feelings.

Similar results were obtained when the children were asked more explicitly about the possibility of hiding their feelings: 'Say you didn't want your mother or father to know that you felt sad. What could you do so they wouldn't know?' Although the proportion of children who proposed some form of emotional masking increased with age in each group, the proportion was much smaller among the hospitalized children.

One plausible explanation of these results is that the emotional status of the children in hospital and the healthy children differs sharply. The hospitalized children are likely to be more distressed, so that they are more sceptical about the possibility of hiding (as well as changing) their feelings. This interpretation implies that the two groups would not differ in their judgements about whether or not *other* people might hide their feelings. This was exactly the issue raised in a further series of questions. One question was especially revealing. The interviewer alleged that he had talked to another child the previous day and 'that other boy said that sometimes, when he was ill, his parents acted cheerful, even when they were very worried about him because he was ill. Do you think he was right or wrong about that?' (For girls the wording was changed to refer to 'that other girl'.)

In the hospitalized group, there were many children who rejected the possibility of parental pretence: this was true for most of the six-year-olds, and almost a third of the ten-year-olds. In the healthy group, on the other hand, the possibility of parental pretence was much more likely to be accepted: fewer than half of the six-year-olds and none of the ten-year-olds denied that parents might try to act cheerfully, if they felt anxious.

Thus, the two groups differed in their replies even when they were questioned about other people, specifically their parents. This means that we cannot explain the hospitalized children's scepticism about the possibility of hiding emotion simply in terms of their own inability to do so in the face of considerable distress.

Nor does it seem feasible to argue that children in hospital will be less likely to encounter parents who attempt to appear cheerful. If anything, we might expect children in hospital to have had more experience of surface cheerfulness because parents will often seek to avoid alarming their children by revealing their own anxieties.

The children's replies to the set of questions about hiding

emotion again suggest that children in hospital conceive of emotion in a less complex or sophisticated way than their healthy peers. They are more inclined to think of an emotional state as automatically visible, and beyond strategic control.

Psychosomatic causality

The fact that children were interviewed about illness offered an opportunity to discuss a hitherto unexplored issue: the link between psyche and soma, or more specifically the link between emotional state and speed of recovery from illness. The interviewer introduced this issue by asking whether trying to feel a particular emotion could make the illness go away more quickly. Children who doubted this possibility were urged to reconsider in two ways; they were asked to consider whether such an influence might be possible for a little illness – a cold or a little flu – and they were asked to comment on a child who had claimed that feeling cheerful would speed recovery. Despite both of these prompts, there still remained a large difference in the replies of the hospitalized and the healthy children. Among the healthy children there was a clear age-change. About one-third of the six-year-olds as compared to two-thirds of the ten-year-olds claimed that such psychosomatic causality was possible. By contrast, only a handful of hospitalized six-year-olds and fewer than a third of hospitalized ten-year-olds allowed that an influence of that nature could be effective.

When children did assert such an influence they often described it, particularly among the healthy older children, in cognitive terms. Not surprisingly, they had some difficulty in pin-pointing the exact mechanism. The following replies from a ten-year-old boy are illustrative:

Boy: 'Cos if you're cheerful, it helps you to think positive.
Interviewer: Think positive?

Boy: Yeah, think like, 'I'm gonna be better tomorrow' – and three days later, you *are* better. It's like hair conditioner, or soap – you think that it's gonna work, so it *does* work. If you think, 'It isn't there', it'll go away.

The reaction of the hospitalized children is typified by the reply of a ten-year-old girl admitted to the hospital with stomach pain:

Girl: . . .Well, if I don't eat too much it seems to feel a little better.
Interviewer: Can feelings make you get better quicker?
Girl: No, I don't think so.
Interviewer: Say you had a flu?'
Girl: No, I can't think of anything.
Interviewer: Another little girl I talked to told me that by trying to feel cheerful when she was ill, she could make herself better sooner. Do you think she was right or wrong about that?
Girl: Wrong, I think, because if you have flu, it doesn't really sort of change and even if you do try to cheer yourself up, I don't think it would really work.

One might explain the scepticism of the hospitalized children by arguing that they would doubt that you could ever be really cheerful when you were ill, so that they never really accepted the premise of the question. This line of argument would suggest that they should accept psychosomatic causation provided it was couched in terms of the *retarding* effect that *negative* feelings might have on recovery. Accordingly, the following question was also put to the children: 'When you are ill do you think feeling a certain feeling ever makes it harder for you to get over the illness and get better?' As with the earlier question, children were prompted to reconsider if they denied such an influence, by asking them to focus on a minor illness and also by asking them to comment on a child who had allegedly told the interviewer that feeling unhappy did slow recovery.

Despite these prompts, and despite the change of premise, a similar pattern re-emerged. The healthy children were more willing to grant the possibility of such psychosomatic causation. When it was acknowledged, it was typically explained in mentalistic terms, particularly by the healthy ten-year-olds, and as before such explanations were somewhat vague despite the confidence with which they were enunciated: 'When you're angry or sad, just thinking about the illness – you just can't stop thinking about the illness, and it just takes much longer to get over. When I'm sad, I just think about the illness all the time, and if it's a flu, it takes longer to get out.'

The sick children, by contrast, continued to reject the idea that emotion could have an impact on the speed of recovery. A ten-year-old suffering from back pain speculated how such a mistaken notion might arise: 'I don't think feelings and the illness have any effect on each other, really. He [the other little boy referred to by the interviewer) might just *think* like: "It's lasting longer," but it couldn't last any longer really.' Other children were more dismissive: 'It's ridiculous to say that being unhappy is going to make your illness last longer. There's just no meaning to that.'

In summary, whether asked about the impact of positive or negative feelings on the course of an illness, the healthy children were willing to entertain the possibility of psychosomatic causation. Depending on the emotion, it could either speed up or slow down recovery. The hospitalized children were more inclined to see their illness as having an autonomous time-course that could not be altered by mental processes.

Interpretations

If we look at the children's replies across the various questions a consistent pattern emerges. Among the healthy children, a familiar picture of developmental change is apparent. As compared with the six-year-olds, the ten-year-olds are more willing to admit that feelings can be mixed, changed and camouflaged. They are also more likely to argue that feelings can alter the course of an illness. According to this later conception, any given emotion has a greater number of causal connections or links. It can be conjoined with another emotion; it can be changed or concealed by strategic intervention; and, in its turn, it can have a causal connection with the body. Among the hospitalized children, this conception of emotion is less prevalent. They claim that feelings about illness will be chiefly negative, that there is little that can be done to ameliorate those feelings, and that they cannot be concealed. They also dismiss the possibility that emotion can alter the rate of recovery. This shift in the conception of emotion was especially noticeable among the hospitalized ten-year-olds but it was also found for some questions among the hospitalized six-year-olds.

How should we interpret the shift? There were several differences between the healthy and the hospitalized children, each of which might have contributed to the variation in their replies. The hospitalized children were ill; they were separated from their parents; they were in a strange environment; and finally, they were assigned an unfamiliar, distressing and passive role, namely the role of patient. The healthy children were not ill, they were not separated from their parents, nor in a strange environment, nor assigned the role of patient.

To help us identify the critical difference between the two groups, we may briefly reconsider the findings from the study of boys entering boarding school, described in the previous chapter. These boys were also in a strange and unfamiliar environment – admittedly one that may be less forbidding than a hospital but certainly one that can be worrying for the new recruit, particularly since he knows he will be there for ten weeks or more at a stretch. The new boarder is also separated from his parents. Indeed, the separation is much more complete and long-lasting for the boarder than for the child in hospital who sees his or her parents during visiting hours, and can frequently expect to return home within one or two weeks. Nevertheless, we found no signs of a shift in the way that boarding school pupils conceive of emotion. Their replies corresponded to what we might have expected for children of that age and, in addition, we found few differences between the replies of the children who had only been at the school for one or two weeks as compared with those who had been there for five or six weeks, even though the latter groups had presumably become more familiar with the school, settled into its routine and made more friends.

The fact that the new boarders showed no obvious shift in their conception of emotion whereas the phenomenon was quite pervasive across a wide range of questions among the hospitalized children strongly suggests that neither parental separation nor an unfamiliar environment is sufficient to produce the shift. This leaves two plausible factors: illness and the patient role. There are arguments both for and against illness playing any direct causal role. It is a commonplace of clinical observation (Bowlby, 1971) that children who are ill become more dependent and turn to an attachment figure with increased frequency. However, there is no obvious reason to suppose that dependency would, in itself, be accompanied by any kind of cognitive shift. Furthermore, the children interviewed in hospital were suffering from a very heterogeneous set of ailments. It is hard to imagine that a bone fracture, appendicitis and a viral infection have any uniform physiological impact. Admittedly, several of the hospitalized children were recovering from an operation that had taken place one or two days earlier, so that the after-effects of a general anaesthetic must be taken into account. However, when we divided the hospitalized children into two sub-groups: those who had undergone surgery versus those who had not, we found a very similar shift in the pattern of replies within each sub-group as compared with the pattern found in the healthy children (Harris and Lipian, 1989).

It seems more plausible, therefore, to search for a difference between the hospitalized and the healthy children at the psychological level. The hospitalized children clearly did not enjoy the role of patient. They complained of feeling sad, bored, worried and fed up. Few of them mentioned anything about the experience that they enjoyed. Moreover, although children were not included in the study if they were experiencing severe pain, the nature of the children's illness meant that in many cases they were experiencing some pain or discomfort. By contrast, the healthy children, tested in school, were presumably feeling cheerful or at least neutral, and they were not experiencing any discomfort. Recall too that the boys at boarding school rarely reported unqualified distress about their new status. They usually said that they felt a mixture of positive and negative feelings and a large proportion acknowledged mixed feelings with minimal prompting from the experimenter.

Accepting for the moment that the patient role and its associated distress and discomfort does provoke a shift in the child's conceptualization of emotion, how might it do so? One possibility is that unalloyed negative emotion has a pervasive bias on the child's train of thought, steering it toward negative memories and associations and away from happier, more optimistic thoughts. Recent research with adults certainly shows that once a depressed or negative mood is induced, various cognitive biases begin to occur. Positive events from the past, particularly those associated with success, are less likely to be recalled (Blaney, 1986). In addition, people who are sad and depressed, or prone to such feelings, are apt to see themselves as a cause of bad events but not good events. This is true of both adults (Brewin, 1985) and children (Seligman and Peterson, 1986). Finally, if a negative mood is induced, people rate the likelihood of a variety of natural calamities (including those quite unrelated to the event that triggered their negative mood) as being greater (Johnson and Tversky, 1983). Overall, a negative mood, particularly a sad or depressed mood, inclines people to recall negative rather than positive events from their past, to expect negative events in the future, and to see themselves as responsible for this bleak state of affairs.

If the children in hospital were distressed or sad, they too would be subject to these negative biases, and they might come into play whenever they were asked a question about their current state or a hypothetical question about some imagined situation. For example, asked to imagine going to the fair with a cold, they would be less likely to recall happy memories. As a result, they would doubt the possibility of feeling positive emotion alongside negative emotion at the fair, so that they would be sceptical about the possibility of mixed feelings. Asked whether their parents might look cheerful (despite actually feeling anxious), they might be sceptical about the possibility of producing even the outer signs of happiness, so that they would deny that parents could hide their anxieties. Finally, fewer positive thoughts and activities would come to mind if they were asked how they could cheer themselves up, so that they would not be optimistic about changing their feelings.

This interpretation does a reasonable job of drawing together the various shifts that we see in the conception of emotion adopted by the children in hospital (Harris and Lipian, 1989). Effectively, they are portrayed as being pessimistic whenever they are asked to evaluate the likelihood of any outcome or behaviour that is positive or appears positive.

There is, however, one result that is difficult to explain with such an interpretation. Recall that the hospitalized children tended to dismiss the possibility of psychosomatic causation. Moreover, they dismissed the possible causal impact of negative feelings as well as positive feelings. According to the line of argument that I have outlined, it is easy to see why they would doubt that feeling more cheerful would speed up recovery. Given a negative or pessimistic bias, they should be inclined to judge feeling cheerful and getting better as less likely, and the happy conjunction of those two events as less likely still. By the same argument, they should be *more* willing to accept the conjunction of negative feelings and a slower recovery. Yet, as we have seen, the results point to exactly the opposite conclusion. The hospitalized children rejected the possibility of psychosomatic causation, in a negative as well as a positive direction.

For this reason, we may consider a second explanation. We may suppose that ideas and associations connected with the role of patient dominate the train of thought of the child in hospital. Children are constantly reminded of their peculiar and upsetting new status. They are often confined to bed, and limited to a small number of passive or low-key distractions, such as watching television or reading. They may receive medication or tests and they may be in pain. Moreover, they are constantly surrounded by the activities of the ward, which will include the coming and going of uniformed doctors and nurses. Under these circumstances, it would not be surprising if children become preoccupied by their immediate situation and find it difficult to imagine themselves engaged in different activities, beyond the confines of the ward. Their patient role has a centripetal effect on their thought processes. Their mental horizon is not shifted in a negative direction; it is simply contracted to their immediate situation.[3]

As a result of this contraction, they find it difficult to imagine themselves or another person acting or feeling in a different setting. For example, they find it hard to imagine the positive feelings that are typically evoked by missing school or going to a funfair. Similarly, they find it difficult to imagine ways in which their current distress or discomfort might be masked, or how they might engage in alternative thoughts or activities that would suppress their thoughts and feelings. In each case, they are being invited to consider a possibility that lies beyond their immediate situation or repertoire, and in each case they reject it as unlikely. According to this interpretation, children who are currently ill might also be more likely to reject the possibility of re-directing their illness by psychosomatic means. Again, they are being asked to consider stepping outside their current passive role of patient to consider a hypothetical situation in which, far from being helpless, they might be agents with the power to alter their rate of recovery, to speed it up or to slow it down.

Whatever the ultimate plausibility of this interpretation, it is one that the boys at boarding school might endorse. Compared with children in hospital, they are fortunate in that they can engage in energetic and absorbing games in the company of others; that active participation helps them to re-define their situation. They cease to think and feel as a homesick person separated from his family, and start to become a member of the school. It is not surprising, therefore, that they recommend such distracting activities as a way to cope with homesickness.

Summary and conclusions

Although it is tempting to assume that children's conception of their emotion is largely dependent on their cognitive maturity, the findings described in this chapter signal the need for caution. When we compared children in hospital with healthy children, we found a consistent difference in their conception of the emotions associated with illness. Whereas the healthy children revealed the usual pattern of age-changes described in earlier chapters, this pattern was attenuated among the children in hospital. They were inclined to doubt that emotions could be mixed or masked or changed, and they assumed that emotion could not re-direct the course of an illness.

These results raise important questions for the future. In particular, we do not know which aspect of hospitalization leads to the observed shift in the child's conception: is it illness per se or is it the associated psychological changes of mood and role? Tentatively accepting that the psychological changes are critical, two interpretations seem worth exploring. First, the child's distress and discomfort might lead to a negative or pessimistic bias, so that the child finds it difficult to acknowledge that any current negative emotion might be less emphatically negative, might be concealed by a cheerful outward display, and might even be transformed. An alternative interpretation is that the immediate situation of the sick child floods consciousness to the point where it is difficult to set aside the status quo in order to contemplate other prospects, including more cheerful prospects.

NOTES

1 These two groups were part of a larger study of healthy children's understanding of the emotional reactions normally associated with illness described in the previous chapter (Lipian, 1985).
2 Fifteen-year-old healthy children (cf. Lipian 1985) were able to offer a bit more detail about psychosomatic causation. They typically argued that one's mood affected the strength of the body or its defences, and that in turn would accelerate or slow one's recovery. For example: 'Well, I think you get yourself into a sort of trap: You convince yourself, if you're depressed or sad about it, that there's nothing you can do – just keep harping on the negative aspects of the illness – and that probably suppresses your defences to a certain extent – at least, it doesn't help your body, or encourage it to actively fight the illness.' (15 years 3 months; healthy female). Very few children below the age of 15 years offered such explanations.
3 A fascinating study carried out in the early 1940s (Barker, Dembo and Lewin, 1943) but sadly neglected ever since offers some support for this line of speculation. The imaginativeness and complexity of children's play with a set of toys was sharply reduced when they were preoccupied by an alternative set of attractive toys, visible on the other side of a barrier but inaccessible.

9

Autism

So far, I have concentrated on the normal course of development for understanding emotion. When that understanding proceeds along normal lines, it is tempting to underestimate its importance. Surely, one might argue, children will vary in the insight that they have into their own emotional lives and those of the people around them; the consequences will not be severe if a particular child exhibits a limited development in that sphere. The case of autism is a reminder of just how devastating abnormal development can be. As I shall outline below, there is now considerable evidence that autistic children have great difficulty in understanding other people's mental states, including their emotional states. Indeed, it has been suggested that this may be one of the central deficits of the autistic syndrome.

Autism is a rare disorder: only two to four children per 10,000 suffer from it although the incidence can rise to 20 per 10,000 if looser criteria are used. The basic syndrome persists throughout childhood and into adulthood, although the symptoms change during development. In adult life, about two-thirds of autistic people are severely handicapped, with the majority in long-term sheltered settings. A minority are able to develop certain compensatory skills, to work, and to sustain a social life. With a normal level of non-verbal intelligence and reasonable language skills, there is an even chance of a good level of social adjustment in adulthood but a small likelihood of complete normality (Rutter and Garmezy, 1983).

The syndrome was first described in 1943 by Leo Kanner, a psychiatrist working in Baltimore. Given the rarity of the disorder, it is a tribute to Kanner's clinical perspicuity that his description remains the basis for current diagnosis. He focused on four major symptoms: an inability to form relationships with other people; a lack of spontaneous play (especially pretend play); serious abnormalities in the development of language and communication; and finally, an obsessive insistence on certain routines or interests.

Follow-up studies have shown the persistence of the disorder and the validity of Kanner's original description. After 28 years, Kanner himself re-examined the 11 children that he had originally diagnosed (Kanner, 1971). Of these, two had managed to secure a regular job, and to enter into community life to some degree. Most of the remaining cases, however, continued to display the same inability to make relationships with other people and varying degrees of social isolation. Bemporad (1979) saw a 31-year-old man whom Kanner had originally diagnosed and provides an especially telling description. There were various indications that the earlier symptoms had persisted into adult life. He showed a lack of empathy and complained that he found other people unpredictable and frightening. Not surprisingly, he tended to structure social encounters rigidly, and during such encounters he was incapable of small talk.

Volkmar and Cohen (1985) were able to obtain a first-hand report of the experience of autism from a young adult. Tony W. had been referred and diagnosed as autistic at 26 months. He had displayed several of the classic features of autism at that age: language was absent, he showed none of the characteristic attachment behaviours toward other people, and he produced repetitive and stereotyped hand movements. At 22 years of age, he now worked as an assembler; he had a few superficial friends although his attempts to secure a girlfriend had failed. Some extracts from his own account give the overall impression (some minor spelling and syntactic errors have been removed):

> I always loved high-tech things planes, rockets. I watched a lot of coverage of the rocket launchings . . . I don't or didn't trust anybody but myself; that's still a problem today. And I was and still am very insecure. I was very cold-hearted too. It was impossible for me to give or receive love from anybody. I often repulse it by turning people off. That is still a problem today, and relating to other people. I liked things over people and didn't care about people at all.

Family factors

Kanner concluded his initial report with the claim that an innate emotional difficulty, rather than any particular feature of the family environment, caused autism: 'We must, then, assume that these children have come into the world with innate inability to form the usual, biologically provided affective contact with people, just as other children come into the world with innate physical or intellectual handicaps.' Nevertheless, there were some early suggestions that the disorder might be partly due to the style of interaction in the child's family rather that to any genetic disorder. In the first place, there were indications that autistic children are more often found in middle-class homes. Second, there was no evidence that autism runs in families, which one would expect, given a genetic basis. On reconsideration, both pieces of evidence are suspect, and current evidence strongly suggests that genetic factors but not family environment do play a crucial role. Recent studies (e.g. Wing, 1980) do not bear out the earlier suggestions of any social class bias. Moreover, it became clear that autistic people rarely have children themselves, so that the failure to observe autism in successive generations of the same family is not surprising.

Autistic people rarely have children, but they do have siblings, and these provide some of the strongest evidence for a genetic component. Of the siblings of autistic children, 2 per 100 are diagnosed as autistic, a low rate admittedly, but at least 50 times higher than the rate observed in the normal population (Rutter, 1967). In a study of 11 autistic children with an identical twin, four of the twins showed the classic symptoms of autism and many of the other twins had intellectual or linguistic handicaps. By contrast, in a comparison group of 10 autistic children with a non-identical twin, none of the twins displayed the full-blown autistic syndrome, and only a few had intellectual or linguistic handicaps (Folstein and Rutter, 1977). This sharp difference between the two sets of twins is difficult to explain in terms of family environment; were treatment by the mother or father a critical factor one would expect a much higher similarity between one twin and the other in the non-identical (DZ) set.

Explanations of autism

The most striking symptom of autism is the difficulty in forming relationships with other people. Recall Kanner's bold pronouncement at the end of his paper: autistic children lack the ability 'to form the usual, biologically provided affective contact with people'. His description of one five-year-old autistic child, Paul, offers a vivid example: 'He behaved as if people did not matter or even exist. It made no difference whether one spoke to him in a friendly or a harsh way. He never looked up at people's faces. When he had any dealings with persons at all, he treated them, or rather parts of them, as if they were objects.'

The writing of autistic adults confirms this clinical picture. As Tony W. wrote: 'It was impossible for me to give or receive love from anybody.' Still, it would be a mistake to think of autistic children as consistently unfeeling or detached. Marian Sigman and her colleagues in Los Angeles have shown that when they are compared with non-autistic children of the same mental age, they show just as much emotion on their face during social interaction, although some of their facial expressions are unusual or difficult to interpret (Yirmiya,

Kasari, Mundy and Sigman, 1987). In addition, when they are briefly separated from their mother or caretaker, they show a normal pattern of behaviour on her return. They move close to her and touch her (Sigman, Mundy, Ungerer and Sherman, 1987). Indeed, one mother of a six-year-old autistic girl that I know finds that her daughter is much more anxious about her absence than her normal four-year-old son. Even if she is only in a different room from her mother, she often returns to check on her mother's presence.

We may conclude that autistic children's difficulties in 'affective contact' do not involve an inability to feel emotion themselves. Their difficulties are more likely to occur in the communication of emotion. Not only are their own emotional expressions unusual, they are also insensitive or unresponsive to the emotional signals that other people display. How might such a deficit arise? As we discussed in chapter 1, the ability to interpret emotional signals usually develops early in life. Even one-year-old children will regulate their approach towards an object in terms of whether they see their caretaker expressing positive encouragement. Consider what would happen if children could not grasp the emotional meaning of other people's facial expressions. They would see people's faces move into a new configuration but for them it would be devoid of significance. Such children would exhibit the lack of empathy that is typical of the autistic child. They would not simply be indifferent to other people's emotions, rather they would have difficulty in grasping that other people have emotional lives at all. Moreover, such incomprehension might well exist even if autistic children themselves exhibit strong emotion and emotional attachments to other people.

Peter Hobson has examined this aspect of the autistic syndrome. He asked whether autistic children have difficulty in seeing that different emotional signals can serve to convey the same emotion (Hobson, 1986a; 1986b). In his first study, children were shown various types of videotape. In one videotape, four different emotions – happiness, anger, fear and sadness – were each conveyed by different facial expressions.

In a second, they were conveyed by appropriate gestures; in a third, by sounds; and finally, in a fourth, by appropriate eliciting events.

Having watched any particular videotape, the children were given five drawings of facial expressions, and asked to pick out the drawing that went with the videotape. For example, having just seen a man making angry gestures, they would be expected to choose the angry face; having just heard a man moaning and sighing, they would be expected to choose the sad face, and so forth.

The autistic children made very few errors on control videotapes containing non-emotional material, so they understood the requirements of the task. Moreover, most of them could manage the simplest part of the emotions task: if they had seen a film of someone producing a facial expression, they selected the appropriate drawing of a facial expression to go with it. At a superficial perceptual level, therefore, they could recognize and re-identify particular facial expressions of emotion. On the more complex matching tasks where perceptual similarity offered no clues, the autistic children made lots of mistakes. For example, when they were asked to choose the facial expression that matched a gesture, a vocalization or an emotional context, they did much worse than normal children or retarded children matched for mental age. They had similar difficulties in a follow-up study when the matching task was turned around so that they had to select the gesture that matched a facial expression or vocalization.

These results give support to Hobson's contention that autistic children have difficulty in understanding that different emotional signals – a gesture, a facial expression, a tone of voice, or even an emotionally-charged situation – can all signify the same emotional state. Moreover, replication studies with autistic adults have shown that this difficulty is not due to slow development; it persists into adulthood even among adults who are able to hold jobs and live in the community (Macdonald et al., 1988). If autistic people do not understand other people's expressions of emotion, they will find it difficult to form normal relationships with them. For example, Peter Hobson describes the following episode. An autistic child heard another screaming and crying. Instead of reacting with distress or sympathy as a normal child might, the autistic child remarked laughingly: 'He is making a funny noise' (Hobson, 1986c).

Hobson's findings are simple and clear. Yet it is not easy to see how a difficulty in interpreting emotion might be linked to the wider difficulties of the autistic child. For example, how would a deficit in reading other people's emotional expressions result in a lack of play, poor language development and an insistence on sameness, all classic symptoms of autism? We need a more wide-ranging theory if we are draw these disparate symptoms together.

Beliefs, desires and emotion

In chapter 3, I argued that the understanding of emotion depends on an understanding of other mental states, particularly desires and beliefs. Perhaps autistic children do not simply misinterpret signs of emotion, but have difficulty in developing that wider conception of mind. Such a deficit would be easier to link to the other symptoms of autism.

Work with normal children has begun to show how that conception is acquired, and what its components are. In a clever experiment, Heinz Wimmer and Josef Perner (1983) presented the following story to normal three- and four-year-olds using suitable dolls and props to depict the sequence of events. Sally comes into the room, puts a marble into her basket and goes outside again. Anne then comes into the room; she takes the marble out of Sally's basket and hides it in her own box in the same room. She too goes out, whereupon Sally returns to look for her marble. Having followed the story to this point, the children are asked two questions to make sure that they have grasped its essentials: 'Where is the marble really?' and 'Where was the marble in the beginning?' Both three- and four-year-olds are able to answer these questions correctly, thereby setting the stage for the critical test question: 'Where will Sally look for her marble?'

Normal children of four years and upward have little difficulty with this question. They realize that Sally will mistakenly think that her marble is still where she put it so that she will look in the basket even though it is now empty. Three-year-olds, by contrast, have much more difficulty. They usually send Sally to look in the box where the marble really is, apparently not realizing that she has no way of knowing about its transfer (Wimmer and Perner, 1983; Perner, Leekam and Wimmer, 1987). Exactly why three-year-olds go wrong is not yet clear. It might be because they are poor at working out that Sally will be misinformed if she did not witness the transfer of the marble. It might be difficult to grasp that Sally now believes in a mental picture of the world that fails to match reality. Finally, it might be difficult to realize that false beliefs are as potent as true ones in guiding behaviour. Whatever the difficulty, we can be sure that it does not arise for four- and five-year-olds because they understand what Sally will think and do. Hence, they must have some conception of the way that beliefs are formed and guide our actions.

How do autistic children perform on this task? Three psychologists working in London, Simon Baron-Cohen, Alan Leslie and Uta Frith, compared a group of autistic children with Down's syndrome children and normal children. The autistic children were intellectually retarded but their non-verbal and verbal intelligence still exceeded that of the two other groups. Nevertheless a sharp difference emerged between the groups on the critical test question. Most of the autistic children (80 per cent) wrongly predicted that Sally would look in the object's new location. In contrast, most of the Down's and normal children (about 85 per cent in each case) correctly predicted that Sally would mistakenly return to the place where she first put the marble (Baron-Cohen, Leslie and Frith, 1985). Even with slightly older and more intelligent autistic children, and even when real people and a real change of location were involved rather than a make-believe story, the difficulty persisted. Most autistic children failed to realize that if they moved a coin from one place to another while the experimenter was briefly out of the room, then the experimenter would come back expecting to find it where it was originally (Leslie and Frith, 1988).

A similar difficulty has also been found when autistic children are asked to order sets of pictures depicting an unexpected transfer or disappearance. For example, one set showed a boy stealing a girl's teddy while her back was turned, and the girl then turning round to discover her unexpected loss. It is important to note that the autistic children did not have a general difficulty with the task of ordering the pictures because when simple physical causality was depicted – for example, a man kicking a boulder which then rolls downhill and falls in the water below – they even did somewhat better than normal or retarded children (Baron-Cohen, Leslie and Frith, 1986).

Can we conclude from these results that autistic children are competent at everyday physics but have little insight into everyday psychology? This is an attractive conclusion because it would help to explain the autistic's problems with social relationships. An inability to make sense of other people's beliefs and desires would make it next to impossible 'to give and receive love'. However, each of the tests described so far has involved an unexpected change of location and a mistaken belief that ensues. How do autistic children perform if they are asked about other psychological states, particularly desires?

Some suggestive findings emerged from the picture-ordering task. Once the children had arranged the pictures into a sequence, they were asked to tell the story in their own words. As compared with the other two groups, the autistic children made many fewer references to the mental states of the story characters, including their desires. Although a normal child might begin a story by saying: 'The boy is putting the sweet in the box *so nobody won't find it*', an autistic child would simply describe the action, and make no reference to the motive behind it. As a result, the narratives of the autistic children were drained of psychological colour. They stuck to a description of the overt behaviour of the story characters. Unlike the normal children, they did not bind the episodes together in terms of the protagonist's desires.[1]

Alongside beliefs, desires are the other crucial component of our everyday conception of mind. For example, as we discussed in chapter 3, our explanations or predictions of a person's emotion must take into account not just what the person expects to happen but also what the person wants to happen. With this in mind, Alison Muncer and I carried out a study in which we assessed autistic children's understanding of both beliefs and desires (Harris and Muncer, 1988).

We again used a simple story format. In each story, John and Mary were about to get a treat or go on an outing but they never agreed with each other. In some stories they *wanted* different things. For example, John might want to go to the fair and Mary to the swimming pool. In other stories, they *expected* different things. For example, John might think they were to get a bar of chocolate whereas Mary might think they were to get an ice-cream. At the end of each story, Mother announced the treat or outing, which inevitably conformed to the wishes or expectations of Mary and confounded those of John or vice versa. We then asked the children to say whether John and Mary had been right or whether they would be pleased with the outcome. To be correct children had to appreciate that only John or Mary was right and only one of them was pleased. In effect, they had to take into account what John and Mary had wanted or expected to happen and compare it with what actually did happen.

The autistic children were on average 11 years of age and their average verbal intelligence was equivalent to that of normal five-year-olds; we used normal five-year-olds, therefore, as the comparison group. Just as Baron-Cohen and his colleagues would expect, the autistic children performed much worse than the normal children despite being about six years older. Moreover, they did equally badly whether they were judging desires or expectations. Apparently, autistic children are not just poor at understanding beliefs; they are also poor at understanding the other major component of our everyday or folk theory of mind, namely desires.

The findings that I described earlier now fall into place. If autistic children do not understand people's motives, no wonder their narratives are surface descriptions with little psychological colour. Stories are built around the goals and plans of the hero. If one cannot understand those goals, the story makes little sense. More generally, it is scarcely surprising that autistic children find other people unpredictable and even frightening. An inability to understand people's beliefs would render their mistaken actions quite puzzling: 'Why on earth is she looking for her toys in that cupboard if it's empty?' An inability to grasp their desires, on the other hand, would make their actions completely incomprehensible. A plan of action would appear to be no more than a series of disconnected movements: 'Why is she moving toward that cupboard . . . why is she now pulling at its door . . . why is she now looking inside?'

To appreciate that tears, a sad facial expression and a sob all signify the same emotional state, it is also necessary to appreciate that each mode of expression can be precipitated by an underlying mental state. As we saw in chapter 3, the situations that lead to sadness (or any emotion) can be quite disparate: the breaking of a toy and the departure of one's mother have no physical features in common. Yet they do have something in common as soon as desires are taken into account. Each of the two situations thwarts a desire. If one cannot understand other people's desires, then their distress or joy, and the various manifestations that accompany those emotions, will appear unrelated. It will be impossible to trace their tears and sobs back to a common cause. At best, they will be sights and sounds that co-occur but for no apparent reason.

How to understand mental states

So far, we have seen that autistic children understand only part of the way that the world works. They understand its physical or mechanical forces but they are bewildered by psychological forces. They have little insight into the desires and beliefs that underlie people's actions and emotions. How does this lacuna come about? Why can they understand one type of causality and not the other? Alan Leslie has proposed an original and intriguing explanation. It suggests how two apparently distinct symptoms of the autistic syndrome – the poor understanding of psychology and the lack of pretend play – might be related to one another (Leslie, 1987).

Leslie's starting point is the claim that adults and also young children can act as if something known to be false were true. Let us start with an illustration that is used by Leslie. A two-year-old child is playing with a banana and briefly holds it up to her ear; she pretends that it is a telephone and starts to talk into the 'receiver'. Because the banana is patently not a telephone, this pretence involves the ability to act temporarily as if something that is false were true. This also applies to other acts of pretence that young children exhibit. Recall the episode described in chapter 3 where two-year-old J. gave a toy farmer a bath; J. acted as if water that turned out to be too hot was filling 'the bath', the little enclosure made out of bricks. Obviously, there was no water and no bath but J. acted as if there were.

We can couch these acts of pretence in terms of statements. The statements 'this banana is a telephone' and 'these bricks are a bath' are patently false, but the child, and anyone else who goes along with the child's fantasy, temporarily regards the statements as true.

The understanding of other people's mental states may also involve, according to Leslie, a willingness to entertain temporarily a proposition that is false. For example, to understand simple hiding games or many fairy tales, children need to appreciate that someone can hold a mistaken belief about a location or identity. The story of Little Red Riding Hood creates suspense because despite being taken aback by Grandma's big eyes and big teeth she does not realize that Grandma is really a wolf.

The understanding of another person's mental state and pretence have important similarities. They both require an ability to entertain statements that are known to be false. More generally, the understanding of many mental states involves an appreciation of the way that the intentional content of such states – the state of affairs that the mental state is directed towards – may not obtain in the actual world. Recall, for example, the stories about John and Mary. What one of them wanted or expected invariably proved to be out of line with what eventually happened.

Leslie goes on to put forward the intriguing hypothesis that autistic children, unlike normal children, cannot temporarily disengage from reality and entertain non-truths instead. Since this disengagement or 'decoupling' is needed both to carry out games of pretence and to understand many mental states, including mistaken beliefs and unfulfilled desires, autistic children will be poor at both. We have already presented evidence showing that autistic children are poor psychologists. Let us now consider their apparent lack of pretend play.

Pretend play

Autistic children play in what strikes the observer as a repetitive and stereotyped manner. They often line up objects or make geometric patterns, but they introduce very little imagination or make-believe into their play. This absence of make-believe play is notable because a well-established sequence of developmental changes (described in chapter 3) is seen among normal children. At around 12 or 13 months, children begin to produce a familiar action such as drinking, eating or sleeping 'in the void', that is to say, in the absence of its normal context. For example, the child sitting on the floor outside of a regular meal-time picks up an empty cup, brings it to the lips and tilts the cup as if drinking from it. These initial make-believe gestures are usually self-referenced (i.e. the child gives itself a drink). At around 18 months of age, the child begins to direct this same pantomime activity to others, particularly dolls. For example, the doll is given something to eat or drink.

At about two or two and a half years of age, children graduate to being a 'play-director'. They play with a doll as if it were an independent agent rather than a passive recipient of their make-believe actions. For example, instead of being given a drink, the doll is credited with a mind of its own and independent action; it is said to want a drink, it is made to search for a cup and to drink from it.

Autistic children do not appear to follow this developmental sequence. Even when they are compared to normal children and Down's syndrome children, matched for verbal IQ, they produce less pretend play (Sigman and Ungerer, 1984). A study carried out by Simon Baron-Cohen (1987) provides a clear demonstration of the autistic child's difficulties. The children were provided with various toys and their spontaneous activities with the toys were categorized. Three of the play categories simply involved manipulation or ordering of the objects but the 'pretend' category involved make-believe actions. For example, dolls might be made to cook with kitchen utensils; the bricks might be lined up to make a railway train; or the child might pretend that someone was at the other end of a toy telephone. Although most of the Down's children (80 per cent) and normal children (90 per cent) produced such pretend play, only two of the autistic children did so. Moreover, the episodes from the autistic children were limited and ambiguous. One pointed to a piece of sponge that was green and cube-shaped and said: 'Are these potatoes? I don't know. They might be peas.' The other pointed to the toy cooker and said: 'Don't touch it. It's hot.' Neither remark was part of any sustained sequence of pretend activity, or involved animation of the toy animals or dolls.

These results corroborate the general picture that we have of the autistic child. They confirm the absence of pretend play, and they show that this is not due to intellectual retardation. Down's children with equally severe intellectual handicaps do engage in pretend play. The findings also support Leslie's assertion that autistic children cannot suspend their disbelief in propositions that have no literal truth in order to act in a pretend mode.

Still, we need to be cautious. The developments in pretend play that I described earlier refer to the child's emerging ability to impute agency and intention. It is conceivable that autistic children rarely produce pretend play, not because they completely lack the ability to do so, but because the type of object-directed play that they prefer can be readily carried on without much call for pretence. Objects can be stacked, spun, lined up and so forth without any need for pretence. A human drama, on the other hand, cannot be staged unless one is prepared to imagine the goals, perceptions, emotions and beliefs of actors in the drama.

This argument implies that we need to make an important distinction between two types of pretence: simple pretence in which physical objects or their properties are conjured up, and advanced pretence in which a mental state is conjured up. Admittedly, in any given play episode, these two types of pretence are often intertwined; recall, for example, the episode in which two-year-old J. announced that the farmer wanted a bath and also produced imaginary water from imaginary faucets. However, the initial emergence of these two types of pretence takes place at different points in development. Pretence with objects emerges by 18 months whereas the attribution of mental states emerges at around 24 months.

Are autistic children equally poor at both types of pretence? Vicky Lewis and Jill Boucher (1988) have shown that they can engage in object-based pretence. The children were given various pairs of objects (e.g. a toy car and a box; a doll and a piece of blue paper) together with an instruction, for example 'make the car go in the garage' or 'make her swim in the swimming pool'. Thus, the children had to pretend that the box was a garage, or that the blue paper was a swimming pool. The autistic children proved to be just as competent as normal children and slow-learning children equated for verbal mental attainment.

If autistic children can manage the simpler object-based pretence, they must have some ability to 'decouple' or disengage from reality and act upon a non-truth, so that a 'decoupling' deficit cannot explain their difficulties in understanding other people. I shall argue instead that they cannot engage in the more advanced mode of pretence, the pretence of mental states, and this is at the root of their difficulties in understanding other people. In chapter 3, I suggested that this type of pretence or simulation is crucial for entering into the hopes and fears of other people, and more generally for developing a theory of mind. To recapitulate briefly, children 'simulate' the mental state of another person. They imagine the desires, beliefs and emotions that the other person has in actuality.

Consider, now, what would happen if a child were congenitally incapable of this type of imaginative projection. He or she would observe the other person's behaviour and expression, but would not be able to imagine the beliefs and desires that guide that behaviour. The behaviour of other people would appear unpredictable, and their emotional expressions would be illegible.

The normal child's pretend play with dolls and toy soldiers provides ample evidence for the existence of this type of projection. Without such a capacity, it would be difficult for the child to develop any conception of other people's mental states, and pretend play that involves the attribution of mental states should rarely occur. This is the pattern that we see in autistic children. Although they can engage in the simpler object-based pretend play, their free play lacks any human drama.

Communication and perspective-taking

We may turn, finally, to the language and communication difficulties of autistic children. These difficulties are particularly informative for two reasons. First, the severity of the autistic child's language handicap has repeatedly proven to be one of the best indicators of whether the child will make reasonable progress during development (Lotter, 1978). Second, as we shall see, there is evidence that communication difficulties can be identified early in life. Whatever disrupts the autistic child's communication with other people makes an early appearance and it does not go away. We need to look carefully at this early disruption of communication and analyse it.

Although autistic children are slow to acquire spoken language, there is no clear indication that their grammar or articulation are deviant (Bartolucci, Pierce and Streiner, 1980; Boucher, 1976). On the other hand, even among those autistics whose language development is advanced, there are persisting difficulties with the pragmatic or social aspects of language. They tend to be poor at initiating conversation, although they may not be unresponsive if another person initiates it (Loveland, Landry, Hughes, Hall and McEvoy, 1988). When they do bring up a topic it is often related to their own preoccupations, and their remarks or questions are usually uttered without cadence or inflection (Rutter and Garmezy, 1983).

When language first emerges in normal children, it takes its place alongside other communicative gestures. For example, at around 12 or 13 months children start to point to an object and to look back and forth between the object and the person whose attention they are trying to direct (Bates, 1976). The implication is that they realize that other people may not be following their gesture, and look to see whether the gesture is being registered and responded to. The combination of pointing plus looking suggests that by one year of age children appreciate that other people can have visual experiences like their own, provided they look in the same direction and that their attention can be directed by gestures such as pointing.

Do autistic children produce such gestures? Marian Sigman and her colleagues in Los Angeles filmed children as they played with an adult. As compared with normal and retarded children, the autistic children were less likely to check that the adult was paying attention to the same object or event as themselves. For example, they pointed less often; they showed objects to the adult less often, and when they were either holding an object or watching a interesting mechanical toy, they rarely looked over to the adult. Indeed, the absence of this visual checking was especially characteristic of the autistic children (Mundy, Sigman, Ungerer and Sherman, 1986; Sigman, Mundy, Sherman and Ungerer, 1986).

Thus, autistic children rarely establish so-called joint attention. They concentrate on an object, apparently unconcerned about whether anyone else is paying attention. Joint attention can be seen as an important precursor to early conversation. A child who could not engage in such joint attention, or who avoided it, would have difficulty in grasping one of the basic pragmatic functions of early language: focus on a common topic or object of interest. This suggests that the autistic child's later difficulties with the pragmatic functions of language originate in communication difficulties that are detectable before the emergence of language.

Why exactly are autistic children poor in establishing joint attention? Ever since Piaget carried out his classic research in which children were asked to imagine different perspectives on a mountain scene (the so-called three-mountains task) visual perspective-taking has been seen as a key component of children's ability to put themselves in another's shoes. Do autistic children find it difficult to imagine what another person can see? This would explain their tendency to fasten on an object, paying little heed to whether anyone else is looking at it as well.

Peter Hobson examined this possibility. As usual, three groups were assessed: autistic children, Down's children and normal children (Hobson, 1984). In one task, the child was asked to say what face of a cube would be visible to a doll positioned at various points around the cube. In another, the child had to position a pipecleaner doll behind a screen so that the doll could not be seen by one or two other figures allegedly trying to find him. The autistic children did surprisingly well. Their performance was in line with their mental age. There was no sign of the marked lag in performance that we described earlier for beliefs and desires. Indeed, a sub-group of older autistic children, approximately 14 years old with a mental age of 11 years, made scarcely any errors on either perspective-taking task.

Combining these various findings, we end up with a puzzle. Like normal children, autistic children can work out what another person can see, but in contrast to normal children they rarely seek to change or check what another person is looking at: they seldom point to an object of interest or check to see whether another person is looking at it.

Simon Baron-Cohen asked whether this paradoxical conclusion holds when the same autistic children are compared on both skills (Baron-Cohen, in press). The children watched while an adult directed his gaze (keeping his head still) at one of various objects dotted around the room and then said which object he was looking at. The task proved trivially easy for all the children including the autistic children. Nevertheless, the usual difficulties with pointing to objects of common interest emerged among the autistic group. They appeared to grasp what the experimenter intended if he pointed to an object that he wanted them to bring him, but when he pointed to an object invisible to the child, as if to say, 'Come and look at this', they failed to understand.

A similar pattern was found when the children's own pointing was observed. Whereas most of the retarded and normal children pointed at objects both to request them and to draw attention to them, the autistic children sometimes pointed to make a request but never pointed in order to draw attention to an object.

This pattern of results confirms the existence of the puzzle. Autistic children do not appear to realize that pointing can be used to direct what someone is looking at, yet they can easily diagnose what another person is looking at. Moreover, they understand one function of pointing, namely to direct another person to bring an object. Why, then, do they not use or understand pointing which is intended to draw attention to an object?

To answer this question, we need to consider the goal of this type of pointing. When we point at an interesting object we are attempting to direct someone to look at something, but that it is not our ultimate intention. We want them to share whatever it is that interests us or has captured our attention. We want them to join in our attitude toward the object, be it one of puzzlement or curiosity or joy; we are not simply intending that they look in a particular direction to receive a given perceptual input. So, it is important to distinguish between two different capacities: the anticipation of another person's reaction to seeing a particular object, and the diagnosis of whether he or she is looking in the right direction to see it.

As Alan Leslie and Uta Frith have pointed out, we can diagnose what another person sees by following his or her line of sight: any object along that line will be visible, provided there is no obstacle. This type of geometric extrapolation is not so different from figuring out the direction in which an object is travelling and whether there is an obstacle in its path (Leslie and Frith, 1988).

If children are to conceive of another person sharing their attitude of curiosity or anxiety about an object, such geometric projection is insufficient. They must be able to imagine the other person sharing their attitude to the object. As I argued earlier, this type of imaginative projection is quite distinctive because it requires the ability to imagine another person's emotional state rather than any physical attribute. The pointing gesture is intended to bring about that emotional state. If the child cannot imagine that state, the pointing gesture is useless, although of course it may serve other goals, such as requesting objects or help. Thus, we may trace the autistic child's neglect of pointing to the same deficit in the capacity for imaginative projection that restricts their pretend play and limits their understanding of beliefs and desires.[2]

We have come full circle. In chapter 1, I described the emergence of emotional understanding in normal children during the first year of life. One important conclusion was that the one-year-old child can appreciate that another person is not simply expressing emotion but is expressing emotion about some object in the environment. Moreover, faced with an uncertain situation, he or she will often look to another person to gauge that person's emotional reaction to the situation. For the normal child, even at this early age, other people embody the permanent possibility of a shared emotional experience. The autistic child moves through the world unable to conceive that possibility.

Summary and conclusions

I have examined abnormal development in this chapter in order to throw the competence of the normal child into relief. One of the key symptoms of autism is an inability to enter into affective contact with other people. Autistic children feel and express emotion, but they have difficulty in making sense of other people's emotions. One possible explanation for that difficulty is that they lack some basic perceptual mechanism that allows the normal child an immediate apprehension of other people's emotional states from their mode of expression – from the gestures, tone of voice and facial expression that they display. However, normal infants respond, often appropriately, to a caretaker's facial expression and tone of voice in the first few months of life, whereas autistic children rarely show signs of their handicap until 12 months and beyond.

At that age, normal infants start not simply to react to the expression of emotion by a caretaker but to show some appreciation that the other person is experiencing an emotion about an object or event in the world around them. They appropriately interpret signs of delight or apprehension directed toward an object and approach or avoid the object in question. They even appear to conceive of the possibility that the other person will express such an emotion: at moments of uncertainty they look toward a caretaker, as if for guidance. Moreover, at around the same age, they begin to understand the meaning of pointing. They start to point at objects themselves, and to follow an adult's point. Both of these behaviours – the emergence of pointing and the monitoring of a caretaker at moments of uncertainty – suggest that the infant is beginning to see other people as creatures who have the potential to adopt an emotional stance – of curiosity, interest or anxiety – towards an object, just as they themselves do.

The available evidence suggests that autistic children fail to achieve this insight into the capacities of other people. In line with the position taken in chapter 3, I have argued that this insight does not depend upon a perceptual mechanism but on an ability to simulate or imagine the emotional state of another person by analogy with the state of the self. Even though autistic children can engage in simple object-based pretend play when prompted to do so, they have particular difficulties with this more complex make-believe or pretend mode. As a result, their appreciation of other people's desires, beliefs and emotions is restricted.

Finally, it is important to stress that my account implies that although the difficulties of autistic children have a cognitive basis, they are not confined to cognition. The emotional experience of autistic children will also be impoverished. Kanner himself commented on their lack of sympathy for others. Recall, in addition, the more complex, social emotions discussed in chapter 4. The full emergence of these emotions depends critically on an ability to imagine the emotional reactions of other people to the achievements or failures of the self, even when those people are absent or uninformed.

Although autistic children may learn to understand what will earn approval and disapproval, in the absence of other people they should experience neither pride nor guilt.

NOTES

1 Baron-Cohen (1988) has obtained further evidence that autistic children stick to the behavioural level. He asked autistic, normal and retarded children what the brain does. Most of the normal and retarded children initially mentioned cognitive functions (e.g. 'thinking', 'dreaming', 'remembering', etc.). Motor functions (e.g. 'It tells you to walk') were mentioned by only a minority of these subjects, following prompting. The opposite pattern emerged among the autistic children. All of them initially mentioned behavioural functions (e.g. 'It makes you move', 'It makes you wake up and go to sleep', 'Running and walking'). Only after prompting did a minority mention mental functions such as thinking.

2 Pointing (accompanied by visual checking) emerges among normal children early in the second year of life. This is, of course, earlier than the attribution of pretend emotional states in make-believe play. How then can the imaginative projection of emotional states play a role in pointing? As noted in chapter 3 (note 6), imaginative projection is likely to be easier and to emerge at an earlier age when it is directed towards animate beings such as a parents or siblings rather than towards inanimate dolls because people are far more similar to the self than dolls.

References

Abramovitch, R., Corter C., and Lando, B. (1979). Sibling interaction in the home. *Child Development*, 50, 997–1003.

Abramovitch, R., Corter, C., and Pepler, D. (1980). Observations of mixed-sex sibling dyads. *Child Development*, 51, 1268–71.

Adlam-Hill, S., and Harris, P. L. (1988). Understanding of display rules for emotion by normal and maladjusted children. Unpublished paper, Department of Experimental Psychology, University of Oxford.

Ainsworth, M. D. S., Blehar, M. C., Waters, E., and Wall, S. (1978). *Patterns of Attachment: A Psychological Study of the Strange Situation*. Hillsdale, NJ: Erlbaum.

Altshuler, J. L. and Ruble, D. N. (1988). Children's awareness of strategies for coping with stress. Unpublished manuscript, Department of Psychology, New York University.

Astington, J. W., Harris, P. L., and Olson, D. R. (1988). *Developing Theories of Mind*. New York: Cambridge University Press.

Baldwin, J. M. (1891). *Handbook of Psychology: Feeling and Will*. New York: Holt.

Band, E. R. and Weisz, J. R. (1988). How to feel better when it feels bad: Children's perspectives on coping with everyday stress. *Developmental Psychology*, 24, 247–53.

Barden, R. C., Zelko, F. A., Duncan, S. W., and Masters, J. C. (1980). Children's consensual knowledge about the experiential determinants of emotion. *Journal of Personality and Social Psychology*, 39, 968–76.

Barker, R. G., Dembo, T., and Lewin, K. (1943). Frustration and regression. In R. G. Barker, J. S. Kounin, and H. F. Wright (eds.), *Child Behavior and Development*. New York: McGraw-Hill.

Baron-Cohen, S. (1987). Autism and symbolic play. *British Journal of Developmental Psychology*, 5, 139–48.

Baron-Cohen, S. (1988). Are autistic children 'Behaviourists'? An examination of their mental–physical and appearance–reality distinctions. Paper presented at the British Psychological Society Developmental Section Conference, Coleg Harlech, Wales.

Baron-Cohen, S. (in press). Perceptual role-taking and protodeclarative pointing in autism. *British Journal of Developmental Psychology*.

Baron-Cohen, S., Leslie, A. M., and Frith, U. (1985). Does the autistic child have a theory of mind? *Cognition*, 21, 37–46.

Baron-Cohen, S., Leslie, A. M., and Frith, U. (1986). Mechanical, behavioural and Intentional understanding of picture stories in autistic children. *British Journal of Developmental Psychology*, 4, 113–25.

Bartolucci, G., Pierce, S. J., and Streiner, D. (1980). Cross-sectional studies of grammatical morphemes in autistic and mentally retarded children. *Journal of Autism and Developmental Disorders*, 10, 39–50.

Bartsch, K., and Wellman, H. M. (1989). From desires to beliefs: First acquisition of a theory of mind. Paper presented in the symposium on 'Children's theory of mind', Society for Research in Child Development Meeting, Kansas, April.

Bates, E. (1976). *Language in Context*. New York: Academic Press.

Batson, C. D. (1987). Prosocial motivation: Is it ever altruistic? In L. Berkowitz (ed.). *Advances in Experimental Social Psychology*, vol. 20. New York: Academic Press.

Beeghly, M., Bretherton, I., and Mervis, C. B. (1986). Mothers' internal state language to toddlers. *British Journal of Developmental Psychology*, 4, 247–61.

Bemporad, J. R. (1979). Adult recollections of a formerly autistic child. *Journal of Autism and Developmental Disorders*, 9, 179–98.

Blaney, P. H. (1986). Affect and memory: A review. *Psychological Bulletin*, 99, 229–46.

Borke, H. (1971). Interpersonal perception of young children: Egocentrism or empathy? *Developmental Psychology*, 5, 263–9.

Boucher, J. (1976). Articulation in early childhood autism. *Journal of Autism and Childhood Schizophrenia*, 6, 297–302.

Bowlby, J. (1971) *Attachment and Loss*, vol.1:*Attachment*. Harmondsworth: Pelican.

Bowlby, J. (1973). *Attachment and Loss*, vol. 2: *Separation, Anxiety and Anger*. London: Hogarth Press.

Boyd, W. (1985). *School Ties*. London: Hamish Hamilton.

Bradshaw, D. L., Campos, J. J., and Klinnert, M. D. (1986). Emotional expressions as determinants of infants' immediate and delayed responses to prohibitions. Paper presented at Fifth International Conference on Infant Studies, Los Angeles.

Bretherton, I., and Beeghly, M. (1982). Talking about internal states: The acquisition of an explicit theory of mind. *Developmental Psychology*, 18, 906–21.

Bretherton, I., Fritz, J., Zahn-Waxler, C., and Ridgeway, D. (1986). Learning to talk about emotions: A functionalist perspective. *Child Development*, 57, 529–48.

Bretherton, I., McNew, S., and Beeghly-Smith, M. (1981). Early person knowledge as expressed in gestural and verbal communication: When do infants acquire a 'theory of mind'? In M. E. Lamb and L. R. Sherrod (eds), *Infant Social Cognition*. Hillsdale, NJ: Erlbaum.

Brewin, C. R. (1985). Depression and causal attributions: What is their relation? *Psychological Bulletin*, *98*, 297–309.

Bühler, C. (1930). *The First Year of Life*. New York: John Day.

Bühler, C. (1939). *The Child and his Family*. London: Harper.

Butterworth, G., and Cochran, E. (1980). Towards a mechanism of joint visual attention in human infancy. *International Journal of Behavioral Development*, 3, 253–70.

Byrne, R., and Whiten, A. (1988). *Machiavellian Intelligence: Social Expertise and the Evolution of Intellect in Monkeys, Apes and Humans*. Oxford: Clarendon Press.

Campos, J. J., Barrett, K. C., Lamb, M. E., Goldsmith, H. H., and Stenberg, C. (1983). Socioemotional development. In M. M. Haith and J. J. Campos (eds) *Infancy and Developmental Psychobiology*. In P. Mussen (ed.), *Handbook of Child Psychology* (vol. 2). New York: John Wiley.

Camras, L. A. (1977). Facial expressions used by children in a conflict situation. *Child Development*, 48, 1431–5.

Camras, L. A. (1980). Children's understanding of facial expressions used in a conflict situation. *Child Development*, 51, 879–85.

Caron, A. J., Caron, R. F., and MacLean, D. J. (1988). Infant discrimination of naturalistic emotional expressions: the role of face and voice. *Child Development*, 59, 604–16.

Caron, R. F., Caron, A. J., and Myers, R. S. (1982). Abstraction of invariant face expressions in infancy. *Child Development*, 53, 1008–15.

Caron, R. F., Caron, A. J., and Myers, R. S. (1985). Do infants see emotional expressions in static faces? *Child Development*, 56, 1552–60.

Chandler, M. J. (1988). Small-scale deceit: Deception as a marker of 2-, 3- and 4-year-olds' early theories of mind. Unpublished paper, Department of Psychology, University of British Columbia, Vancouver, BC, Canada.

Chandler, M. J., and Greenspan, S. (1972). Ersatz egocentrism: A reply to H. Borke. *Developmental Psychology*, 7, 104–6.

Cohn, J. F., and Tronick, E. Z. (1983). Three-month-old infants' reactions to simulated maternal depression. *Child Development*, 54, 185–93.

Cohn, J. F., and Tronick, E. Z. (1987). Mother–infant face-to-face interaction: The sequence of dyadic states. *Developmental Psychology*, 23, 66–77.

Colby, A., Kohlberg, L., Gibbs, J., and Lieberman, M. (1983). A longitudinal study of moral judgement. Monographs of the Society for Research in Child Development, 200.

Cole, P. M. (1986). Children's spontaneous control of facial expression. *Child Development*, 57, 1309–21.

Cooley, C. H. (1902). *Human Nature and the Social Order*. New York: Charles Scribner's Sons.

Craik, K. (1943). *The Nature of Explanation*. Cambridge: Cambridge University Press.

Cummings, E. M. (1987). Coping with background anger in early childhood. *Child Development*, 58, 976–84.

Cummings, E. M., Hollenbeck, B., Iannotti, R., Radke-Yarrow, M., and Zahn-Waxler, C. (1986). Early organization of altruism and aggression: Developmental patterns and individual differences. In C. Zahn-Waxler, E. M. Cummings. and R. Iannotti (eds) *Altruism and Aggression*. Cambridge: Cambridge University Press.

Cummings, E. M., Iannotti, R. J., and Zahn-Waxler, C. (1985). Influence of conflict between adults on the emotions and aggression of young children. *Developmental Psychology*, 21, 495–507.

Darwin, C. (1872). *The Expression of the Emotions in Man and Animals*. London: Murray.

Davidson, P., Turiel, E., and Black, A. (1983). The effects of stimulus familiarity on the use of criteria and justifications in children's social reasoning. *British Journal of Developmental Psychology*, 1, 49–65.

DeLoache, J. S., and Plaetzer, B. (1985). Tea for two: Joint mother–child symbolic play. Presented at the meeting of the Society for Research in Child Development, Toronto, April 1975.

Denham, S. A. (1986). Social cognition, prosocial behaviour, and emotion in preschoolers: Contextual validation. *Child Development*, 57, 194–201.

DePaulo, B. M., and Jordan, A. (1982). Age changes in deceiving and detecting deceit. In R. S. Feldman (ed.), *Development of Nonverbal Behavior in Children*. New York: Springer-Verlag.

Dias, M., and Harris, P. L. (1988). The effect of make-believe play on deductive reasoning. *British Journal of Developmental Psychology*, 6, 207–21.

DiLalla, L. F. and Watson, M. W. (1988). Differentiation of fantasy and reality: Preschoolers' reactions to interruptions in their play. *Developmental Psychology*, 24, 286–91.

Donaldson, S. K. and Westerman, M. A. (1986). Development of children's understanding of ambivalence and causal theories of emotions. *Developmental Psychology*, 22, 655–62.

Dunn, J. (1984). *Sisters and Brothers*. London: Fontana.

Dunn, J. (1988). *The Beginnings of Social Understanding*. Oxford: Blackwell.

Dunn, J., and Kendrick, C. (1979). Interaction between young siblings in the context of family relationships. In M. Lewis and L. A. Rosenblum (eds). *The Child and its Family*. New York: Plenum Press.

Dunn, J., and Kendrick, C. (1982). *Siblings: Love, Envy and Understanding*. Cambridge, Mass.: Harvard University Press.

Dunn, J., Kendrick, C., and MacNamee, R. (1981). The reaction of first-born children to the birth of a sibling: Mother's reports. *Journal of Child Psychology and Psychiatry*, 22, 1–18.

Dunn, J., and Munn, P. (1985). Becoming a family member: Family conflict and the development of social understanding in the first year. *Child Development*, 50, 306–18.

Dunn, J., and Munn, P. (1986). Siblings and the development of prosocial behaviour. *International Journal of Behavioral Development*, 9, 265–84.

Dunn, J., and Munn, P. (1987). Development of justifications in disputes with mother and children. *Developmental Psychology*, 23, 791–8.

Eisenberg, N., and Miller, P. A. (1987). The relation of empathy to prosocial and related behaviors. *Psychological Bulletin*, 101, 91–119.

Ekman, P. (1973). Cross-cultural studies of facial expression. In P. Ekman (ed.), *Darwin and Facial Expression.* New York: Academic Press.

Ekman, P. (in press). The argument and evidence about universals in facial expressions of emotion. In H. Wagner and A. Manstead (eds). *Handbook of Psychophysiology: Emotion and Social Behaviour*. London: John Wiley.

Ekman, P., and Friesen, W. (1971). Constants across culture in the face and emotion. *Journal of Personality and Social Psychology*, 17, 124–9.

Ekman, P., and Friesen, W. V. (1974). Detecting deception from the body or face. *Journal of Personality and Social Psychology*, 29, 288–98.

Ekman, P., and Friesen, W. V. (1975). *Unmasking the Face: A Guide to Recognizing Emotions from Facial Clues*. Englewood Cliffs, NJ: Prentice-Hall.

Ekman, P., and Friesen, W. V. (1978). *Facial Action Coding Systems*. Palo Alto, Calif.: Consulting Psychologists Press.

Ekman, P., Sorenson, E. R., and Friesen, W. V. (1969). Pan-cultural elements in facial displays of emotions. *Science*, 164, 86–8.

Estes, D., Wellman, H. M., and Woolley, J. D. (in press). Children's understanding of mental phenomena. In H. W. Reese (ed.), *Advances in Child Development and Behaviour*. Orlando, Fla.: Academic Press.

Field, T. M., Vega-Lahr, N., Scafadi, F., and Goldstein, S. (1986). Effects of maternal unavailability on mother–infant interaction. *Infant Behavior and Development*, 9, 473–8.

Field, T. M., Woodson, R., Cohen, D., Greenberg, R., Garcia, R., and Collins, K. (1983). Discrimination and imitation of facial expressions by term and preterm neonates. *Infant Behavior and Development*, 6, 485–9.

Field, T. M., Woodson, R., Greenberg, R., and Cohen, D. (1982). Discrimination and imitation of facial expression by neonates. *Science*, 218, 179–81.

Fisher, S., Frazer, N., and Murray, K. (1986). Homesickness and health in boarding school children. *Journal of Environmental Psychology*, 6, 35–47.

Fodor, J. A. (1987). *Psychosemantics*. Cambridge, Mass.: Bradford.

Folstein, S., and Rutter, M. (1977). Infantile autism: A genetic study of 21 twin pairs. *Journal of Child Psychology and Psychiatry*, 18, 297–321.

Ganchrow, J. R., Steiner, J. E., Daher, M. (1983). Neonatal facial expressions in response to different qualities and intensities of gustatory stimuli. *Infant Behavior and Development*, 6, 473–84.

Gardner, D., Harris, P. L., Ohmoto, M., and Hamazaki, T. (1988). Japanese children's understanding of the distinction between real and apparent emotion. *International Journal of Behavioral Development*, 11, 203–18.

George, C., and Main, M. (1979). Social interaction of young abused children: Approach, avoidance and aggression. *Child Development*, 50, 306–18.

Gnepp, J., McKee, E., Domanic, J. A. (1987). Children's use of situational information to infer emotion: Understanding emotionally equivocal situations. *Developmental Psychology*, 23, 114–23.

Gordon, R. M. (1986). Folk psychology as simulation. *Mind and Language*, 1, 156–71.

Gordon, R. M. (1987). *The Structure of Emotions*. Cambridge: Cambridge University Press.

Graham, S. (1988). Children's developing understanding of the motivational role of affect: An attributional analysis. *Cognitive Development*, 3, 71–88.

Graham, S., Doubleday, C., and Guarino, P. A. (1984). The development of relations between perceived controllability and the emotions of pity, anger, and guilt. *Child Development*, 55, 561–5.

Graham, S., and Weiner, B. (1986). From an attributional theory of emotion to developmental psychology: A round-trip ticket? *Social Cognition*, 4, 152–79.

Gross, D., and Harris, P. L. (1988). Understanding false beliefs about emotion. *International Journal of Behavioral Development*, 11, 475–88.

Gusella, J. L., Muir, D., and Tronick, E. Z. (1988). The effect of manipulating maternal behavior during an interaction on three- and six-month-olds' affect and attention. *Child Development*, 59, 1111–24.

Hardman, C. E. (1981). The psychology of conformity and self-expression among the Lohorung Rai of East Nepal. In P. Heelas and A. Lock (eds), *Indigenous psychologies*. London: Academic Press.

Harré, R. (1987). *The Social Construction of Emotions*. Oxford: Blackwell.

Harris, P. L. (1983). Children's understanding of the link between situation and emotion. *Journal of Experimental Child Psychology*, 36, 490–509.

Harris, P. L. (1985). What children know about the situations that provoke emotion. In M. Lewis and C. Saarni (eds), *The Socialization of Emotions*. New York: Plenum Press.

Harris, P. L., Donnelly, K., Guz, G. R., and Pitt-Watson, R. (1986). Children's understanding of the distinction between real and apparent emotion. *Child Development*, 57, 895–909.

Harris, P. L. and Gross, D. (1988). Children's understanding of real and apparent emotion. In J. W. Astington, P. L. Harris, and D. R. Olson, (eds), *Developing Theories of Mind*. New York: Cambridge University Press.

Harris, P. L. and Guz, G. R. (1986). Models of emotion: How boys report their emotional reactions upon entering an English boarding school. Unpublished paper, Department of Experimental Psychology, University of Oxford.

Harris, P. L., Guz, G. R., and Lipian, M. S. (1985). Thoughts and feelings: Children's conception of their time-course and mutual influence. Unpublished paper, Department of Experimental Psychology, University of Oxford.

Harris, P. L., Guz, G. R., Lipian, M. S., and Man-Shu, Z. (1985). Insight into the time-course of emotion among Western and Chinese children. *Child Development*, 56, 972–88.

Harris, P. L., Johnson, C. N., Hutton, D., Andrews, G., and Cook, T. (1989). Young children's theory of mind and emotion. *Cognition and Emotion*, 3.

Harris, P. L., and Lipian, M. S. (1989). Understanding emotion and experiencing emotion. In C. Saarni and P. L. Harris (eds), *Children's Understanding of Emotions*. New York: Cambridge University Press.

Harris, P. L., Marriott, C., and Whittall, S. (1988). Monsters, ghosts and witches: Testing the limits of the fantasy–reality distinction in young children. Paper presented at the European Conference of Developmental Psychology, Budapest, Hungary.

Harris, P. L., Morris, J. E., and Meerum Terwogt, M. (1986). The early acquisition of spatial adjectives: a cross-linguistic study. *Journal of Child Language*, 13, 335–52.

Harris, P. L., and Muncer, A. (1988). Autistic children's understanding of beliefs and desires. Paper presented at the British Psychological Society Developmental Section Conference, Coleg Harlech, Wales.

Harris, P. L. and Olthof, T. (1982). The child's concept of emotion. In G. E. Butterworth and P. Light (eds), *Social Cognition*, Brighton, UK: Harvester.

Harris, P. L., Olthof, T., and Meerum Terwogt, M. (1981). Children's knowledge of emotion. *Journal of Child Psychology and Psychiatry*, 22, 247–61.

Harris, P. L., Olthof, T., Meerum Terwogt, M., and Hardman, C. E. (1987). Children's knowledge of the situations that provoke emotion. *International Journal of Behavioral Development*, 10, 319–44.

Harter, S. (1977). A cognitive–developmental approach to children's expression of conflicting feelings and a technique to facilitate such expression in play therapy. *Journal of Consulting and Clinical Psychology*, 45, 417–32.

Harter, S. (1983). Children's understanding of multiple emotions: a cognitive–developmental approach. In W. F. Overton, (ed.), *The Relationship between Social and Cognitive Development*. Hillsdale, NJ: Erlbaum.

Harter, S., and Buddin, B. (1987). Children's understanding of the simultaneity of two emotions: A five-stage developmental acquisition sequence. *Developmental Psychology*, 23, 388–99.

Harter, S., and Whitesell, N. (1989). Developmental changes in children's emotion concepts. In C. Saarni and P. L. Harris (eds), *Children's Understanding of Emotions*. New York: Cambridge University Press.

Harter, S., Wright, K., and Bresnick, S. (1987). A developmental sequence of the understanding of pride and shame. Paper presented at the Society for Research in Child Development Biennial Meeting, Baltimore, Md., April.

Haviland, J. M. and Lelwica, M. (1987). The induced affect response: 10-week-old infants' responses to three emotional expressions. *Developmental Psychology*, 23, 97–104.

Hendry, J. (1984). Becoming Japanese: A social anthropological view of child rearing. *Journal of the Anthropological Society of Oxford*, 15, 101–18.

Hendry, J. (1986). *Becoming Japanese: A Social Anthropological Approach to Pre-school Education.* Manchester: Manchester University Press.

Hess, R. D., Kashiwagi, K., Azuma, H., Price, G. G., and Dickson, W. P. (1980). Maternal expectations for mastery of developmental tasks in Japan and the United States. *International Journal of Psychology*, 15, 259–71.

Hiatt, S., Campos, J. J., and Emde, R. N. (1979). Facial patterning and infant emotional expression: Happiness, surprise and fear. *Child Development*, 50, 1020–35.

Hobson, R. P. (1984). Early childhood autism and the question of egocentrism. *Journal of Autism and Developmental Disorders*, 14, 85–104.

Hobson, R. P. (1986a). The autistic child's appraisal of expressions of emotion. *Journal of Child Psychology and Psychiatry*, 27, 321–42.

Hobson, R. P. (1986b). The autistic child's appraisal of expressions of emotion: A further study. *Journal of Child Psychology and Psychiatry*, 27, 671–80.

Hobson, R. P. (1986c). The autistic child's concept of people. *Communication*, 20, 12–17.

Hoffman, M. (1970). Moral development. In P. H. Mussen (ed.), *Carmichael's Manual of Child Psychology* (3rd edn, vol. 2). New York: John Wiley.

Hoffman, M. L. (1981). Perspectives on the difference between understanding people and understanding things: The role of affect. In J. Flavell and L. Ross (eds), *Social Cognitive Development.* Cambridge: Cambridge University Press.

Hoffman, M. L. and Saltzstein, H. D. (1967). Parent discipline and the child's moral development. *Journal of Personality and Social Psychology*, 5, 45–57.

Hoffman-Plotkin, D., and Twentyman, C. T. (1984). A multimodal assessment of behavioral and cognitive deficits in abused and neglected preschoolers. *Child Development*, 55, 795–802.

Hornik, R., Risenhoover, N., and Gunnar, M. (1987). The effects of maternal positive, neutral, and negative affective communications on infant responses to new toys. *Child Development*, 58, 937–44.

Howell, S. (1981). Rules not words. In P. Heelas and A. Lock (eds), *Indigenous Psychologies*. London: Academic Press.

Izard, C. E. (1979). The maximally discriminative facial movement scoring system. Unpublished manuscript, University of Delaware.

Izard, C. E., Hembree, E. A., Dougherty, L. M., and Spizzirri, C. (1983). Changes in 2- to 19-month-old infants' responses to acute pain. *Developmental Psychology*, 19, 418–26.

Izard, C. E., Huebner, R., Risser, D., McGinnes, G., and Dougherty, L. (1980). The young infant's ability to produce discrete emotion expressions. *Developmental Psychology*, 16, 132–40.

Johnson, C. N. (1988). Theory of mind and the structure of conscious experience. In J. W. Astington, P. L. Harris, and D. R. Olson (eds), *Developing Theories of Mind*. New York: Cambridge University Press.

Johnson, E. J., and Tversky, A. (1983). Affect, generalization, and the perception of risk. *Journal of Personality and Social Psychology*, 45, 20–31.

Jordano, R. (1986). The effects of adult emotion on young children. M.Sc. thesis, Department of Experimental Psychology, University of Oxford.

Kaitz, M., Meschulach-Sarfaty, O., Auerbach, J., and Eidelman, A. (1988). A reexamination of newborns' ability to imitate facial expressions. *Developmental Psychology*, 24, 3–7.

Kanner, L. (1943). Autistic disturbance of affective contact. *The Nervous Child*, 2, 217–50.

Kanner, L. (1971). Follow-up study of eleven autistic children originally reported in 1943. *Journal of Autism and Childhood Schizophrenia*, 2, 9–33.

Klinnert, M. (1984). The regulation of infant behavior by maternal facial expression. *Infant Behavior and Development*, 7, 447–65.

Klinnert, M., Campos, J. J., Sorce, J., Emde, R. N., and Svejda, M. (1983). Emotions as behavior regulators: Social referencing in infancy. In R. Plutchik and H. Kellerman (eds), *Emotions in Early Development*, vol. 2: *The Emotions*. New York: Academic Press.

Koriat, A., Melkman, R., Averill, J. R., and Lazarus, R. S. (1972). The self-control of emotional reactions to a stressful film. *Journal of Personality*, 40, 601–19.

Kuczaj, S. A., II (1981). Factors influencing children's hypothetical reference. *Journal of Child Language*, 8, 131–7.

Kuczaj, S. A., II, and Daly, M. J. (1979). The development of hypothetical reference in the speech of young children. *Journal of Child Language*, 6, 563–79.

Kuhl, P. K. (1987). The special-mechanisms debate in speech research: Categorization tests on animals and infants. In S. Harnad (ed.), *Categorical Perception*. Cambridge: Cambridge University Press.

Kuhl, P. K. and Meltzoff, A. (1982). The bimodal perception of speech in infancy. *Science*, 218, 1138–41.

Laird, J. (1974). Self-attribution of emotion: The effects of expressive behavior on the quality of emotional experience. *Journal of Personality and Social Psychology*, 29, 475–86.

Laird, J. D., Wagenar, J. J., Halal, M., and Szegda, M. (1982). Remembering what you feel: Effects of emotion on memory. *Journal of Personality and Social Psychology*, 42, 646–57.

Lamb, M. E., Hwang, C. P., Frodi, A. M., and Frodi, M. (1982). Security of mother– and father–infant attachment and its relation to sociability with strangers in traditional and non-traditional Swedish families. *Infant Behavior and Development*, 5, 355–67.

Lazarus, R. (1975). The self-regulation of emotion. In L. Levi (ed.), *Emotions – Their Parameters and Measurement*. New York: Raven Press.

Leslie, A. M. (1987). Pretense and representation: The origins of 'theory of mind'. *Psychological Review*, 94, 412–26.

Leslie, A. M., and Frith, U. (1988). Autistic children's understanding of seeing, knowing and believing. *British Journal of Developmental Psychology*, 6, 315–24.

Lewis, M. (1989). Cultural differences in children's knowledge of emotion scripts. In C. Saarni and P. L. Harris (eds), *Children's Understanding of Emotions*. New York: Cambridge University Press.

Lewis, V., and Boucher, J. (1988). Spontaneous, instructed and elicited play in relatively able autistic children. *British Journal of Developmental Psychology*, 6, 325–39.

Lipian, M. S. (1985). Ill-conceived feelings: Developing concepts of the emotions associated with illness in healthy and acutely ill children. Unpublished doctoral dissertation, Yale University.

Lotter, V. (1978). Follow-up studies. In M. Rutter and E. Schopler (eds), *Autism: A Reappraisal of Concepts and Treatment.* New York: Plenum Press.

Loveland, K. A., Landry, S. H., Hughes, S. O., Hall, S. K., and McEvoy, R. E. (1988). Speech acts and the pragmatic deficits of autism. *Journal of Speech and Hearing Research, 31,* 593–604.

Lutz, C. (1982). The domain of emotion words in Ifaluk. *American Ethnologist*, 9, 113–28

Lutz, C. (1987). Goals, events, and understanding in Ifaluk emotion theory. In D. Holland and N. Quinn (eds), *Cultural Models in Language and Thought.* Cambridge: Cambridge University Press.

MacDonald, H., Rutter, M., Howlin, P., Rios, P., Le Couteur, A., Evered, C., and Folstein, S. (1988). Recognition and expression of emotional cues by autistic and normal adults. Unpublished paper, Department of Child and Adolescent Psychiatry, Institute of Psychiatry, University of London.

Main, M., and George, C. (1985). Responses of abused and disadvantaged toddlers to distress in agemates: A study in the day care setting. *Developmental Psychology*, 21, 407–12.

Main, M., and Goldwyn, R. (1985). *Adult attachment classification system.* Unpublished manuscript, Department of Psychology, University of California, Berkeley.

Matsumo, D. (1987). The role of facial response in the experience of emotion: More methodological problems and a meta-analysis. *Journal of Personality and Social Psychology*, 52, 769–74.

Meerum Terwogt, M., Koops, W., Oosterhoff, T., and Olthof, T. (1986). Development in processing of multiple emotional situations. *Journal of General Psychology*, 11, 109–21.

Meerum Terwogt, M., Schene, J., and Harris, P. L. (1986). Self-control of emotional reactions by young children. *Journal of Child Psychology and Psychiatry*, 27, 357–66.

Meltzoff, A. N., and Moore, M. K. (1977). Imitation of facial and manual gestures by human neonates. *Science*, 198, 75–8.

Meltzoff, A. N., and Moore, M. K. (1983). Newborn infants imitate adult facial gestures. *Child Development*, 54, 702–19.

Miller, S. M., and Green, M. L. (1985). Coping with stress and frustration: Origins, nature and development. In M. Lewis and C. Saarni (eds), *The Socialization of Emotions*. New York: Plenum Press.

Miyake, K., Chen, S.-J., and Campos, J. J. (1985). Infant temperament, mother's mode of interaction and attachment in Japan: An interim report. In I. Bretherton and E. Waters (eds), *Growing Points of Attachment Theory and Research*. Monographs of the Society for Research in Child Development, 209.

Mundy, P., Sigman, M., Ungerer, J., and Sherman, T. (1986). Defining the social deficits of autism: The contribution of non-verbal communication measures. *Journal of Child Psychology and Psychiatry*, 27, 657–69.

Murphy, L. B. (1937). *Social Behaviour and Child Personality*. New York: Columbia University Press.

Nunner-Winkler, G., and Sodian, B. (1988). Children's understanding of moral emotions. *Child Development*, 59, 1323–38.

Perner, J. (1988). Higher-order beliefs and intentions in children's understanding of social interaction. In J. W. Astington, P. L. Harris, and D. R. Olson (eds), *Developing Theories of Mind*. New York: Cambridge University Press.

Perner, J., Leekam, S., and Wimmer, H. (1987). Three-year-olds' difficulty in understanding false belief: Cognitive limitation, lack of knowledge, or pragmatic misunderstanding? *British Journal of Developmental Psychology*, 5, 125–37.

Piaget, J. (1962). *Play, Dreams and Imitation*. New York: Norton.

Reissland, N. (1985). The development of concepts of simultaneity in children's understanding of emotions. *Journal of Child Psychology and Psychiatry*, 26, 811–24.

Reissland, N. (1988a). Neonatal imitation in the first hour of life: Observations in rural Nepal. *Developmental Psychology*, 24, 464–69.

Reissland, N. (1988b). The development of emotion in young children. Unpublished doctoral thesis, Department of Experimental Psychology, University of Oxford.

Rosaldo, M. Z. (1980). *Knowledge and Passion*. Cambridge: Cambridge University Press.

Rubin, K. H., Fein, G. G., and Vandenberg, B. (1983). Play. In E. M. Hetherington (ed.), *Handbook of Child Psychology*, vol. IV: *Socialization, Personality and Social Development*. New York: John Wiley.

Rutter, M. (1967). Psychotic disorders in early childhood. In A. J. Coppen and A. Walk (eds), *Recent Developments in Schizophrenia*. Ashford, England: Headley Bros.

Rutter, M. and Garmezy, N. (1983). Developmental psychopathology. In E. M. Hetherington (ed.), *Handbook of Child Psychology*, vol. IV: *Socialization, Personality, and Social Development*. New York: John Wiley.

Saarni, C. (1984). Observing children's use of display rules: Age and sex differences. *Child Development*, 55, 1504–13.

Scaife, M., and Bruner, J. (1975). The capacity for joint visual attention in the infant. *Nature*, 253, 265–6.

Seidner, L. B., Stipek, D. J., and Feshbach, N. D. (1988). A developmental analysis of elementary school-aged children's concepts of pride and embarrassment. *Child Development*, 59, 367–77.

Seligman, M. E. P. and Peterson, C. (1986). A learned helplessness perspective on childhood depression: Theory and research. In M. Rutter, C. E. Izard, and P. B. Read (eds), *Depression in Young People*. New York: Guilford.

Shatz, M., Wellman, H. M., and Silber, S. (1983). The acquisition of mental verbs; A systematic investigation of the first reference to mental state. *Cognition*, 14, 301–21.

Shweder, R. A., Mahapatra, M., and Miller, J. G. (1987). Culture and moral development. In J. Kagan (ed.), *The Emergence of Morality in Young Children*. Chicago: University of Chicago Press.

Shweder, R. A., Turiel, E., and Much, N. C. (1981). The moral intuitions of the child. In J. H. Flavell and L. Ross (eds), *Social Cognitive Development*. New York: Cambridge University Press.

Siegel, M., and Storey, R. M. (1985). Daycare and children's conceptions of moral and social rules. *Child Development*, 56, 1001–8.

Sigman, M., Mundy, P., Sherman, T., and Ungerer, J. A. (1986). Social interaction of autistic, mentally retarded and normal children and their caregivers. *Journal of Child Psychology and Psychiatry*, 27, 647–55.

Sigman, M., Mundy, P., Ungerer, J. A., and Sherman, T. (1987). The development of social attachments in autistic children. Paper presented at the Society for Research in Child Development

Biennial Meeting, Baltimore, Md., April.

Sigman, M., and Ungerer, J. A. (1984). Attachment behaviors in autistic children. *Journal of Autism and Developmental Disorders*, 14, 231–44.

Slade, A. (1986). Symbolic play and separation-individuation: A naturalistic study. *Bulletin of the Menninger Clinic*, 50, 541–63.

Smetana, J. G. (1981). Preschool children's conception of moral and social rules. *Child Development*, 52, 1333–6.

Smetana, J. G. (1984). Toddlers' social interactions regarding moral and conventional transgressions. *Child Development*, 55, 1767–76.

Smetana, J. G. (1985). Preschool children's conceptions of transgressions: Effects of varying moral and conventional domain-related attributes. *Developmental Psychology*, 21, 18–29.

Smetana, J. G., Kelly, M., and Twentyman, C. T. (1984). Abused, neglected and nonmaltreated children's conceptions of moral and socio-conventional transgressions. *Child Development*, 55, 277–87.

Song, M.-J., Smetana, J. G., and Kim, S. Y. (1987). Korean children's conceptions of moral and conventional transgressions. *Developmental Psychology*, 23, 577–82.

Sorce, J. F., Emde, R. N., Campos, J. J., and Klinnert, M. D. (1985). Maternal emotional signaling: Its effects on the visual cliff behavior of 1-year-olds. *Developmental Psychology*, 21, 195–200.

Spiegler, D. L., and Caron, R. F. (1986). Intermodal perception of emotions by infants. Paper presented at Fifth International Conference on Infant Studies, Los Angeles.

Stein, N. L., and Levine, L. (1987). Thinking about feelings: The development and organization of emotional knowledge. In R. E. Snow and M. Farr (eds), *Aptitude, Learning, and Instruction*, vol. 3: *Cognition, Conation, and Affect*. Hillsdale, NJ: Erlbaum.

Stenberg, C., Campos, J. J., and Emde, R. (1983). The facial expression of anger in seven month old infants. *Child Development*, 54, 178–84.

Stewart, R. B. (1983). Sibling attachment relationship: Child–infant interactions in the strange situation. *Developmental Psychology*, 19, 192–99.

Stewart, R. B., and Marvin, R. S. (1984). Sibling relations: The role of conceptual perspective-taking in the ontogeny of sibling caregiving. *Child Development*, 55, 1322–32.

Strayer, J. (1980). A naturalistic study of empathic behaviors and their relation to affective states and perspective-taking skills in preschool children *Child Development*, 51, 815–22.

Taylor, D. A., and Harris P. L. (1983). Knowledge of the link between emotion and memory among normal and maladjusted boys. *Developmental Psychology*, 19, 832–8.

Taylor, D. A., and Harris, P. L. (1984). Knowledge of strategies for the expression of emotion among normal and maladjusted boys: A research note. *Journal of Child Psychology and Psychiatry*, 24, 141–5.

Termine, N. T., and Izard, C. E. (1988). Infants' responses to their mothers' expressions of joy and sadness. *Developmental Psychology*, 24, 223–9.

Thompson, R. A. (1989). Causal attributions and children's emotional understanding. In C. Saarni and P. L. Harris (eds), *Children's Understanding of Emotions*. New York: Cambridge University Press.

Thompson, R., and Hoffman, M. L. (1980). Empathy and the arousal of guilt in children. *Developmental Psychology*, 15, 155–6.

Tolmie, A. (1988). Children's knowledge of feelings: differences between emotions and non-emotions. Paper presented at the British Psychological Society Developmental Section Conference, Coleg Harlech, Wales.

Trabasso, T., Stein, N. L., and Johnson, L. R. (1981). Children's knowledge of events: A causal analysis of story structure. In G. Bower (ed.), *Learning and Motivation*, vol. 15. New York: Academic Press.

Trickett, P. K., and Kuczynski, L. (1986). Children's misbehaviors and parental discipline strategies in abusive and nonabusive families. *Developmental Psychology*, 22, 115–23

Turiel, E. (1983). *The Development of Social Knowledge*. Cambridge: Cambridge University Press.

Underwood, B., and Moore, B. (1982). Perspective-taking and altruism. *Psychological Bulletin*, 91, 143–73.

Volkmar, F. R., and Cohen, D. J. (1985). The experience of infantile autism: A first-person account by Tony W. *Journal of Autism and Developmental Disorders*, 15, 47–54.

Walker, A. (1982). Intermodal perception of expressive behaviors by human infants. *Journal of Experimental Child Psychology*, 33, 514–35.

Walker-Andrews, A. S. (1986). Intermodal perception of expressive behaviors: Relation of eye and voice? *Developmental Psychology*, 22, 373–7.

Wellman, H. M. (1988). First steps in the child's theorizing about the mind. In J. Astington, P. L. Harris, and D. R. Olson (eds), *Developing Theories of Mind*. New York: Cambridge University Press.

Wellman, H. M., and Estes, D. (1986). Early understanding of mental entities: A reexamination of childhood realism. *Child Development*, 57, 910–23.

Whiten, A., and Byrne, R. (1988). Tactical deception in primates. *Behavioral and Brain Sciences*, 11, 233–73.

Wimmer, H., and Perner, J. (183). Beliefs about beliefs: Representations and constraining function of wrong beliefs in young children's understanding of deception. *Cognition*, 13, 103–28.

Wing, L. (1980). Childhood autism and social class: A question of selection. *British Journal of Psychiatry*, 137, 410–17.

Winton, W. M. (1986). The role of facial response in self-reports of emotion: A critique of Laird. *Journal of Personality and Social Psychology*, 50, 808–12.

Wolf, D. (1982). Understanding others: A longitudinal case study of the concept of independent agency. In G. E. Forman (ed.), *Action and Thought*, New York: Academic Press.

Wolf, D. P., Rygh, J., and Altshuler, J. (1984). Agency and experience: Actions and states in play narratives. In I. Bretherton (ed.), *Symbolic Play*, Orlando, Fla.: Academic Press.

Yirmiya, N., Kasari, C. Mundy, P., and Sigman, M. (1987). Facial expressions of emotion: Are autistic children different from mentally retarded and normal children? Paper presented at the Society for Research in Child Development Biennial Meeting, Baltimore, Md., April.

Yuill, N. (1984). Young children's coordination of motive and outcome in judgments of satisfaction and morality. *British Journal of Developmental Psychology*, 2, 73–81.

Zahn-Waxler, C., and Radke-Yarrow, M. (1982). The development of altruism: Alternative research strategies. In N. Eisenberg-Berg (ed.), *The Development of Prosocial Behaviour*. New York: Academic Press.

Zahn-Waxler, C., Radke-Yarrow, M., and Brady-Smith, J. (1977). Perspective-taking and prosocial behavior. *Developmental Psychology*, *13*, 87–8.

Zahn-Waxler, C., Radke-Yarrow, M., and King, R. A. (1979). Child rearing and children's prosocial dispositions towards victims of distress. *Child Development*, *50*, 319–30.

Author index

Subject index